# The Diabetic Food Bible

## The Complete Low-GI Nutrition Guide

*What You Really Need to Know to Balance Blood Sugar,*

*Manage Prediabetes and Type 2 Diabetes,*

*Keeping the Food you Love*

Adam J. Clark

# Table of Contents

# Part I
# Understanding Type 2 Diabetes

## THE BASICS OF BLOOD GLUCOSE AND DIABETES

## *A Brief Lesson on Blood Glucose*

Imagine walking through a lush garden full of vibrant, life-giving plants. This garden is your body, a miraculous ecosystem dependent on a delicate balance to thrive. In this ecosystem, blood glucose plays a crucial role, much like sunlight does for the garden, providing the energy necessary for life.

The primary form of sugar in your blood is called blood glucose, or blood sugar. It comes from the food you eat and is the main energy source for your body. Your body's ability to manage this sugar is vital for your health. Let's break this down into simpler terms:

**What Is Blood Glucose?** Glucose is a simple sugar that circulates in your bloodstream. It's derived from the carbohydrates in your diet — from your morning toast to the pasta in your dinner. Upon digestion, these carbohydrates are broken down into glucose and other sugars.

**The Journey of Glucose:** After you eat, glucose enters your bloodstream. This signals your pancreas to release insulin, a hormone that acts like a key, unlocking your body's cells so they can absorb glucose and use it for energy.

**Why It's Important:** Every cell in your body needs energy to perform its functions — whether it's repairing tissue, powering your muscles, or sending signals through your brain. Glucose is their fuel.

**Maintaining Balance:** Just as a garden needs the right amount of sunlight, your body needs to maintain its blood glucose levels within a narrow range. Too much or too little can lead to health issues. The process of keeping blood glucose levels in check is primarily managed by insulin and another hormone called glucagon, working in concert to keep you balanced and healthy.

Understanding blood glucose is the first step towards appreciating the complexity and importance of managing diabetes. It sets the foundation for our journey through diet and lifestyle choices that support healthy blood sugar levels, without stepping into the realms of treatment options or specific dietary strategies covered later in this guide.

In essence, managing blood glucose is about nurturing your body's garden, ensuring it receives just the right amount of 'sunlight' to thrive. By grasping this concept, you're better equipped to make informed choices about your health and well-being.

## *The Path to Diabetes: Insulin Resistance and the Impact of Nutrition*

In our journey through the garden of our body, understanding how each element interacts is crucial to maintaining its health. One such pathway, often veiled in complexity, is the road to diabetes, particularly type 2 diabetes. This condition is intricately linked with insulin resistance and the profound impact of our nutritional choices.

Imagine insulin as a key once again, but this time, the locks to the cells in our body become rusty and difficult to open. This is insulin resistance. When the body's cells don't respond as effectively to insulin, glucose can't enter the cells as easily, and it begins to build up in the blood.

Delving deeper into the concept of insulin resistance, let's expand on the analogy of a key and a lock, which simplifies a complex biochemical process affecting millions. In this scenario, insulin is the key produced by the pancreas, and the cell receptors act as locks on the surface of cells throughout our body. These locks need to open for glucose—the body's primary energy source derived from the food we eat—to enter the cells.

## *Understanding Insulin Resistance*

- **The Rusty Lock Mechanism:** Over time, due to various factors such as poor diet, lack of exercise, and genetic predispositions, these cell receptors become less responsive to insulin. It's akin to a lock that has become rusty. No matter how well the key is cut (or how much insulin is present), it struggles to turn the lock smoothly. This resistance makes it increasingly difficult for glucose to be absorbed by the cells, leading to higher levels of both glucose and insulin in the bloodstream.
- **The Pancreas Under Pressure:** In response to this resistance, the pancreas begins to work overtime, producing more insulin in an attempt to overcome the cells' decreased responsiveness. Imagine a locksmith trying to force a rusty lock to work by applying more pressure or creating more keys in hopes one will work better. Initially, this might help manage blood glucose levels, but over time, it places a significant strain on the pancreas.
- **Complications of Continuous Strain:** Continually demanding extra insulin from the pancreas can lead to its overexertion, and eventually, it might not be able to produce sufficient insulin to manage blood sugar levels effectively. This state of hyperinsulinemia (high insulin levels in the blood) and hyperglycemia (high blood sugar levels) sets the stage for prediabetes and, if unaddressed, can progress to type 2 diabetes.
- **Feedback Loop and Further Resistance:** High levels of insulin in the blood can lead to further insulin resistance, creating a vicious cycle. The body's cells become even less responsive to insulin due to the constant high levels, akin to how continuously applying force to a rusty lock can cause further damage, making it even more challenging to open.

**Role of Nutrition:** Our diet plays a pivotal role in this scenario. Consuming large amounts of processed foods, sugars, and unhealthy fats can contribute to the body's increased insulin resistance. These foods can cause inflammation and signal the body to release more insulin, exacerbating the problem.

**Impact of Excess Glucose:** With more glucose circulating in the blood due to insulin resistance, the body faces various health risks, including the potential to develop type 2 diabetes. This condition doesn't develop overnight but results from prolonged periods of insulin resistance and pancreatic strain.

**Prevention Through Diet:** The silver lining is the significant impact that dietary choices have on managing and potentially preventing insulin resistance. By favoring whole foods, rich in fiber, and low in added sugars and unhealthy fats, we can help maintain more stable blood glucose levels and reduce the burden on our insulin-producing cells.

## The Risks of Untreated Diabetes

Venturing deeper into the garden of our health, we encounter the risks of untreated diabetes, a path we must navigate with care and knowledge. The tale of untreated diabetes is not just a single story but a collection of potential narratives that affect every part of the garden, from the smallest plant to the largest tree.

**High Blood Sugar Levels:** At the core of untreated diabetes lies persistently high blood sugar. Over time, this excessive sugar acts like a flood in our garden, overwhelming and damaging various plants (body cells and organs). This can lead to a cascade of complications, affecting nearly every system in the body.

**Damage to Blood Vessels:** One of the first casualties in this scenario are the blood vessels. High glucose levels can injure the vessel walls, leading to cardiovascular problems. This includes increased risk for heart disease, heart attack, and stroke, akin to the main water lines of our garden becoming clogged or damaged, disrupting the flow of life-giving water to essential areas.

**Nerve Damage (Neuropathy):** Excess glucose can also harm the nerves, leading to neuropathy. Imagine the garden's communication system sending distorted signals or, at times, none at all. This can result in numbness, tingling, or pain, typically starting in the hands and feet and potentially affecting other parts of the body.

**Kidney Damage (Nephropathy):** The kidneys, the garden's filtration system, can become overwhelmed by the effort to filter the excess sugar. Over time, this strain can lead to kidney failure, a severe complication requiring dialysis or kidney transplantation.

**Vision Problems:** High blood sugar can harm the eyes' delicate blood vessels, which can result in diseases like diabetic retinopathy. This is similar to the garden's lighting system becoming dimmer or malfunctioning, affecting our ability to see the beauty of the garden clearly.

**Risk of Infections:** High blood sugar levels can weaken the body's ability to fight infections, making even a small wound or infection potentially serious. In our garden analogy, this is akin to the garden's defense mechanisms being compromised, making it more vulnerable to pests and diseases.

**Slow Healing:** When diabetes is uncontrolled, the healing process after injury or surgery can be slower than usual. This is like the natural regenerative processes of our garden being slowed down, affecting its resilience and ability to recover from damage.

## Distinguishing Between Prediabetes and Diabetes

Understanding the distinction between these two conditions is akin to a gardener knowing the difference between a plant that's showing the first signs of distress and one that's already in a state of prolonged neglect. Both situations call for attention, but the strategies and outcomes may differ significantly.

**What is Prediabetes?** Prediabetes is like the garden's early warning system. It happens when a person's blood sugar is higher than usual but not high enough to be considered diabetic. Think of it as the soil becoming less fertile - not barren, but showing signs that it's not as healthy as it should be. It's a critical juncture where intervention can prevent further damage.

**Blood Sugar Levels:** In technical terms, prediabetes is diagnosed when fasting blood sugar levels are between 100 to 125 mg/dL, or when the Hemoglobin A1C, a measure of average blood sugar over the past 2-3 months, is between 5.7% and 6.4%.

**Transitioning to Diabetes:** Diabetes, particularly type 2 diabetes, represents a more advanced stage of blood sugar imbalance. If prediabetes is akin to the soil's fertility waning, diabetes is when the soil becomes barren in patches, affecting the garden's overall health. Blood sugar levels consistently above the thresholds for prediabetes, fasting blood glucose over 126 mg/dL or an A1C over 6.5%, mark this transition.

**Prediabetes: The Subtle Signals** Prediabetes is akin to a garden at the cusp of distress. The signs are there, but they're not always easy to spot:

- **Slight Thirst Increase:** You might find yourself reaching for the water jug a bit more often than usual, but not enough to raise alarms. It's like noticing that the soil is dry more quickly than it used to be.
- **Mild Fatigue:** A general feeling of being tired can be present, similar to how a garden looks a bit less vibrant, but it's easy to attribute this to a busy week or poor sleep.
- **Blurry Vision:** Occasionally, your vision might be a bit blurrier than usual, like a subtle haze over the garden on a humid day, making it hard to focus on the details of the leaves or flowers.

These symptoms are easy to dismiss individually, much like we might overlook a single wilted leaf or a slightly drooping flower. However, they are early whispers from our body, signaling that it's time to pay closer attention to our health.

**Diabetes: The Clear Distress Signals** As prediabetes progresses to diabetes, the symptoms become more pronounced and harder to ignore, signaling a garden in undeniable distress:

- **Increased Thirst and Frequent Urination:** A significant increase in thirst is often accompanied by a noticeable need to urinate more frequently. This is the body's way of trying to rid itself of excess glucose, similar to a garden that's become waterlogged from too much rain, attempting to drain the excess.
- **Unexplained Weight Loss:** Despite eating the same amount or even more, you might start losing weight without trying. It's as if the garden begins to lose its leaves and blooms despite receiving enough water and sunlight, an indicator that it's not able to utilize these resources effectively.
- **Fatigue:** The fatigue that comes with diabetes is more pronounced than the mild tiredness of prediabetes. It's the kind of exhaustion that feels as if the garden's vitality is sapped, leaving it listless and devoid of energy.
- **Vision Becoming More Blurry:** What was once a slight blur becomes more noticeable, making everyday tasks more challenging. It's akin to the garden's haze thickening, obscuring the beauty and detail of the plants within.

**Why the Distinction Matters:** Recognizing the difference between prediabetes and diabetes is crucial. It's about understanding the opportunity to nurture the garden back to health before it's too late. With lifestyle changes such as diet, exercise, and weight management, prediabetes can often be reversed, preventing the progression to diabetes.

**The Importance of Diagnostic Tests**

In our exploration of health, akin to tending to a garden, the use of diagnostic tests represents the tools and techniques we employ to understand the soil's condition, the health of our plants, and the environment they're growing in. These tools are not merely for the sake of gathering information but are essential in guiding our decisions and actions to ensure the garden thrives. Similarly, the importance of diagnostic tests in the context of managing blood sugar and diagnosing diabetes cannot be overstated. They are critical in pinpointing where we are on the path of glucose management and what steps we need to take to either maintain our health or steer it back on course.

- **Fasting Plasma Glucose Test (FPG):** This test measures blood sugar levels after an overnight fast. It's like checking the soil's moisture level before watering the garden—it tells us if there's a deficiency that needs addressing. An FPG level of 100 to 125 mg/dL indicates prediabetes, while 126 mg/dL or higher suggests diabetes.
- **Oral Glucose Tolerance Test (OGTT):** The OGTT goes a step further, measuring blood sugar before and after consuming a sweet drink. This test is akin to assessing how well the soil drains and retains water after a heavy rain. It helps to see how your body handles a glucose challenge. A 2-hour blood sugar level of 140 to 199 mg/dL post-drink points to prediabetes, and 200 mg/dL or higher can indicate diabetes.
- **Hemoglobin A1c Test (A1C):** This test provides a snapshot of your average blood sugar levels over the past 2-3 months, offering a broader view of the garden's health over a season. An A1C of 5.7% to 6.4% is considered prediabetes, while an A1C of 6.5% or higher on two separate tests suggests diabetes.

- **The Role of Regular Monitoring:** Just as a gardener regularly checks on their plants, monitoring blood sugar levels over time is crucial. It helps in detecting changes early, allowing for timely adjustments in diet, exercise, and possibly medication. Regular testing can be the compass that guides the management of your blood sugar levels, ensuring you're heading in the right direction.

## Deciding Whether to Get Tested for Diabetes

Deciding to get tested for diabetes is not about succumbing to fear but about embracing empowerment. It's a decision to take control of one's health narrative, much as a gardener takes charge of their garden's story through attentive care and informed decisions.

This choice, seemingly simple, is in fact a critical crossroads on the path of health awareness and proactive disease prevention. It's akin to deciding whether to perform a soil test to understand its nutrient composition, pH level, and moisture content — crucial data that informs every subsequent decision about plant care, watering schedules, and fertilization needs. Concerning diabetes, this decision is guided by understanding risk factors, recognizing symptoms, and acknowledging the importance of early detection.

**Understanding Risk Factors:** Just as a gardener must know the signs of nutrient deficiency or pest infestation, recognizing the risk factors for diabetes is the first step. These include:

- Being overweight or obese, which can strain the body's ability to use insulin effectively.
- A family history of diabetes, suggesting a possible genetic predisposition.
- Being 45 years of age or older, although diabetes can occur at any age.
- having a sedentary lifestyle that involves little to no exercise.
- Excessive blood pressure and excessive cholesterol levels can increase the risk.

These factors, much like the indicators of soil health, signal the need for closer scrutiny — in this case, through diagnostic testing.

**Recognizing Symptoms:** Occasionally, the garden sends clear distress signals — wilting leaves, discolored petals, stunted growth. Similarly, certain symptoms might suggest the presence of diabetes or prediabetes, prompting the need for testing. These symptoms include excessive thirst, frequent urination, unexplained weight loss, and persistent fatigue. However, it's crucial to note that prediabetes often occurs without noticeable symptoms, making the decision to test based on risk factors all the more important.

**The Importance of Early Detection:** Early detection of diabetes or prediabetes can be likened to catching a garden pest before it inflicts widespread damage. It opens the door to effective management strategies that can significantly delay or even prevent the progression of diabetes. Through lifestyle changes such as diet modification, increased physical activity, and, if necessary, medication, the impact of diabetes on one's life can be minimized.

## Overview of Treatment Strategies

Adopting a comprehensive approach to diabetes management, integrating lifestyle changes, medication as needed, regular monitoring, and ongoing education and support, can help individuals maintain their garden of health. This holistic strategy empowers individuals to take control of their diabetes, fostering a life of balance and wellness. The selection and implementation of treatment strategies for managing blood sugar and diabetes is akin to choosing the right tools and techniques to nurture and restore balance. Just as a gardener must understand the specific needs of their garden, from the soil to the climate, individuals navigating the management of diabetes must be equipped with a clear understanding of the various strategies at their disposal. This overview aims to shed light on these tools, presenting them in a way that's accessible and actionable.

**Lifestyle Adjustments:** The cornerstone of managing diabetes lies in lifestyle changes. These modifications are like the daily care we give to our garden, essential for its overall health and resilience.

**Diet:** Emphasizing a diet rich in whole foods, fiber, and nutrients while limiting processed foods, sugars, and unhealthy fats can help manage blood sugar levels.

**Exercise:** Regular physical activity helps improve insulin sensitivity, making it easier for your body to manage glucose levels.

**Weight Management:** Achieving and maintaining a healthy weight is crucial, as excess weight can contribute to insulin resistance.

**Medication:** Sometimes, lifestyle changes alone are not enough to control blood sugar levels. Medications can be thought of as supplements for our garden, providing additional resources when natural methods fall short.

**Metformin:** Often the first medication prescribed for type 2 diabetes, metformin helps lower glucose production in the liver and improve insulin sensitivity.

**Insulin Therapy:** Some individuals may require insulin therapy to help their body use glucose effectively. This is akin to adding a new, vital nutrient to the soil to aid in the absorption and use of essential elements. **Other Medications:** Various other medications can be prescribed to help manage blood sugar levels, each with specific roles in the treatment plan, much like different fertilizers or amendments that address specific soil deficiencies.

**Monitoring Blood Sugar:** Regular monitoring is critical in managing diabetes, acting as the garden journal where observations about plant health, soil condition, and the effects of weather are recorded. It helps track the effectiveness of the treatment plan and any need for adjustments.

**Home Blood Glucose Monitoring:** Using a home glucose monitor to track blood sugar levels can inform daily decisions about diet, activity, and medication.

**Continuous Glucose Monitoring (CGM):** Some people may benefit from a continuous glucose monitor (CGM), which offers real-time information on blood sugar levels all day long.

**Education and Support:** Understanding diabetes and how to manage it is crucial. Support groups and educational programs can be likened to gardening clubs or classes, where sharing knowledge and experiences enriches everyone's understanding and skills.

**Regular Medical Check-Ups:** Routine visits to healthcare professionals ensure that the treatment plan remains effective and adjusts to changing needs over time, much like periodic soil tests ensure the garden remains fertile and balanced.

# NUTRITION AND DIABETES MANAGEMENT

## *The Role of Carbohydrates*

In our journey to understand the garden of our health, the role of carbohydrates stands out as both foundational and nuanced. Carbohydrates, or carbs as they're often called, are like the sunlight for our garden—they provide the primary energy source that fuels our body's daily activities. However, not all sunlight is the same, and similarly, carbohydrates come in various forms, each affecting our garden's health in different ways. The role of carbohydrates in managing diabetes is akin to managing the amount and type of sunlight our garden receives. Just as too much direct sunlight can scorch our plants, too many simple sugars can harm our health. Yet, just as plants need sunlight to grow, our bodies need carbohydrates to function. The secret lies in choosing the right types of carbs, in the right amounts, to nourish our garden without overwhelming it.

**Types of Carbohydrates:** In general, there are three primary categories of carbohydrates: sugars, starches, and fiber. Every one has a distinct function in our diet.

- **Sugars:** These are the most basic type of carbs and provide you energy right away.
- Imagine them as the morning light that wakes up the garden. However, too much can overwhelm the plants, akin to the effects of excessive simple sugars on our body.
- **Starches:** Think of starches as the full sunlight of the day. They are complex carbohydrates that the body breaks down into glucose, providing sustained energy. Foods like potatoes, grains, and legumes are rich in starches.

- **Fiber:** Fiber is the part of plant foods that the body can't digest. It's akin to the shade in our garden, necessary for balance. Fiber helps control how sugars are used by the body, which in turn helps to control blood sugar and hunger.

**Impact on Blood Sugar:** Understanding how different types of carbohydrates impact blood sugar is crucial for managing diabetes. Simple sugars cause quick spikes in blood glucose levels, while complex carbohydrates, like those found in whole grains and vegetables, result in a slower, more manageable rise.

**The Importance of Balance:** Incorporating a balance of carbohydrates into the diet is essential. This doesn't mean avoiding all carbs, as they're a vital energy source, but choosing the right types and amounts.

- **Choosing Complex Carbohydrates:** Opting for whole, unprocessed carbohydrate sources with low GI values can support blood sugar management. These foods provide not only energy but also essential nutrients and fiber.
- **Portion Control:** Even with healthier carbs, portion control is key. It's about finding the right amount of sunlight that our garden needs—not too little but not too much.

## *Understanding Carbohydrates: Types and Management in a Diabetes-Friendly Diet*

Carving out a diabetes-friendly diet starts with a fundamental understanding of carbohydrates, the main source of energy for our bodies, and yet, in the context of diabetes, a nutrient to be approached with mindfulness and knowledge. This journey into the world of carbohydrates is akin to learning the language of our garden's needs, enabling us to nourish it thoughtfully and effectively.

### The Spectrum of Carbohydrates

Sugars, starches, and fibers that can be found in fruits, cereals, vegetables, and dairy products are known as carbohydrates, or just carbs for short. They are classified into two main types: simple and complex, a distinction based on their chemical structure and the speed at which they are digested and absorbed.

- **Simple Carbohydrates:** The body uses simple carbohydrates, sometimes known as sugars, for energy quickly and readily. They are found naturally in foods like fruits (fructose) and milk (lactose) but are also added to many processed foods in the form of table sugar (sucrose) or high-fructose corn syrup. While they can provide a quick energy source, they often lead to rapid spikes in blood glucose levels, which can be particularly problematic for individuals managing diabetes.
- **Complex Carbohydrates:** The longer molecular chains of these carbohydrates make them harder for the body to absorb and break down. Because of the delayed digestion, glucose is released into the bloodstream more gradually, providing a more consistent supply of energy. Legumes, starchy vegetables, and whole grains are good sources of complex carbs.

### The Role of Fiber

Fiber is one type of complex carbohydrate that needs specific consideration. Fiber is not broken down by the body way other carbohydrates are. As it moves through the digestive system, it aids in controlling how sugars are used by the body as well as appetite and blood sugar levels. There are two types of fiber: soluble (dissolves in water) and insoluble (does not dissolve in water) which can help food pass through your digestive system more easily and encourage regularity.

### Managing Carbohydrates in a Diabetes-Friendly Diet

Understanding and managing carbohydrates is not about elimination but about balance and choice. Here are some strategies for incorporating carbs in a way that supports blood sugar management:

- **Choose Low-GI Foods:** Choose for carbohydrates that absorb and digest more slowly. Good options include whole grains, legumes, some fruits, and non-starchy veggies.
- **Watch Portion Sizes:** When taken in excess, even healthful carbohydrates can cause blood sugar increases. Pay attention to portion proportions, particularly when consuming foods that have a higher GI.
- **Balance Your Meals:** Incorporate a balance of carbohydrates, protein, and healthy fats in each meal to help moderate blood sugar levels. Protein and fat have little to no direct impact on blood glucose levels and can help you feel full and satisfied.
- **Don't Forget About Fiber:** High-fiber foods not only help control blood sugar levels but also contribute to overall digestive health. Aim to include a variety of fiber-rich foods in your diet, such as vegetables, fruits, whole grains, and legumes.
- **Consider the Whole Meal:** When evaluating the impact of carbohydrates on blood sugar, consider the entire meal. The digestion and absorption of carbs can be affected by the presence of protein, fat, and fiber.

## Navigating the Glycemic Index and Glycemic Load

Understanding the Glycemic Index (GI) and Glycemic Load (GL) becomes crucial, much like knowing exactly how much sunlight and water each plant needs. These scientific measures help us predict how different carbohydrate-containing foods impact our blood sugar levels, allowing for a more tailored approach to managing diabetes.

**The Glycemic Index:** Carbohydrates are ranked by the GI from 0 to 100 according to how quickly they affect blood sugar levels. Foods having a high GI (more than 70) absorb and digest more quickly, which results in a sudden rise in blood sugar. For example, white bread has a GI of around 75, while a regular soda's GI can be as high as 63. On the other hand, foods with a low GI (55 or less) absorb more slowly, causing blood sugar levels to rise gradually. Lentils, for instance, boast a GI of approximately 32, and apples are rated around 36.

- **High-GI Foods:** These often include processed or refined foods devoid of fiber. A slice of white bread (GI of 75) or a bowl of cornflakes (GI of 93) can lead to rapid spikes in blood sugar, akin to a sudden flood in a garden that overwhelms the plants.
- **Low-GI Foods:** Foods rich in fiber, such as whole grains, legumes, and non-starchy vegetables, generally have a lower GI. For example, barley has a GI of about 28, and chickpeas come in at around 30. Incorporating these foods into your diet is similar to providing your garden with a steady, gentle supply of water and sunlight, ensuring the plants grow steadily without the risk of damage.

**The Glycemic Load:** The GL refines the GI by accounting for the amount of carbohydrates in a standard serving of food, giving a more accurate picture of a food's impact on blood sugar levels. The formula to calculate GL is (GI × the amount of carbohydrate per serving) / 100. This measure helps us understand not just the type of carbohydrate we're consuming but also how much of it.

- **Calculating Glycemic Load:** For example, if you eat a medium apple with a GI of 36 and containing about 25 grams of carbohydrates, the GL would be (36 × 25) / 100 = 9. This low GL indicates a small impact on blood sugar.

- **Interpreting Glycemic Load:** A GL of 10 or under is considered low, meaning it has a minor effect on blood sugar levels. A GL between 11 and 19 is medium, and a GL of 20 or above is high. For instance, a serving of watermelon has a GI of 72 but a low GL of 7.2 due to its high water content and relatively low carbohydrate content per serving.

## The Role of Proteins

Delving deeper into the role of proteins within our nutritional garden reveals the multifaceted ways in which this essential nutrient supports our body, particularly in the context of managing diabetes. Proteins, with their complex structure and diverse functions, are akin to the varied species in a garden that contribute to its overall health and resilience. Their importance in a balanced diet cannot be overstated, especially for those navigating the challenges of diabetes

### Building and Repair

First and foremost, proteins are the building blocks of the body. Just as bricks and mortar come together to build a sturdy wall, amino acids—the components of proteins—combine to form muscle, bone, skin, and other tissues. This structural role is crucial not only for growth and development but also for the repair and maintenance of body tissues. For individuals with diabetes, this repair function is vital, considering the risk of complications that can arise from the condition, affecting various organs and systems.

- **Muscle Maintenance:** Regular protein intake helps maintain muscle mass, which is particularly important for metabolism. A robust metabolism can aid in managing body weight, a key factor in controlling diabetes.
- **Healing and Recovery:** For those with diabetes, healing from wounds or surgery can be slower. Adequate protein intake supports the body's healing process, ensuring that repairs are made efficiently and effectively.

### Hormonal and Enzymatic Functions

Proteins play a critical role in the creation and action of enzymes and hormones. These proteins act as messengers and catalysts, guiding and speeding up nearly every biochemical process in the body. In the garden analogy, enzymes and hormones are like the water and nutrients that facilitate plant growth; they ensure that everything runs smoothly and efficiently.

- **Insulin Production:** Insulin itself is a protein, and its production and function are essential for blood sugar regulation. Understanding the dietary intake of proteins and its effect on insulin is key for individuals with diabetes.
- **Digestive Enzymes:** Proteins are responsible for the formation of many digestive enzymes, which help break down the food we eat into absorbable nutrients, supporting overall digestion and nutrient uptake.

**Impact on Blood Sugar and Satiety**

One of the most significant aspects of protein intake for diabetes management is its effect on blood sugar levels and satiety. Unlike carbohydrates, proteins do not cause quick spikes in blood glucose levels. Instead, they provide a more sustained source of energy, helping to stabilize blood sugar levels over time.

- **Blood Sugar Stability:** By promoting a slow and steady release of glucose into the bloodstream, proteins can help prevent the blood sugar spikes and crashes often associated with carbohydrate-rich meals.
- **Satiety and Weight Management:** Proteins are more satiating than carbohydrates or fats, meaning they can help you feel full longer. This can reduce overall calorie intake, aiding in weight management—a crucial aspect of diabetes management.

**Choosing the Right Proteins**

The source of protein is as important as the quantity. For a healthful diet, especially for those managing diabetes, it's essential to choose proteins that are low in saturated fat and calories.

- **Lean Animal Proteins:** Options such as chicken breast, turkey, lean cuts of beef, and fish are excellent choices. Fish, particularly fatty types like salmon, also provide omega-3 fatty acids, which have cardiovascular benefits.
- **Plant-based Proteins:** Beans, lentils, chickpeas, tofu, and tempeh are not only good sources of protein but also fiber, which can further aid in blood sugar management. Plant-based proteins often come with lower levels of saturated fats and cholesterol, making them a heart-healthy choice.

**The Broader Context**

Integrating proteins into a diabetes-friendly diet involves considering the broader nutritional context—balancing protein intake with healthy fats, carbohydrates, vitamins, and minerals to ensure a holistic approach to health and well-being. This balance is crucial, much like the ecological balance in a garden, where diverse plant life supports a healthy, vibrant ecosystem.

## The Importance of Fats

Fats, often unjustly vilified in the narrative of nutrition, are akin to the foundational elements of a garden's ecosystem, such as the organic matter that enriches the soil or the pollinators that ensure the garden's productivity. They play a crucial role in our health, serving as a major source of energy, aiding in the absorption of vital nutrients, and providing insulation and protection for our organs. Just as a garden thrives with a diversity of elements, our bodies require a balanced intake of various types of fats to function optimally, especially in the context of managing conditions like diabetes.

**The Vital Roles of Fats**

- **Energy Source:** Fats are the most energy-dense macronutrient, providing 9 calories per gram, compared to 4 calories per gram from proteins and carbohydrates. They are like the slow-burning logs in a fire, offering sustained energy over longer periods, crucial for endurance and daily functioning.

- **Nutrient Absorption:** Certain vitamins, namely A, D, E, and K, are fat-soluble, meaning they require fat for their absorption into the body. Consuming fats alongside these vitamins ensures that our "garden" can absorb all the "nutrients" it needs to thrive.
- **Cell Structure and Function:** Fats are essential components of cell membranes, influencing their flexibility and the movement of materials in and out of cells. This is akin to the garden's boundaries and paths, which determine how nutrients and water circulate.
- **Hormone Production:** Many hormones are derived from cholesterol, a type of fat. These hormones regulate a vast array of physiological processes, from metabolism to immune function, similar to how a garden's health is influenced by the balance of natural hormones in plants and soil.

## Understanding Different Types of Fats

Just as gardens require a balance of various elements, our bodies benefit from a balanced intake of different types of fats. However, not all fats are created equal:

- **Unsaturated Fats:** These are the "heroes" of the fat world, including both monounsaturated and polyunsaturated fats. They can improve blood cholesterol levels, easing inflammation and stabilizing heart rhythms. Monounsaturated fats are found in olive oil, avocados, and nuts, while polyunsaturated fats are abundant in fish, flaxseeds, and walnuts. They're akin to the beneficial organisms in the garden that promote health and vitality.
- **Saturated Fats:** Found in red meat, butter, and coconut oil, saturated fats can raise LDL (bad) cholesterol levels in the blood, contributing to heart disease. Like the occasional pest in the garden, a small amount can be managed, but an overabundance can lead to problems.
- **Trans Fats:** These are the true villains in the story of fats. Often found in processed and fried foods, trans fats can raise LDL cholesterol levels while lowering HDL (good) cholesterol, increasing the risk of heart disease. In our garden analogy, they are akin to the invasive species that disrupt the ecosystem's balance.

## Balancing Fat Intake

In managing diabetes and promoting heart health, the quality and quantity of fats consumed are crucial. Opting for unsaturated fats over saturated and trans fats can support insulin sensitivity and reduce the risk of heart disease. This is akin to nurturing a garden by choosing plants that enrich the soil, support pollinators, and maintain ecological balance.

Incorporating healthy fats into the diet doesn't just provide metabolic benefits; it also enhances the flavors and textures of food, making meals more satisfying and enjoyable—much like the way diverse plantings can enhance the beauty and productivity of a garden.

## Understanding Umami

Umami is a taste that signifies the presence of glutamate, an amino acid that occurs naturally in many foods. When proteins are broken down through cooking, fermentation, or ripening, glutamate is released, giving foods a distinct savory flavor that deepens the overall eating experience. This flavor enhancer does more than just tantalize the taste buds; it plays a crucial role in satiety, the sense of fullness, which can aid in managing weight and regulating appetite—key factors in diabetes management.

## Sources of Umami

The natural sources of umami are varied, each bringing its unique profile to the table:

- **Tomatoes:** Ripe tomatoes are rich in glutamate, with sun-dried tomatoes offering a concentrated source of umami. They're like the full sun that bathes the garden, enriching it with vitality.

- **Mushrooms:** Especially varieties like shiitake, mushrooms are umami powerhouses. They add depth to dishes, akin to the rich, fertile soil that nurtures the garden.
- **Aged Cheeses:** Parmesan is a prime example of umami in dairy, where aging concentrates the glutamate.
- **Seaweed:** Often used in Japanese cuisine, seaweed is not only a sustainable source of umami but also brings a bounty of minerals, reflecting the diverse microelements that benefit the garden.
- **Fermented Foods:** Soy sauce, miso, and fermented fish sauce are traditional ways to add umami to dishes. Fermentation, like composting in the garden, transforms basic ingredients into rich sources of flavor and nutrients.

### The Role of Umami in Health and Diabetes Management

The significance of umami extends beyond culinary pleasure, offering benefits particularly relevant to diabetes management:

- **Enhances Satiety:** Umami flavors can increase the feeling of fullness, which helps in controlling portion sizes and reducing overall calorie intake.
- **Promotes Healthy Eating:** By enriching the flavor profile of foods without adding excessive calories, fats, or sugars, umami can make healthy foods more palatable and satisfying.
- **Nutrient Absorption:** Foods rich in umami are often sources of important nutrients and antioxidants, supporting overall health and well-being.

### Culinary Strategies to Incorporate Umami

Incorporating umami into your diet doesn't require complicated recipes or exotic ingredients. Simple strategies can enhance your meals with this savory depth:

- **Use Tomato Paste:** A spoonful of tomato paste can deepen the flavors of soups, stews, and sauces.
- **Incorporate Mushrooms:** Adding mushrooms to dishes not only brings umami but also texture and nutrition.
- **Experiment with Fermented Condiments:** A dash of soy sauce or miso can transform a bland dish into a savory delight.
- **Choose Aged Cheeses:** Sprinkling a bit of grated Parmesan on dishes can add a burst of flavor without the need for large quantities.

## *Essential Vitamins and Minerals for Managing Diabetes*

Incorporating a diet rich in essential vitamins and minerals is like nurturing a garden with the right balance of nutrients, sunlight, and water. Each plays a unique role in maintaining the body's health, supporting metabolic processes, and ensuring the garden of our body can thrive, even in the face of challenges like managing diabetes. Just as certain nutrients in the soil support the growth and health of plants, vitamins and minerals play critical roles in supporting our body's metabolic processes, including the regulation of blood sugar levels. Understanding these essential vitamins and minerals, and knowing how to incorporate them into our diet, is akin to a gardener knowing exactly what their garden needs to flourish.

**Magnesium:** Magnesium is like the water that quenches the garden's thirst. This mineral is essential for more than 300 enzymatic processes in the body, including the metabolism of glucose. Research has demonstrated a correlation between reduced levels of insulin and fasting glucose and a higher dietary magnesium consumption. Whole grains, nuts, seeds, and dark leafy greens are among the foods high in magnesium. Including these meals can help lower blood sugar and increase insulin sensitivity.

**Chromium:** Chromium works in the garden of our body much like pollinators, helping to enhance insulin's action and facilitate glucose to enter the cells. This trace element may help some people with type 2 diabetes improve their blood sugar control. Sources of chromium include broccoli, potatoes, meats, and whole-grain products. Though chromium supplements are available, it's best to consult with a healthcare provider before starting them, as the whole food sources often provide a balanced intake.

**Vitamin E:** Vitamin E, with its antioxidant properties, is like the mulch that protects the garden, guarding the body's cells against damage and supporting immune health. This is particularly important for those with diabetes, as higher levels of oxidative stress are common.

**Vitamin D:** Vitamin D is the sunlight that strengthens the plants. It's essential for bone health and immune function and plays a role in insulin production and sensitivity. Low levels of vitamin D are common in people with type 2 diabetes. Fatty fish, like salmon and mackerel, fortified foods, and sunlight exposure can help boost vitamin D levels.

**Omega-3 Fatty Acids:** Omega-3 fatty acids are like the beneficial insects of the garden, providing protection and support to the plants. They are not vitamins or minerals but are essential fats that play a critical role in heart health, which is crucial for individuals with diabetes, who are at an increased risk for heart disease. Sources of omega-3s include fatty fish, flaxseeds, chia seeds, and walnuts.

**Vitamin B12:** Vitamin B12 is akin to the compost that enriches the soil, supporting the health of the garden's nervous system and aiding in the production of energy. Metformin, a common diabetes medication, can sometimes lead to a deficiency in this crucial vitamin. Sources of B12 include meat, fish, poultry, and dairy products. For those on a plant-based diet, fortified foods or supplements might be necessary.

**Zinc:** Zinc is like the stakes that support young plants, vital for the immune system's health and wound healing, processes that can be compromised in individuals managing diabetes. Foods rich in zinc include beef, poultry, seafood, beans, and nuts.

# DEBUNKING MYTHS AROUND DIABETES

The battle against diabetes is not just fought with medication and diet changes; it's also a battle against misinformation. As we delve into debunking myths around diabetes, it's crucial to distinguish between what's commonly believed and what science tells us, especially regarding genetic vs. lifestyle influences.

## *Common Misconceptions*

### Myth 1: Eating Too Much Sugar Causes Diabetes

The belief that consuming too much sugar directly causes diabetes is overly simplistic and misleading. While a diet high in calories from any source contributes to weight gain—a risk factor for type 2 diabetes—it's not sugar alone that's the culprit. Type 2 diabetes develops when the body becomes resistant to insulin or when the pancreas stops producing enough insulin. However, a diet high in refined sugars can contribute to insulin resistance, thus indirectly affecting diabetes risk.

### Myth 2: Diabetes Is Not a Serious Condition

Some individuals believe that diabetes is a minor medical condition that is readily treated with medicine. This misconception undermines the serious nature of diabetes, which, if not managed properly, can lead to severe complications such as heart disease, stroke, kidney failure, blindness, and lower limb amputation. Understanding the gravity of diabetes is crucial for motivating individuals to adopt healthier lifestyle choices.

### Myth 3: Diabetics Can't Eat Carbohydrates

Carbohydrates are often seen as the enemy for individuals with diabetes. However, the body needs carbohydrates for energy. The key is to select healthier options like whole grains, fruits, and vegetables, and to manage portion sizes. Completely eliminating carbohydrates can lead to other health issues and deprive the body of essential nutrients.

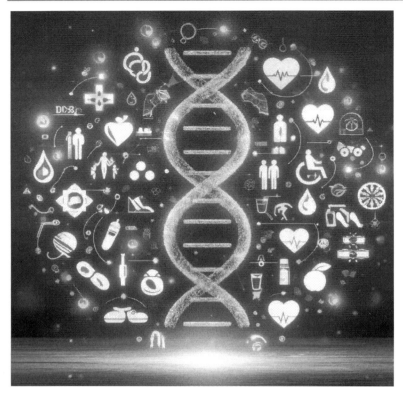

### The Role of Genetics in Diabetes

It's undeniable that genetics play a role in the development of type 2 diabetes. If you have a family history of diabetes, your risk of developing the condition is higher. Scientists have identified various genetic markers that are associated with an increased susceptibility to diabetes. However, having these genetic markers does not guarantee that you will develop diabetes; lifestyle factors also play a significant role.

### Lifestyle's Impact on Diabetes

Type 2 diabetes risk is significantly influenced by lifestyle factors. It is important to consider factors including body weight, physical activity, and food. For example, weight gain and insulin resistance may result from a diet heavy in processed foods and low in fruits, vegetables, and whole grains. Physical inactivity makes the issue worse by contributing to an increase in body fat, particularly in the abdominal region, which is a known risk factor for diabetes. On the other hand, even for those who have a genetic tendency, regular physical activity combined with a healthy diet can greatly lower the chance of acquiring type 2 diabetes.

### The Power of Lifestyle Changes

Evidence from numerous studies underscores the effectiveness of lifestyle changes in managing and even reversing type 2 diabetes. For example, the Diabetes Prevention Program study in the United States demonstrated that lifestyle interventions, including moderate weight loss and regular physical activity, reduced the development of diabetes by 58% over three years. This finding is a testament to the power of lifestyle choices in influencing health outcomes, emphasizing that while genetics cannot be changed, lifestyle is modifiable.

### Integrating Genetic Knowledge and Lifestyle Modifications

Understanding the interplay between genetics and lifestyle is crucial for effective diabetes management and prevention. While we cannot alter our genetic makeup, we can adopt healthier lifestyles to mitigate the genetic risk. This approach involves:

- Choosing a diet rich in whole foods, low in processed foods, and balanced in macronutrients.
- Getting regular exercise, with a weekly minimum of 150 minutes of moderate aerobic exercise.
- Monitoring and maintaining a healthy body weight.
- Regularly checking blood glucose levels to ensure they are within the target range.

# Part II
# Dietary Strategies for Managing Diabetes

## CRAFTING A DIABETES-FRIENDLY DIET

### *Deciphering the Food Pyramid*

Understanding the food pyramid in the context of managing diabetes is akin to learning the intricate layers of a thriving garden ecosystem. Each layer or section of the pyramid serves a specific purpose, contributing to the overall health and balance of the diet, just as each layer of a garden contributes to its biodiversity and resilience. Here, we delve deep into the structure of the food pyramid, exploring how each segment plays a pivotal role in crafting a diabetes-friendly diet.

**The Foundation: Whole Grains, Fruits, and Vegetables**

At the base of the food pyramid lie the whole grains, fruits, and vegetables. This foundation is crucial for a diabetes-friendly diet, emphasizing the importance of fiber, vitamins, and minerals.

- **Whole Grains:** Whole grains are the bedrock of healthy eating, providing slow-releasing energy that helps maintain stable blood sugar levels. Nutrients like iron, fiber, and B vitamins are found in foods like brown rice, quinoa, barley, and whole wheat. The fiber in whole grains aids digestion and helps control blood sugar by slowing the absorption of glucose into the bloodstream. Incorporating a variety of whole grains into meals ensures a steady supply of energy and nutrients, much like a rich, fertile soil supports diverse plant life.

- **Fruits and Vegetables:** Rich in colors and flavors, fruits and vegetables are akin to the diverse flora that populates a garden, providing a range of nutrients and antioxidants that protect the body from oxidative stress, a condition often exacerbated by diabetes. The fiber content in these foods not only aids in blood sugar management but also supports digestive health. Leafy greens, berries, citrus fruits, and cruciferous vegetables are particularly beneficial, offering high nutritional value with lower glucose impact. Eating a rainbow of fruits and vegetables ensures a wide range of antioxidants and phytochemicals, akin to cultivating a garden with a variety of plants to promote ecological balance.

### The Second Layer: Lean Proteins and Dairy

Moving up the pyramid, lean proteins and dairy products form the next layer, supporting muscle health and bone density.

- **Lean Proteins:** Proteins are the structural components of our body, much like the sturdy trees and shrubs that give structure to a garden. Lean meats, poultry, fish, and plant-based proteins such as lentils, beans, and tofu provide the essential amino acids needed for repair and growth, without the excess fat that can exacerbate insulin resistance. Including a source of lean protein in every meal can help maintain muscle mass, which is crucial for metabolism and weight management.
- **Dairy:** Dairy products, especially those low in fat, are rich in calcium and vitamin D, essential for bone health. In the context of a diabetes-friendly diet, choosing low-fat or non-fat options can provide these benefits without the added risk of weight gain. Fortified dairy alternatives, such as almond milk or soy milk, can also be excellent sources of these nutrients, offering variety for those with dietary restrictions.

### The Top Layer: Fats, Oils, and Sweets

At the peak of the food pyramid are fats, oils, and sweets, elements to be used sparingly in a diabetes-friendly diet.

- **Healthy Fats:** Not all fats are created equal. Monounsaturated and polyunsaturated fats, found in olive oil, avocados, nuts, and seeds, are like the beneficial insects of the garden, supporting health without harming the balance. These fats can improve heart health and enhance the absorption of fat-soluble vitamins, making them an important part of diabetes management. However, moderation is key, as all fats are high in calories.
- **Sweets and Added Sugars:** Just as a garden might have a few decorative elements that don't contribute to its productivity, sweets and added sugars can be occasional indulgences in a balanced diet. However, for individuals managing diabetes, these foods should be consumed rarely, as they can cause rapid spikes in blood sugar levels. Finding natural ways to satisfy sweet cravings, such as through fruits or small amounts of dark chocolate, can be a healthier approach to including these flavors in the diet.

### Hydration: The Underlying Necessity

Beneath all layers of the food pyramid lies the essential need for hydration. Water is to the body what rain is to a garden — absolutely essential. Staying well-hydrated helps manage blood sugar levels, aids digestion, and supports overall health. Herbal teas and water-infused with fruits or cucumber can also be refreshing ways to meet hydration needs without adding sugar.

## *Mastering Serving Sizes*

It's crucial to tailor dietary choices and serving sizes to individual needs, often with the guidance of healthcare professionals. Let's refine the earlier information with a focus on precision and alignment with recommendations often suggested for type 2 diabetes management.

### Tailoring the Food Pyramid for Type 2 Diabetes

For individuals managing type 2 diabetes, the food pyramid is adjusted to emphasize foods that support blood sugar control and minimize those that can cause spikes.

- **Vegetables:** Non-starchy vegetables should be the foundation, with recommendations often suggesting at least 3-5 servings per day. A serving size is generally 1 cup raw or 1/2 cup cooked.

- **Fruits:** Whole fruits are preferred over juices due to their fiber content, with a typical serving being a small piece (like an apple) or 1/2 cup chopped. Limit to 2-4 servings per day, considering their carbohydrate content.
- **Whole Grains:** Opt for whole grains over processed ones to enhance fiber intake. A serving size might be 1 slice of whole-grain bread or 1/2 cup of cooked grains like quinoa or brown rice. Guidelines often suggest 3-6 servings per day, distributed throughout to avoid blood sugar spikes.
- **Proteins:** Lean protein choices are recommended, with a serving size of 2-3 ounces of cooked meats (about the size of a deck of cards) or a similar portion of plant-based protein. Including some protein at each meal can aid in satiety and blood sugar stabilization.
- **Dairy:** Low-fat or non-fat dairy options are preferred to manage calorie and fat intake. A serving is 1 cup of milk or yogurt. Limit to 2-3 servings per day.

## Specific Serving Sizes and Daily Intake

When managing type 2 diabetes, it's not just about the type of food but also the quantity and the overall balance of nutrients throughout the day.

- **Carbohydrates:** Total daily intake should be consistent. The American Diabetes Association suggests that starting with about 45-60 grams of carbohydrates per meal is a good place to begin, adjusting based on blood sugar monitoring and individual needs.
- **Fiber:** Aim for at least 25 to 30 grams of fiber per day, which can help manage blood sugar levels. This is naturally covered by consuming ample vegetables, fruits, and whole grains.
- **Proteins:** Incorporate lean proteins to make up 10-20% of your daily calorie intake. This helps with satiety without significantly impacting blood sugar levels.
- **Fats:** Focus on healthy fats, particularly those rich in omega-3 fatty acids, while limiting saturated and trans fats. Total fat intake should be tailored to individual caloric needs and usually should not exceed 30% of total daily calories.

## Adjusting for Individual Needs

It's crucial for individuals with type 2 diabetes to work with healthcare providers to determine the best dietary plan for their specific health status, lifestyle, and metabolic needs. Factors such as age, activity level, weight goals, and other health conditions play a significant role in defining the ideal dietary approach.

Monitoring blood sugar levels in response to meals is an effective way to understand how different types and amounts of food affect individual glucose control. This ongoing process of adjustment and learning allows for a tailored approach that supports both blood sugar management and overall health.

In managing type 2 diabetes, precision in dietary choices, serving sizes, and nutrient balance is not a one-size-fits-all matter. It's a personalized strategy developed over time, akin to cultivating a unique garden that flourishes under specific care and conditions.

## *Navigating Low Blood Sugar Levels: Strategies for Stability*

Navigating the realm of low blood sugar levels, or hypoglycemia, requires a nuanced understanding and a strategic approach, much like navigating a dense forest with its varying landscapes and unpredictable weather patterns. Hypoglycemia presents a significant challenge for those managing diabetes, yet, with the right knowledge and tools, it can be managed effectively, ensuring stability and well-being.

## Understanding Hypoglycemia

At its core, hypoglycemia occurs when blood sugar levels fall below the normal range, typically under 70 mg/dL. It's akin to the garden's water levels dropping too low—the vital sustenance for plants diminishes, signaling an urgent need for replenishment. Recognizing the early signs is crucial for prompt action. Symptoms may include:

- Shakiness or nervousness
- Sweating or chills
- Irritability or impatience
- Confusion or difficulty concentrating

- Rapid heartbeat
- Hunger or nausea
- Fatigue
- Blurred vision

## Immediate Steps for Raising Blood Sugar

When signs of hypoglycemia appear, quick-acting carbohydrates are the immediate remedy, acting like emergency rain showers that quickly revive the garden. These include:

- Glucose tablets or gels, specifically designed for rapid absorption
- Fruit juice or regular (not diet) soda, about 4 ounces
- Hard candies, jellybeans, or gummy candies, though absorption rates may vary
- Honey or syrup, about a tablespoon

The goal is to consume 15-20 grams of quick-acting carbohydrates and then recheck blood sugar levels after 15 minutes, repeating the process if levels remain low. This strategy is the equivalent of methodically watering parched plants until they show signs of revival.

## Sustained Blood Sugar Management

After stabilizing blood sugar with quick-acting carbs, it's important to ensure lasting stability. If the next meal is more than an hour away, follow up with a more substantial snack or meal that includes both carbohydrates and protein, akin to adding a layer of mulch to help retain the garden's moisture. Examples include:

- A small sandwich with lean meat
- Crackers with cheese
- A handful of nuts and a piece of fruit
- Yogurt with a sprinkle of nuts or granola

## Preventing Hypoglycemia

Prevention is always preferable to treatment, like preparing the garden before the dry season begins. Strategies include:

- **Regular Monitoring:** Keeping a close eye on blood sugar levels allows for timely adjustments to diet, activity, and medication. Think of it as the daily walk-through of the garden to check soil moisture levels.
- **Balanced Meals and Snacks:** Incorporating a mix of carbohydrates, proteins, and fats in each meal or snack helps ensure a steady release of glucose into the bloodstream, similar to a well-balanced ecosystem that self-regulates and sustains its inhabitants.
- **Understanding Carbohydrate Counting:** Being aware of how different types and amounts of carbohydrates affect blood sugar levels can help in planning meals and snacks to prevent lows.
- **Adjusting for Physical Activity:** Physical activity can lower blood sugar levels for several hours afterward. Adjusting carbohydrate intake or medication before exercise can help maintain stable blood sugar levels, much like adjusting water levels in anticipation of a hot day.

## Education and Communication

Educating oneself about the nuances of managing diabetes and hypoglycemia is critical, as is clear communication with healthcare providers. It's akin to seeking the wisdom of experienced gardeners or horticulturists who can offer guidance tailored to your garden's specific needs.

- **Workshops and Support Groups:** Joining diabetes education programs or support groups provides valuable insights and shared experiences from others navigating similar paths.
- **Healthcare Team Collaboration:** Regular check-ins with a healthcare team ensure that the management plan remains effective and adjusts to changing needs, just as a garden evolves over time.

## Technology in Management

Advancements in diabetes management technology, such as continuous glucose monitors (CGMs), offer real-time insights into blood sugar levels, acting like sophisticated irrigation systems that monitor and adjust water levels as needed, ensuring the garden remains vibrant and healthy.

**Emotional and Psychological Considerations**

Managing hypoglycemia also involves addressing the emotional and psychological impacts. The fear of low blood sugar can be significant, affecting quality of life. Building a support network, practicing mindfulness, and seeking professional counseling if needed are important steps, much like cultivating a garden provides a sanctuary for relaxation and reflection.

In navigating low blood sugar levels, the goal is to maintain a balance, ensuring that the body, like a well-tended garden, thrives in all conditions. Through a combination of immediate action, preventative strategies, education, and the use of technology, individuals can manage hypoglycemia effectively, leading to a healthier and more balanced life.

# ENHANCING YOUR DIETARY APPROACH

Enhancing your dietary approach to managing diabetes is akin to refining your gardening skills: it's about fine-tuning the balance of elements to foster the most healthful and enjoyable environment possible. Let's delve deeper into how principles of portion control, diversity on your plate, mindful eating practices, and tips for elevating the dining experience can act as the cornerstones of conscious consumption, mirroring the meticulous care a gardener puts into nurturing their garden.

## *Portion Control Principles*

Portion control is the cornerstone of a strategic approach to managing diabetes, akin to the meticulous attention a gardener pays to the exact requirements of sunlight, water, and nutrients necessary for each plant's growth. It transcends the simple concept of eating less and delves into the nuanced understanding of quantity and its impact on the body's blood sugar levels and overall health. This principle is about nurturing your body with the right amount of food, much like a garden thrives under the watchful eye of a knowledgeable gardener.

**Visual Cues for Portion Control**

Visual cues serve as a practical and straightforward method to manage portions without the need for scales or measuring cups, akin to how a gardener intuitively knows how to space plants for optimal growth. For example, envisioning a serving of meat or fish as the size of a deck of cards helps gauge an appropriate portion, providing enough protein for sustenance without overindulgence. Similarly, a fist or a cupped hand can represent a serving size for carbohydrates, such as rice or pasta, offering a visual benchmark that aids in preventing overconsumption, which is crucial for maintaining stable blood sugar levels.

Expanding on this, consider other everyday items as guides for different food groups: a tennis ball for a serving of fruit or a checkbook for a portion of fish. These comparisons become tools in your dietary toolbox, enabling you to build meals that are balanced and in harmony with your body's needs, much like a gardener uses tools to maintain the garden's health.

**The Art of Reading Labels**

Reading labels is an invaluable skill in portion control, offering a window into the contents of packaged foods, akin to reading a detailed map before embarking on a journey. Nutritional labels provide essential information on serving sizes, calorie counts, and nutrient breakdowns, enabling informed decisions about what and how much to eat. This practice equips you with the knowledge to understand how a particular food fits into your daily nutritional goals, similar to how a gardener reads seed packets to understand the growth requirements of different plants.

Moreover, labels can reveal hidden sugars, fats, and sodium levels, allowing you to avoid foods that might spike your blood sugar or undermine your health goals. Just as a gardener would choose seeds that are best suited to their garden's conditions, reading labels helps you choose foods that align with your dietary needs.

**The Plate Method: A Blueprint for Balanced Meals**

The Plate Method is a visual guide that simplifies meal planning, much like a garden layout guides plant placement. By dividing your plate into sections, you can easily create meals that support blood sugar management and overall health. Half of the plate should be filled with non-starchy vegetables, such as leafy greens, peppers, or broccoli, providing a rich source of vitamins, minerals, fiber, and antioxidants with minimal impact on blood sugar levels. These vegetables are the garden's foliage, offering variety and color while enriching the soil (your body) with essential nutrients.

One quarter of the plate should contain lean protein sources, such as chicken, fish, tofu, or beans. Protein is essential for building and repairing tissues and does not directly raise blood sugar levels, making it a crucial component of a diabetes-friendly diet. This section of the plate is akin to the garden's trees and shrubs, providing structure and stability.

Whole grains and starchy vegetables such as corn, sweet potatoes, quinoa, and brown rice are to be served with the remaining quarter. These foods are energy sources, akin to the sun's energy, vital for the garden's growth. They contain fiber, which slows the absorption of glucose into the bloodstream, helping to maintain stable blood sugar levels.

## Diversifying Your Plate: The Spectrum of Nutritious Choices

Expanding the diversity of your diet not only enhances the nutritional value of your meals but also contributes to a more engaging and enjoyable eating experience, mirroring the richness and vitality found in a well-tended, biodiverse garden. Just as a garden bursting with a variety of plants attracts beneficial insects and promotes a healthier ecosystem, a diet filled with a spectrum of foods can boost your overall health, improve metabolic functions, and may even reduce the risk of chronic diseases, including diabetes.

**Colorful Vegetables and Fruits: A Kaleidoscope of Nutrients**

The palette of vegetables and fruits available to us is as broad and vibrant as the colors we see in nature. Each color in our produce is not just for show; it signifies an array of phytonutrients, vitamins, and minerals that play critical roles in our body's functioning.

- **Green:** Leafy greens like spinach, kale, and broccoli are rich in vitamins A, C, E, and K, and contain antioxidants that support eye health and may reduce cancer risk.
- **Red:** Tomatoes, red peppers, and strawberries are loaded with lycopene and anthocyanins, antioxidants that protect against heart disease and improve brain function.
- **Yellow and Orange:** Carrots, sweet potatoes, and oranges are high in beta-carotene, which the body converts to vitamin A, essential for immune function, eye health, and skin integrity.
- **Blue and Purple:** Blueberries, eggplants, and blackberries get their hues from anthocyanins, which have anti-inflammatory properties and can help lower the risk of heart disease, stroke, and cancer.
- **White:** Garlic, onions, and cauliflower may not be colorful, but they're packed with allicin, sulforaphane, and other compounds that have antiviral and anticancer effects.

Including a "rainbow" on your plate not only maximizes the nutritional impact of your meals but also makes dining a more delightful sensory experience.

**Variety of Proteins: Building Blocks of Life**

Proteins are fundamental to building and repairing tissues, making enzymes and hormones, and maintaining bone health. By rotating your protein sources, you ensure a broad spectrum of essential nutrients and reduce the risk of developing intolerances or imbalances associated with consuming too much of one type.

- **Animal-based Proteins:** Options like poultry, fish, and lean meats are high-quality protein sources containing all nine essential amino acids. Fish, especially fatty types like salmon and mackerel, are also rich in omega-3 fatty acids, which are beneficial for heart health.

- **Plant-based Proteins:** Beans, lentils, tofu, tempeh, and quinoa are excellent sources of protein for vegetarians and vegans. They're not only packed with fiber but also with unique phytonutrients and antioxidants. Incorporating plant-based proteins can lower blood pressure, reduce cholesterol levels, and improve kidney function.

**Whole Grains: Foundations of Fiber**

A balanced diet must include whole grains since they are a great source of fiber and nutrients that support healthy digestion and blood sugar regulation. Whole grains, as opposed to refined grains, preserve the entire seed, including the bran, germ, and endosperm, providing the complete range of nutritional advantages.

- **Varieties to Explore:** Far beyond just whole wheat, the world of whole grains includes barley, brown rice, oats, quinoa, bulgur, and millet, each bringing its unique taste, texture, and nutritional profile.
- **Nutritional Powerhouses:** Whole grains are high in dietary fiber, which encourages satiety and supports a healthy gut flora, minerals like iron, magnesium, and selenium, and B vitamins, which are essential for brain function and energy production.

## *Mindful Eating Practices: Savoring Every Bite with Intention*

Mindful eating is about being fully present during meals, appreciating the flavors, textures, and sensations of your food, much like a gardener takes time to sit back and enjoy the beauty of their garden. It involves slowing down and listening to your body's hunger and fullness cues.

- **Eat Slowly:** Take time to chew your food thoroughly, allowing you to savor the flavors and helping with digestion. This practice is like watering plants slowly, ensuring the water seeps deeply into the soil.
- **Eliminate Distractions:** Just as a gardener removes weeds to prevent them from choking out the plants, eliminate distractions during meals to focus on the eating experience.
- **Appreciate Your Food:** Take a moment before eating to appreciate the look and smell of your food, acknowledging the effort that went into preparing it, much like admiring a well-tended garden.

Meal timing is a critical component of effective blood sugar management in type 2 diabetes. By understanding and implementing strategies around optimal meal times, individuals can significantly improve their blood sugar control and overall health. Adopting a consistent eating schedule, focusing on nutritious, balanced meals, and avoiding late-night eating are foundational steps in harmonizing your body's natural rhythms with your diabetes management goals. Meal timing plays a crucial role in managing blood sugar levels. Eating at consistent times each day helps regulate the body's internal clock, improving metabolic functions including insulin release and glucose processing. Disruptions in this rhythm, such as skipping meals or eating late at night, can lead to increased blood glucose levels and decreased insulin sensitivity.

### Morning: The Foundation of Your Day

- **Breakfast:** Often referred to as the most important meal of the day, breakfast should not be skipped, especially by individuals with type 2 diabetes. Consuming a nutritious breakfast within an hour of waking up can jumpstart your metabolism and stabilize blood sugar levels throughout the day. Opt for foods low in glycemic index to avoid spikes in blood glucose.
- **Mid-Morning Snacks:** If you experience a dip in energy or blood sugar levels mid-morning, a small, healthy snack can help. Focus on a combination of protein, healthy fats, and fibers to maintain energy and blood sugar levels until lunch.

### Afternoon: Sustaining Energy and Blood Sugar Levels

- **Lunch:** Eating lunch around the same time each day helps maintain a stable blood glucose level. It should include a balance of carbohydrates, proteins, and fats to ensure sustained energy release and blood sugar control. Avoid heavy, high-carbohydrate meals that can lead to post-lunch blood sugar spikes.
- **Afternoon Snacks:** An afternoon snack is beneficial for preventing late-day energy crashes and managing hunger before dinner. Similar to mid-morning snacks, focus on balanced nutrition.

### Evening: Preparing for Rest

- **Dinner:** Dinner should be consumed at least 2-3 hours before bedtime to ensure proper digestion and to prevent blood sugar spikes during the night. A lighter meal, lower in carbohydrates and calories, can help maintain blood sugar levels and support a healthy weight.
- **Post-Dinner Snacking:** Discourage late-night snacking, especially on foods high in sugar or refined carbohydrates. If a snack is necessary, choose options with minimal impact on blood sugar levels.

### The Impact of Late-Night Eating

Eating late at night can disrupt the natural rhythm of insulin secretion and blood sugar regulation. Late-night meals or snacks can lead to higher fasting blood glucose levels the following morning and increased difficulty in managing blood sugar levels throughout the next day.

### Understanding Your Body's Signals

- Recognizing signs of hunger and fullness can help you make informed decisions about when to eat. Eating in response to true hunger signals, rather than emotional cues or boredom, supports better blood sugar management.
- Monitoring blood sugar levels before and after meals can provide valuable insights

into how your body responds to different foods and meal timings, allowing for more personalized meal planning.

**Practical Tips for Meal Timing**

- **Consistency is Key:** Aim to eat your meals and snacks at the same times daily to help regulate your body's internal clock.
- **Plan Ahead:** Preparing meals and snacks in advance can prevent last-minute choices that might not be conducive to blood sugar management.
- **Listen to Your Body:** Pay attention to your body's hunger and fullness signals to guide your eating schedule, adjusting as necessary to accommodate your daily routine.

# Part III
# The Comprehensive Diabetes-Friendly Food Guide

## FOODS TO EMBRACE

## *Whole Grains and Their Benefits*

Whole grains are not just another food group; they are a critical component of a balanced, diabetes-friendly diet. By making whole grains a staple in your meals, you're not only enjoying delicious and versatile foods but also leveraging their full spectrum of health benefits. Remember, managing diabetes is not just about restricting certain foods; it's about embracing those that nourish and sustain you. Whole grains stand out as one of nature's gifts in this journey, offering a blend of nutrients that support your health on multiple levels.

In the journey towards managing Type 2 Diabetes, understanding the role of whole grains in your diet is like discovering a treasure trove of benefits hidden in plain sight. Whole grains, in their most unrefined state, retain the germ, bran, and endosperm, offering a full spectrum of health advantages, especially for individuals navigating the challenges of diabetes.

## What Are Whole Grains?

Whole grains encompass a variety of foods from all grain families, including wheat, barley, oats, rye, brown rice, millet, quinoa, and others. Unlike their refined counterparts, whole grains are processed minimally, preserving their nutritional integrity.

## Nutritional Profile: A Closer Look

- **Fiber**: The high fiber content in whole grains plays a pivotal role in diabetes management. It slows down the digestion process, leading to a gradual rise in blood sugar levels rather than a spike. This helps in maintaining stable blood glucose levels, crucial for those with Type 2 Diabetes.
- **Vitamins and Minerals**: Whole grains are a powerhouse of essential vitamins and minerals, including B vitamins, iron, magnesium, and selenium. These nutrients support overall health, from energy production to immune defense and bone health.
- **Phytochemicals and Antioxidants**: These compounds are nature's defense against inflammation and oxidative stress, conditions often exacerbated in diabetes. By including whole grains in your diet, you're enlisting natural allies to protect your cells and tissues.

## The Benefits of Whole Grains in a Diabetes-Friendly Diet

1. **Improved Blood Sugar Control**: The fiber in whole grains prevents rapid blood sugar spikes, offering a steadier energy source and aiding in blood sugar regulation.
2. **Heart Health**: People with diabetes have a higher risk of heart disease. Whole grains contribute to heart health by improving cholesterol levels, reducing blood pressure, and diminishing the risk of heart disease.
3. **Weight Management**: The fiber content also contributes to a feeling of fullness, helping prevent overeating and supporting weight management efforts, a crucial aspect of diabetes management.
4. **Digestive Health**: The dietary fiber aids in maintaining gut health, promoting regular bowel movements and helping prevent constipation.

## Incorporating Whole Grains into Your Diet

- **Breakfast**: Start your day with oatmeal or a whole grain cereal. Add some nuts and berries for extra fiber and antioxidants.
- **Lunch and Dinner**: Substitute white rice, bread, and pasta with their whole grain versions. Quinoa, barley, and brown rice are excellent choices that add variety and nutrition.
- **Snacks**: Choose whole grain crackers, popcorn, or a small portion of dark rye bread with avocado. These snacks are not only satisfying but also diabetes-friendly.

## A Note of Caution

While whole grains are beneficial, portion control is key. Consuming too much of even a good thing can lead to weight gain and impact blood sugar levels. Aim for balance and moderation, integrating whole grains with a variety of other nutritious foods to create a well-rounded diet.

## *The Right Choices in Breads, Cereals, and Flours*

## Breads: Choosing Wisely

When it comes to bread, not all slices are created equal. The market is flooded with options, from white to whole wheat to artisanal rye, making the choice seem daunting. However, the aim should be to select breads made from whole grains. These breads have a lower GI, thanks to their high fiber content, which slows the absorption of sugar into the bloodstream.

- **Whole Grain over Refined**: Look for breads labeled "100% whole grain" or "100% whole wheat." These contain the entire grain kernel, offering the full spectrum of nutrients and fiber. Avoid "white" or "enriched" bread, as these have been stripped of their nutritional value.
- **Fiber Content**: Aim for breads with at least 3 grams of fiber per slice. This not only aids in glucose management but also supports digestive health.
- **Minimal Ingredients**: The best breads have a short ingredient list, highlighting whole grains, water, yeast, and salt. Beware of added sugars and preservatives.

### Cereals: A Mindful Morning Start

Breakfast cereals can be a minefield for those with type 2 diabetes. Many popular options are loaded with added sugars and refined grains, leading to blood sugar spikes. However, choosing the right cereal can provide a nutritious start to the day.

- **Whole Grain Cereals**: Choose cereals like brown rice, whole wheat, or whole oats that have a whole grain listed as the first component. In general, these cereals have a lower GI and more nutrients.
- **Sugar Content**: Always check the nutrition label for sugar content. Aim for cereals with less than 5 grams of sugar per serving. Better yet, choose unsweetened options and add your own fruit for natural sweetness.
- **High Fiber**: Similar to bread, a high-fiber cereal (at least 5 grams per serving) can slow the absorption of glucose, providing a steady energy source throughout the morning.

### Flours: The Foundation of Healthy Baking

Flour is the foundation of many recipes, from bread to pancakes to cookies. The type of flour used can significantly impact the nutritional profile and GI of the final product.

- **Whole Wheat Flour**: This is a straightforward substitute for white flour in most recipes, offering more fiber and nutrients.
- **Almond and Coconut Flour**: These low-carb, high-fiber alternatives are excellent for baking and suitable for those managing diabetes. They add a rich, nutty flavor to recipes.
- **Legume-based Flours**: Flours made from chickpeas, lentils, or beans are high in protein and fiber, making them excellent options for blood sugar management.

### Practical Tips for Incorporating These Choices

- **Start Gradually**: If you're used to white bread or sugary cereals, transition slowly. Mix half white flour with half whole wheat flour in recipes, or mix a lower-sugar cereal with your usual choice.
- **Read Labels Carefully**: Nutrition labels and ingredient lists are your best tools for making informed choices. Look beyond marketing claims and assess the real nutritional value.
- **Experiment with Recipes**: Use these healthier ingredients as an opportunity to explore new recipes and flavors. Whole gr

## *Starchy vs. Non-Starchy Vegetables*

Navigating the world of vegetables can sometimes feel like walking through a lush, vibrant forest, full of variety and nutrition, yet complex in its diversity. In the realm of type 2 diabetes management, understanding the distinction between starchy and non-starchy vegetables is essential. This knowledge empowers individuals to make choices that support blood sugar control while still enjoying a rich tapestry of flavors and nutrients.

### Understanding the Difference

**Starchy Vegetables:** These are packed with carbohydrates, the nutrient that has the most direct impact on blood sugar levels. While not inherently bad, starchy vegetables release glucose more rapidly into the bloodstream, necessitating mindful consumption. **Examples include:** Potatoes (white, sweet), Corn, Peas (green peas, split peas), Winter Squashes (butternut, acorn, pumpkin), Plantains, Yams

**Non-Starchy Vegetables:** Generally lower in carbohydrates and calories, non-starchy vegetables have a minimal impact on blood glucose levels, making them an excellent choice for people managing diabetes. They are abundant in fiber, antioxidants, vitamins, and minerals.

**Examples include:** Leafy Greens (spinach, kale, arugula, romaine lettuce), Broccoli, Cauliflower, Bell Peppers (red, yellow, green), Zucchini and Summer Squash, Asparagus, Cucumbers, Tomatoes, Mushrooms, Green Beans, Brussels Sprouts

**The Role of Fiber**

One of the key factors distinguishing starchy and non-starchy vegetables is their fiber content. Fiber slows the absorption of sugar into the bloodstream, providing a steadier energy source and helping to maintain more stable blood glucose levels. Non-starchy vegetables are particularly high in fiber, making them invaluable in a diabetes-friendly diet. For instance, a cup of cooked spinach packs about 4 grams of fiber, while broccoli provides about 5 grams per cup.

**Balancing Your Plate**

Incorporating a mix of starchy and non-starchy vegetables into your diet is about balance. Here are some practical tips to get you started:

- **Portion Control for Starchy Vegetables:** Enjoy starchy vegetables in moderation. A good rule of thumb is to limit the portion size to about half a cup or a small potato per meal. This allows you to enjoy the nutritional benefits without significantly spiking your blood sugar.
- **Fill Half Your Plate with Non-Starchy Vegetables:** Aim for non-starchy vegetables to fill half of your plate. This not only helps control blood sugar levels but also increases your intake of vital nutrients and antioxidants.
- **Incorporate Variety:** Eating a wide range of vegetables ensures you get a broad spectrum of vitamins, minerals, and antioxidants. Try to include a rainbow of colors on your plate to maximize nutrient intake.

**Examples and Ideas for Incorporation**

**For Starchy Vegetables:**

- Roasted sweet potatoes with a sprinkle of cinnamon and a touch of olive oil.
- Mashed cauliflower (a non-starchy alternative) with a portion of peas for a comforting side dish.
- A small serving of corn mixed with black beans, cilantro, and lime for a diabetic-friendly salad.

**For Non-Starchy Vegetables:**

- A stir-fry featuring broccoli, bell peppers, snap peas, and carrots, lightly seasoned and served over a small portion of brown rice.
- A salad packed with leafy greens, cherry tomatoes, cucumber, and a vinaigrette dressing.
- Zucchini noodles (zoodles) as a low-carb alternative to pasta, topped with marinara sauce and grilled chicken.

**Considerations When Preparing Vegetables**

- **Cooking Methods Matter:** Steaming, grilling, roasting, and raw preparations preserve the nutritional integrity of vegetables more than boiling or frying.
- **Beware of Additions:** Dressings, sauces, and toppings can add significant amounts of sugar, fat, and calories. Opt for herbs, spices, and lemon juice to enhance flavors without impacting blood sugar adversely.
- **Experiment with Substitutions:** Use non-starchy vegetables as substitutes in traditional recipes. For example, try cauliflower rice instead of white rice or spaghetti squash in place of pasta.

## *Lean Proteins: From Land and Sea*

Incorporating lean proteins from both land and sea into one's diet is a cornerstone of managing and potentially reversing type 2 diabetes. Proteins play a critical role in our health by building, maintaining, and repairing tissues in our body. Unlike foods high in refined carbohydrates and sugars, which can spike blood sugar levels, lean proteins provide a more stable source of energy without dramatically affecting blood glucose levels. Here, we delve into the benefits of lean proteins and offer guidance on incorporating these essential nutrients into your diet, focusing on variety, preparation, and balance.

**Understanding Lean Proteins**

Lean proteins are sources of protein that contain lower amounts of fat, making them a healthier choice for individuals managing diabetes. They help in feeling full and satisfied, reducing the likelihood of overeating, which is crucial for maintaining a healthy weight. Proteins do not raise blood sugar levels as carbohydrates do, making them a vital part of a diabetic-friendly diet.

**From the Land: Poultry, Meat, and Plant-Based Options**

When selecting proteins from land animals, opt for cuts that are lower in fat:

- **Chicken and Turkey**: Look for breast meat, either skinless or with skin removed before cooking, as these are the leanest parts.
- **Beef and Pork**: Choose cuts labeled "loin" or "round" as these tend to have less fat. Grass-fed beef is also a healthier option due to its higher omega-3 content.
- **Game Meats**: Venison, bison, and other game meats are naturally leaner than traditional beef and pork.

Example: Chicken or turkey breast (skinless), Lean cuts of beef (sirloin, tenderloin), Pork loin or tenderloin, Bison, venison.

**From the Sea: Fish and Shellfish**

Seafood is an excellent source of lean protein, particularly fatty fish that are high in omega-3 fatty acids, which have been shown to improve cardiovascular health—a concern for many with type 2 diabetes.

- **Fatty Fish**: Salmon, mackerel, sardines, and trout are rich in omega-3 fatty acids.
- **White Fish**: Cod, haddock, and tilapia are lean options with a mild flavor, suitable for a variety of dishes.
- **Shellfish**: Shrimp, crab, and lobster can be lean protein choices if prepared without added fats like butter.

Example: Salmon, mackerel, sardines (fatty fish), Cod, halibut, tilapia (white fish), Shrimp, scallops

**Incorporating Lean Proteins into Your Diet**

- **Balance Your Plate**: Aim to fill a quarter of your plate with lean protein, a quarter with whole grains or starchy vegetables, and half with non-starchy vegetables. This balance supports blood sugar control and overall health.
- **Variety is Key**: Rotate between different protein sources to ensure a range of nutrients. Each type of lean protein offers unique vitamins and minerals.
- **Mindful Preparation**: How you prepare your proteins can significantly impact their healthfulness. Grilling, baking, steaming, or broiling are excellent methods that add minimal fat. Avoid frying or preparing proteins with heavy sauces or batters.
- **Portion Control**: A serving size of meat is about 3 ounces, roughly the size of a deck of cards. For plant-based proteins, serving sizes can vary, so it's important to check nutrition labels.

**Examples of Protein-Rich Meals**

- **Grilled Chicken Salad**: A mix of greens, vegetables, and grilled chicken breast, dressed with olive oil and vinegar.
- **Salmon and Quinoa**: Oven-baked salmon served alongside quinoa and steamed broccoli.

## *Legumes: Beans, Peas, and Lentils*

In the quest for managing type 2 diabetes, legumes — including beans, peas, and lentils — emerge as nutritional powerhouses, offering a bounty of benefits for those seeking to embrace a healthier diet. These humble foods, often overlooked in favor of more glamorous fare, pack a punch when it comes to nutritional value, offering a complex array of nutrients that can help stabilize blood sugar, enhance satiety, and support overall health. Let's delve deeper into why these legumes deserve a starring role in your diet and how you can incorporate them into your meals.

**The Nutritional Profile of Legumes**

Legumes are a category of plants that produce a pod with seeds inside. Common legumes include beans (such as black, pinto, and kidney beans), peas (like chickpeas and black-eyed peas), and lentils. These foods are incredibly nutrient-dense, offering:

- **High Fiber**: Legumes are rich in both soluble and insoluble fiber, which can slow down digestion and absorption, helping to manage blood sugar levels.
- **Low Glycemic Index (GI)**: Thanks to their fiber content, legumes have a low GI, making them ideal for blood sugar management.
- **Protein**: Offering a plant-based source of protein, legumes can help maintain muscle mass, which is crucial for a healthy metabolism.
- **Vitamins and Minerals**: They are packed with nutrients such as iron, magnesium, potassium, and folate, supporting overall health and well-being.

**Incorporating Legumes into Your Diet**

Embracing legumes in your diet is not only beneficial for managing diabetes but can also add variety and depth to your meals. Here are some practical tips and ideas:

**Start with Familiar Foods**

- **Chili**: Use kidney beans or black beans in a hearty vegetable chili.
- **Hummus**: Chickpeas are the main ingredient in hummus, which can be used as a dip or spread.
- **Salads**: Toss lentils or chickpeas into your salads for added protein and fiber.

**Experiment with International Cuisine**

- **Indian Dishes**: Lentils are a staple in Indian cooking, used in dishes like dal.
- **Mexican Favorites**: Black beans can be used in tacos, burritos, and quesadillas.
- **Middle Eastern Meals**: Chickpeas are used in falafel and various stews.

**Use Them as a Meat Substitute**

Legumes can be a great substitute for meat in many recipes, offering protein without the saturated fat. They work well in burgers, meatloaf, and pasta sauces.

**Tips for Preparing and Cooking Legumes**

- **Soaking**: For dried beans, soaking them overnight can reduce cooking time and improve digestibility.
- **Rinsing**: Canned legumes can be high in sodium. Rinse them under cold water to reduce sodium content.
- **Cooking**: Lentils and split peas don't require soaking and can be cooked relatively quickly compared to beans.

**Nutritional Considerations**

While legumes are incredibly healthy, portion control is still key, especially for those managing diabetes. Although they have a low GI, consuming large amounts in one sitting can lead to blood sugar spikes. Aiming for about a half-cup serving size is a good start.

**Legumes List and Examples**

To get you started, here's a list of legumes to explore: Black beans, Pinto beans, Kidney beans, Navy beans, Cannellini beans, Chickpeas (garbanzo beans), Black-eyed peas, Split peas, Green peas, Green lentils, Red lentils, Brown lentils, Black lentils.

The selection of the right types of dairy or dairy alternatives can have a significant impact on your health, particularly in how it relates to blood sugar management and overall nutritional balance. Understanding the benefits and considerations of each can empower you to make informed choices that align with your health goals.

### Dairy: A Nutrient-Dense Option

Dairy products are renowned for their nutritional density, providing a rich source of calcium, vitamin D, and protein. These nutrients play a crucial role in bone health, muscle function, and metabolic regulation. However, when selecting dairy products, it's crucial to consider their fat content and how they fit into a diabetes-friendly diet.

- **Low-fat or Skim Milk**: Opt for low-fat or skim versions to enjoy the benefits of milk without the added saturated fat, which can be detrimental to heart health.
- **Greek Yogurt**: A standout for its high protein content, Greek yogurt can help with satiety and blood sugar stabilization. Look for plain versions with no added sugar.
- **Cheese**: While cheese can be a good source of protein and calcium, opt for low-fat versions and be mindful of portion sizes due to its calorie density.

### Plant-Based Alternatives: A Versatile Choice

For those looking to reduce or eliminate dairy from their diet, plant-based alternatives offer a versatile and often nutrient-rich option. These alternatives are made from a variety of sources, including nuts, grains, and legumes, and are often fortified with vitamins and minerals to enhance their nutritional profile.

- **Almond Milk**: Low in calories and sugar, almond milk is a popular choice. Ensure it's unsweetened and fortified with calcium and vitamin D.
- **Soy Milk**: Made from soybeans, it's a good source of protein and essential fatty acids. Opt for fortified, unsweetened versions to get the most benefit.
- **Oat Milk**: Rich in fiber and naturally sweet, oat milk can be a comforting choice. However, it's essential to choose versions with no added sugars.
- **Cashew Milk**: Creamy and rich, unsweetened cashew milk can be a delightful addition to your diet, providing healthy fats and a low sugar content.

### Navigating Dairy and Plant-Based Alternatives

Incorporating dairy or plant-based alternatives into your diet requires attention to labels and an understanding of how different products can impact your blood sugar and overall health.

### Tips for Selection:

- **Read Labels Carefully**: Look for products with no added sugars, as these can lead to unexpected blood sugar spikes.
- **Check for Fortification**: Especially with plant-based alternatives, ensure they are fortified with calcium, vitamin D, and other nutrients typically found in dairy.
- **Mind the Portions**: Even healthy alternatives can contribute to excessive calorie intake if not consumed in moderation.

### Incorporating into Your Diet:

- **Smoothies**: Use low-fat dairy or unsweetened plant-based milks as a base for nutritious smoothies, combining with berries, leafy greens, and a source of protein like Greek yogurt or silken tofu.
- **Cereal and Oatmeal**: Opt for unsweetened plant-based milks to add to your whole grain cereals or oatmeal, providing a creamy texture without added sugars.

- **Cooking and Baking**: Replace dairy milk with plant-based alternatives in recipes, adjusting for sweetness and consistency as needed.

**Examples of Nutrient-Rich Choices**

**Dairy:**

- Skim milk: A low-fat option providing calcium and vitamin D.
- Low-fat cottage cheese: Offers protein with minimal added fats.
- Plain, low-fat Greek yogurt: High in protein and probiotics for gut health.

**Plant-Based Alternatives:**

- Unsweetened almond milk: Low in calories, fortified with vitamins.
- Fortified soy milk: A protein-rich alternative similar in nutrition to cow's milk.
- Unsweetened oat milk: Offers fiber and a naturally sweet taste for those monitoring their sugar intake.

## Healthy Fats: MUFAs and Omega-3 Fatty Acids

For individuals managing type 2 diabetes, incorporating healthy fats such as MUFAs and Omega-3 fatty acids into the diet can offer numerous benefits, from improving heart health to potentially aiding in blood sugar control. However, it's crucial to distinguish between the types of fats, focusing particularly on the benefits of Monounsaturated Fatty Acids (MUFAs) and Omega-3 Fatty Acids. These fats are not only beneficial for blood sugar control but also for overall heart health, which is particularly important for individuals managing diabetes, given the increased risk of heart disease associated with the condition.

**Understanding Healthy Fats**

**Monounsaturated Fatty Acids (MUFAs)** are a type of fat found in various oils and foods. Studies suggest that diets high in MUFAs can improve blood cholesterol levels, which can decrease the risk of heart disease. Additionally, MUFAs may benefit insulin levels and blood sugar control, which can be incredibly beneficial for those with type 2 diabetes.

**Omega-3 Fatty Acids** are a type of polyunsaturated fat and are essential fats, meaning the body can't make them, and they must be obtained through diet. Omega-3s are known for their anti-inflammatory properties and their role in heart health. They can help reduce triglycerides, lower blood pressure, and decrease the risk of heart disease.

**Foods Rich in MUFAs**

To incorporate more MUFAs into your diet, consider adding the following foods:

- **Nuts and Seeds**: Nuts including macadamia nuts, cashews, almonds, and peanuts are great sources of MUFAs. These beneficial fats are also present in seeds, such as pumpkin and sesame seeds.
- **Avocados**: This fruit is not only rich in MUFAs but also brings fiber and essential nutrients to your meals.
- **Oils**: Olive oil, canola oil, and peanut oil are high in MUFAs and can be used in cooking or dressings.
- **Olives**: Both black and green olives are good sources of MUFAs and can be added to salads or enjoyed as a snack.

**Foods High in Omega-3 Fatty Acids**

For Omega-3 fatty acids, focus on incorporating:

- **Fatty Fish**: Sardines, trout, mackerel, and salmon are all great providers of Omega-3 fatty acids. Two servings of fatty fish should be your weekly goal.
- **Flaxseeds and Chia Seeds**: These seeds are not only high in Omega-3s but also fiber, which can aid in blood sugar control.
- **Walnuts**: A handful of walnuts provides a significant amount of Omega-3 fatty acids.
- **Plant Oils**: Flaxseed oil and canola oil are plant-based sources of Omega-3s.

**Incorporating Healthy Fats into Your Diet**

Adding MUFAs and Omega-3s to your diet doesn't have to be complicated. Here are some simple strategies:

- **Cook with Olive Oil**: Instead of butter or other saturated fats, use olive oil for cooking or salad dressings.
- **Snack on Nuts**: Nuts are a great snack that can help you feel full, thanks to their healthy fat and protein content.
- **Add Avocado to Your Meals**: Whether it's adding slices to a sandwich or salad or making guacamole, avocados are a versatile way to incorporate MUFAs.
- **Include Fatty Fish in Your Diet**: Replace some meat servings with fatty fish to boost your Omega-3 intake.
- **Sprinkle Seeds on Your Meals**: Flaxseeds or chia seeds can be added to yogurt, oatmeal, or smoothies for a dose of Omega-3s.

Nutritional Considerations

While MUFAs and Omega-3s are beneficial, portion control is essential. Fats are calorie-dense, so it's important to consume them in moderation to avoid weight gain. Additionally, when choosing fish, be mindful of mercury content, especially in larger fish like swordfish and king mackerel. Choose fish that has less mercury, such as salmon and sardines.

providers. Embrace these nutritious fats as part of a balanced, diabetes-friendly diet to support your health journey.

## Nuts, Seeds, and Their Oils

Nuts, seeds, and their oils represent a category of foods that, despite their small size, are mighty in nutritional value and health benefits, especially for individuals managing type 2 diabetes. Rich in essential nutrients, healthy fats, and antioxidants, these natural treasures can play a significant role in a balanced, diabetes-friendly diet. This section delves into the importance of incorporating nuts, seeds, and their oils into your meals, providing practical advice and examples to guide you on this nutritious journey.

**Understanding Nuts and Seeds**

Nuts and seeds are dense in nutrients, providing a rich source of healthy fats, primarily monounsaturated and polyunsaturated fats, which are beneficial for heart health and blood sugar control. They also contain protein, fiber, vitamins, minerals, and antioxidants, making them an excellent addition to any diet, particularly for those focusing on blood sugar management.

**Key Nutrients in Nuts and Seeds:**

- **Healthy Fats**: Essential for brain health and reducing inflammation.
- **Protein**: Important for muscle repair and growth.
- **Fiber**: Slows the absorption of sugar into the bloodstream.
- **Vitamins and Minerals**: Such as magnesium, potassium, and zinc, which play roles in everything from energy production to immune function.
- **Antioxidants**: Help combat oxidative stress and reduce the risk of chronic diseases.

**The Role of Nuts and Seeds in Blood Sugar Control**

The combination of healthy fats, protein, and fiber in nuts and seeds can help slow digestion and the absorption of carbohydrates, leading to a more gradual rise in blood sugar levels. This makes them an excellent snack choice for people with diabetes, as they can help maintain steady blood sugar levels throughout the day.

**Incorporating Nuts, Seeds, and Their Oils into Your Diet**

Adding nuts and seeds to your diet is easy and can be incredibly delicious. Here are some practical tips and examples:

**Snacking:**

- **Raw or Roasted Nuts**: Almonds, walnuts, and cashews make great snacks. To limit your consumption of sodium, choose unsalted varieties.
- **Seed Mixes**: A mix of sunflower seeds, pumpkin seeds, and chia seeds can offer a crunchy, nutritious snack.

**Cooking and Baking:**

- **Salads**: Sprinkle chopped nuts or seeds over salads for added texture and nutrients.
- **Baking**: Use almond flour or ground flaxseeds as a low-carb, high-fiber alternative to traditional flour.
- **Cooking**: Use nut oils, like walnut or almond oil, for their flavor and health benefits in dressings and light sautéing.

## Types of Nuts and Seeds to Embrace

Here's a list of nuts, seeds, and their oils to explore:

**Nuts:** Pecans, Macadamia nuts, Walnuts, Cashews, and Almonds

**Seeds:** sesame, flax, pumpkin, sunflower, and chia

**Oils:** Walnut, almond, flaxseed, and extra virgin olive oils

Each type of nut, seed, and oil offers unique flavors and nutritional profiles, encouraging you to experiment with them in your cooking and snacking.

## Nutritional Considerations

While nuts and seeds are incredibly healthy, they are also high in calories, so portion control is essential. A small handful of nuts (about 1 ounce) or a tablespoon of seeds is a good serving size. When it comes to their oils, remember that while they are healthy, they are still fats, and moderation is key.

## Recipes and Ideas

Incorporating nuts, seeds, and their oils into your diet doesn't have to be complicated. Here are a few ideas to get you started:

- **Breakfast**: Sprinkle chia seeds over Greek yogurt or incorporate flaxseeds into your morning smoothie.
- **Lunch**: Add a handful of almonds to your chicken salad for a crunchy texture.
- **Dinner**: Dress your salads with a homemade vinaigrette using extra virgin olive oil.
- **Snacks**: Keep a small bag of mixed nuts and seeds for an on-the-go snack.

## *The Colorful World of Fruits with Low Glycemic Index*

Incorporating low-GI fruits into your diet can be a delightful way to manage blood sugar levels while enjoying the natural sweetness and nutritional benefits fruits offer. The key lies in selecting fruits with a low glycemic index (GI), which can add vibrancy, flavor, and essential nutrients to your diet without causing rapid spikes in your blood sugar levels. Understanding the glycemic index is crucial for anyone looking to manage diabetes effectively. The GI measures how quickly food raises blood glucose levels; foods with a low GI (55 or less) are digested more slowly, causing a gradual rise in blood sugar.

### The Benefits of Low-GI Fruits

Low-GI fruits are a treasure trove of vitamins, minerals, fiber, and antioxidants, offering multiple health benefits:

- **Blood Sugar Control**: They provide a slower, more controlled release of glucose into the bloodstream.
- **Increased Satiety**: High in fiber, these fruits can help you feel full longer, aiding in weight management.
- **Nutrient-Rich**: Packed with essential nutrients, they support overall health beyond diabetes management.

### Choosing the Right Fruits

When incorporating fruits into a diabetes-friendly diet, selection is key. Here's a guide to some of the best low-GI fruits:

### Berries

- **Strawberries**: Delightful and versatile, they're excellent in salads or as a snack.
- **Blueberries**: Packed with antioxidants, they're great in smoothies or as a yogurt topping.
- **Raspberries**: Fiber-rich, perfect for adding texture and flavor to oatmeal or desserts.

### Citrus Fruits

- **Oranges**: A juicy snack that's also a wonderful addition to salads.
- **Lemons and Limes**: Ideal for flavoring water or tea without added sugar.

### Stone Fruits

- **Cherries**: With a GI score of 22, they're a sweet, low-GI option.
- **Plums**: Fresh or dried into prunes, plums are a good source of fiber.
- **Peaches**: Delicious whether fresh, grilled, or added to cereals.

### Others

- **Apples**: With a fiber-rich skin, they're a portable, healthy snack.
- **Pears**: Offer a sweet, juicy treat, and are excellent when added to salads or eaten as is.
- **Kiwi**: A small fruit packed with flavor and vitamin C.

### Incorporating Low-GI Fruits into Your Diet

Adopting a diet that includes low-GI fruits requires more than just knowing which fruits to choose; it's also about how to incorporate them into your meals and snacks in a balanced way.

- **Portion Control:** Even low-GI fruits can impact blood sugar levels if consumed in large quantities. Aim for moderate portions — a small apple, a half-cup of berries, or a medium-sized peach.
- **Pairing with Proteins or Healthy Fats:** Combining fruits with proteins or healthy fats can further slow the absorption of glucose. Savor berries with Greek yogurt or apple slices with almond butter.
- **Fresh is Best:** While fresh fruits are ideal, frozen fruits without added sugars are a good alternative. Be cautious with dried fruits and canned fruits, as they can be higher in sugars.
- **Be Creative:** Use fruits to add natural sweetness to meals without extra sugar. Top salads with orange segments, add diced apples to oatmeal, or blend berries into smoothies.

### Recipe Ideas

Here are some simple ideas to get you started:

- **Berry Salad**: Mix fresh strawberries, blueberries, and raspberries. Drizzle with lemon juice and a touch of mint for a refreshing salad.
- **Kiwi Parfait**: Layer sliced kiwi with plain Greek yogurt and a sprinkle of chia seeds for a nutrient-dense snack.
- **Peach Smoothie**: Blend fresh peaches, a handful of spinach, unsweetened almond milk, and a scoop of protein powder for a balanced breakfast.

## *Fresh Herbs and Spices for Flavorful Cooking*

Transforming your meals with the vibrant colors, textures, and aromas of fresh herbs and spices is not just a journey for your senses; it's a healthful path, especially for individuals managing type 2 diabetes. Embracing these natural flavor enhancers can significantly reduce reliance on salt, sugar, and unhealthy fats, which are often our default choices for adding taste to our dishes. These natural wonders offer a simple yet effective strategy for enhancing the nutritional value of your meals, making every dish an opportunity to nourish your body and soul.

### The Health Benefits of Herbs and Spices

Herbs and spices are more than just flavoring agents; they are packed with antioxidants, vitamins, and minerals essential for maintaining good health. For example:

- **Cinnamon** is known to improve insulin sensitivity and lower blood sugar levels.

- **Turmeric**, with its active compound curcumin, has strong anti-inflammatory properties and can aid in reducing blood sugar levels.
- **Ginger** contains anti-inflammatory properties and can aid in glycemic management.
- **Garlic** has been shown to improve cholesterol levels and lower blood pressure.

Including a variety of herbs and spices in your diet can contribute to overall health and support diabetes management by enhancing the flavor of your food without adding unnecessary calories or harmful additives.

## Incorporating Herbs and Spices into Your Diet

Here are some practical ways to incorporate these potent plants into your daily meals:

### Start with Familiar Herbs and Spices

- **Basil**: Adds a fresh flavor to salads, soups, and tomato-based dishes.
- **Cinnamon**: Can be sprinkled on oatmeal, yogurt, or used in baking.
- **Mint**: Refreshing in salads, drinks, or mixed into yogurt.
- **Rosemary**: Perfect for seasoning chicken, fish, or roasted vegetables.

### Experiment with New Flavors

- **Turmeric**: Gives a warm, earthy flavor and a golden color to curries and rice dishes.
- **Cumin**: Adds a smoky note to meat dishes, soups, and stews.
- **Coriander**: Offers a lemony, floral taste to salads, dressings, and marinades.
- **Cardamom**: Enhances the flavor of coffee, tea, and baked goods.

### Create Your Own Spice Blends

Mixing your own spice blends not only allows you to customize flavors to your liking but also avoids the added salt and sugar found in many store-bought blends.

### Tips for Using Fresh Herbs and Spices

- **Storage**: Fresh herbs can be kept in the refrigerator, wrapped in a damp paper towel, and stored in a plastic bag. Most spices should be stored in a cool, dark place.
- **Pairing**: Experiment with pairing different herbs and spices with various foods. For example, cilantro pairs well with lime for a Mexican flair, while dill complements the delicate flavors of fish.
- **Add at the Right Time**: Add hardy herbs like rosemary and thyme early in the cooking process; delicate herbs like basil and cilantro should be added just before serving to preserve their flavor.

### Examples of Diabetes-Friendly Dishes with Herbs and Spices

- **Cinnamon-Spiced Apple Slices**: A sprinkle of cinnamon on sliced apples for a healthy, flavorful snack.
- **Turmeric Lentil Soup**: A comforting soup with the anti-inflammatory benefits of turmeric.
- **Garlic and Rosemary Roasted Chicken**: A simple yet delicious way to add depth of flavor to chicken.
- **Mint and Cucumber Water**: A refreshing drink to stay hydrated without added sugars.

### Beneficial Herbs:

- **Basil**: Enhances the taste of salads, soups, and tomato dishes.
- **Cilantro**: Perfect in Mexican, Indian, and Asian cuisines.
- **Dill**: Adds a fresh flavor to fish, potatoes, and yogurt-based sauces.
- **Mint**: Refreshing in drinks, salads, and Middle Eastern dishes.
- **Parsley**: Brightens flavors in soups, salads, and pasta dishes.
- **Rosemary**: Ideal for meats, bread, and Italian cuisine.
- **Thyme**: Excellent in soups, stews, and with poultry.
- **Sage**: Pairs well with pork, beans, and stuffing.
- **Oregano**: A staple in Italian, Mexican, and Mediterranean cooking.
- **Chives**: Offers a mild onion flavor to salads, soups, and potato dishes.

- **Tarragon**: Has a bittersweet taste, great with chicken, eggs, and in sauces.
- **Lemongrass**: Adds a citrus flavor to Asian dishes and teas.

**Beneficial Spices:**

- **Cinnamon**: Can help regulate blood sugar levels, used in both sweet and savory dishes.
- **Cumin**: Adds a smoky note to Mexican, Indian, and Middle Eastern dishes.
- **Turmeric**: Known for its anti-inflammatory properties, used in curries and rice.
- **Ginger**: Aides digestion and adds heat to stir-fries, desserts, and teas.
- **Garlic**: Improves cholesterol levels and enhances flavor in a myriad of dishes.
- **Cardamom**: Sweet and spicy, great in baked goods and Indian dishes.
- **Coriander**: Offers a lemony taste to soups, salads, and meat dishes.
- **Nutmeg**: A warm spice for baking, spinach, and sweet potato dishes.
- **Cloves**: Has a strong, sweet flavor, used in baking and with meats.
- **Fennel Seeds**: Anise-flavored, good with fish and in Italian sausages.
- **Mustard Seeds**: Brings a spicy kick to curries and pickled items.
- **Paprika**: Ranges from sweet to hot, colors and flavors meats and stews.
- **Black Pepper**: Enhances virtually any dish with its sharp bite.
- **Cayenne Pepper**: Adds heat and metabolism-boosting properties to dishes.
- **Star Anise**: Licorice flavor, used in Vietnamese and Chinese cooking.
- **Saffron**: Offers a unique flavor and color to Mediterranean and Middle Eastern dishes.

# FOODS TO CONSUME WITH CAUTION

## Understanding Sugars and Sweeteners

Navigating the world of sugars and sweeteners can be a complex journey, especially for individuals managing type 2 diabetes. The key lies in understanding which sugars and sweeteners can impact your blood sugar levels and how to consume them with caution.

Here, we'll delve into the nuances of sugars and sweeteners, providing you with the knowledge to make informed decisions about your diet.

### The Basics of Sugars and Sweeteners

**Sugars** come in various forms, from natural sugars found in fruits (fructose) and milk (lactose) to added sugars used in processed foods. The latter are the ones to watch out for, as they can quickly spike blood glucose levels.

**Sweeteners**, on the other hand, include a wide range of substances used to give a sweet taste without the calorie content of sugar. They can be natural or artificial, with varying effects on blood sugar and health.

### Understanding Natural Sugars

Natural sugars, while part of a whole food's nutritional package, still need to be consumed judiciously. For instance:

- **Fruits**: While they provide fiber, vitamins, and minerals, their fructose content means portion control is essential. Berries, cherries, and apples have lower glycemic indexes compared to tropical fruits like pineapples and mangoes.
- **Milk**: Contains lactose, a natural sugar, so it's wise to monitor intake.

### The Impact of Added Sugars

Added sugars are prevalent in many processed foods and can significantly affect blood glucose levels. Key sources include:

- **Sodas and sweetened beverages**: One of the largest sources of added sugars in the American diet.
- **Baked goods**: Cookies, cakes, and pastries often contain high amounts of added sugars.
- **Candies and sweets**: Almost entirely made of sugar.

- **Processed foods**: Added sugars can be found in unexpected places, like breads, sauces, and salad dressings.

The American Heart Association recommends limiting added sugars to no more than 6 teaspoons (24 grams) per day for women and 9 teaspoons (36 grams) for men. For those managing diabetes, even stricter control may be necessary.

## Navigating Sweeteners

Sweeteners can be a contentious topic. They offer the sweetness of sugar without the calories, but their effect on health and blood glucose levels can vary.

**Artificial Sweeteners:** Artificial sweeteners like aspartame, sucralose, and saccharin have been deemed safe by regulatory agencies, yet their impact on appetite, cravings, and gut health remains debated. While they don't directly raise blood sugar levels, they may influence your body's response to sugar and affect diabetes management.

**Natural Sweeteners:** Natural sweeteners, such as stevia and monk fruit extract, are derived from plants and may offer a safer alternative to artificial sweeteners. They have minimal impact on blood glucose levels, making them a better choice for those with diabetes.

**Sugar Alcohols:** Sugar alcohols, such as erythritol and xylitol, have a sweet flavor but are lower in calories than sugar. They have a lesser effect on blood sugar but can cause digestive issues in some people.

## Guidelines for Consumption

When incorporating sugars and sweeteners into your diet, consider the following guidelines:

- **Read Labels Carefully**: Be on the lookout for hidden sugars in processed foods. Names like sucrose, high-fructose corn syrup, and dextrose indicate added sugars.
- **Prioritize Whole Foods**: Opt for natural sources of sweetness, like fruits, where the fiber content helps mitigate blood sugar spikes.
- **Exercise Portion Control**: Even with lower-GI fruits and natural sweeteners, keeping portions in check is crucial.
- **Be Mindful of Sweeteners**: Choose natural sweeteners over artificial ones and use them sparingly. Remember, the goal is to reduce your overall sweet taste preference.
- **Monitor Your Blood Sugar**: Observing how your blood sugar responds to different sugars and sweeteners can help you make better dietary choices.

## Making Informed Choices

Remember, managing diabetes doesn't mean you have to forgo all things sweet; it's about making informed choices that support your wellbeing.

## *Navigating Processed Foods*

While the convenience of processed foods can be tempting, their impact on health, especially for individuals managing type 2 diabetes, is too significant to overlook. In today's fast-paced society, the convenience of processed foods is undeniable, but their impact on health, particularly blood sugar levels, requires careful consideration. Understanding what constitutes processed foods, recognizing their potential effects on your health, and learning how to make wiser choices can empower you in managing your diabetes more effectively.

## Understanding Processed Foods

Firstly, it's crucial to differentiate between minimally processed foods and heavily processed ones. Minimally processed foods, such as pre-chopped vegetables or roasted nuts, retain most of their inherent nutritional value and are generally safe and beneficial. On the other hand, heavily processed foods often contain added sugars, unhealthy fats, and a high amount of sodium, all of which can adversely affect blood sugar levels, weight, and overall health.

## Common Heavily Processed Foods Include:

- Pre-packaged meals and snacks

- Frozen pizzas and microwave dinners
- Canned soups high in sodium
- Breakfast cereals with added sugars
- White breads and pastas made from refined flour
- Sodas, sweetened beverages, and energy drinks
- Packaged cakes, cookies, and pastries

**The Impact on Health**

Heavily processed foods can have a significant impact on your health, especially for those with type 2 diabetes:

- **Blood Sugar Spikes**: High in refined sugars and flours, these foods can lead to rapid spikes in blood sugar levels.
- **Weight Gain**: The high calorie content and low nutritional value can contribute to weight gain, a risk factor for worsening diabetes control.
- **Heart Health**: Trans fats and high sodium levels in processed foods can increase the risk of heart disease.
- **Nutrient Deficiency**: Consuming processed foods can lead to a lack of essential nutrients, as these foods often lack vitamins, minerals, and fiber found in whole foods.

**Navigating Processed Foods with Caution**

While it might not always be possible to avoid processed foods entirely, there are strategies to minimize their impact on your health:

**Read Labels Carefully**

- **Check for Sugar Content**: Look for hidden sugars listed under various names like fructose, sucrose, maltose, and corn syrup.
- **Examine Fat Content**: Avoid trans fats and limit saturated fats by choosing foods with healthy fats like those from nuts, seeds, and avocados.
- **Watch Sodium Levels**: Choose low-sodium options to help maintain healthy blood pressure levels.

**Make Healthier Choices**

- **Opt for Whole Grains**: Choose whole-grain bread, pasta, and cereals over those made with refined flour.
- **Select Low-Sugar Options**: Look for snacks and beverages with little to no added sugars.
- **Choose Lean Proteins**: Opt for lean cuts of meat, poultry, and fish, and avoid processed meats like sausages and deli meats.

**Prepare Meals at Home**

Cooking meals at home allows for complete control over ingredients, enabling you to make healthier choices that align with managing diabetes effectively.

**Example Foods to Approach with Caution**

While navigating processed foods, consider these examples and the potential healthier alternatives:

- **Frozen Pizzas**: High in sodium and refined carbohydrates. A healthier option would be homemade pizza using whole wheat crust and plenty of vegetables.
- **Canned Soups**: Often laden with sodium. Opt for homemade soups with fresh ingredients and control the amount of salt used.
- **Sweetened Breakfast Cereals**: Typically high in added sugars. Choose whole-grain cereals with no added sugars, or better yet, make oatmeal and add fresh fruit for sweetness.
- **Sodas and Sweetened Beverages**: Major contributors to sugar intake. Better options are water, herbal teas without added sugar, or sparkling water with a dash of fruit juice.

In managing type 2 diabetes, understanding the role of fats in our diet is crucial. Not all fats are created equal, and some, particularly when consumed in excess, can contribute to health issues including heart disease, which individuals with diabetes are at increased risk for. Identifying and limiting certain types of fats can play a significant role in maintaining a balanced, healthful diet and controlling blood sugar levels.

**Saturated Fats:** Animal products and certain plant oils are the main sources of saturated fats. Moderation is vital, even though they are no longer the evil they were previously believed to be. Consuming a lot of saturated fats can increase LDL (bad) cholesterol levels, which increases the risk of heart disease. Saturated fat-containing foods include:

- Red meat (beef, lamb, pork)
- Butter
- Cheese and other dairy products made from whole or 2% milk
- Coconut oil
- Palm oil

Reducing consumption of these foods and opting for leaner meats, low-fat dairy products, and using oils high in unsaturated fats for cooking can help manage saturated fat intake.

**Trans Fats:** When it comes to bad fats, trans fats are the main offenders. They are created through a process called hydrogenation, which makes oils solid at room temperature and extends their shelf life. Trans fats can increase LDL cholesterol while decreasing HDL (good) cholesterol, exacerbating heart disease risk. The FDA has taken steps to eliminate artificial trans fats from the food supply, but they can still be found in:

- Margarine (stick forms)
- Packaged snacks (e.g., chips, crackers)
- Commercially baked goods (e.g., pastries, cookies, doughnuts)
- Fried foods

You may steer clear of trans fats by looking for "partially hydrogenated oils" on food labels. Opting for fresh or home-cooked foods instead of processed items can significantly reduce trans fat consumption.

**Omega-6 Fatty Acids:** An unbalanced intake of omega-6 and omega-3 fatty acids is not always harmful, but it might exacerbate chronic illnesses and inflammation. Omega-6s are typically abundant in the typical American diet and can be found in:

- Vegetable oils (such as corn, safflower, soybean, and sunflower oils)
- Many processed and fast foods

Balancing omega-6 intake with more omega-3s, found in fatty fish, flaxseeds, and walnuts, can support better health outcomes.

**Making Healthier Choices:**
- **Choose Lean Proteins**: Opt for lean cuts of meat, and consider incorporating more plant-based protein sources into your diet, such as beans, lentils, and tofu, which are low in saturated fat.
- **Select Low-Fat Dairy**: Choose milk, yogurt, and cheese made from skim or 1% milk to reduce saturated fat intake.
- **Cook with Healthier Oils**: Use oils high in unsaturated fats, such as olive oil or canola oil, for cooking and salad dressings.
- **Increase Omega-3s**: Include more omega-3-rich foods in your diet, like salmon, chia seeds, and walnuts, to help balance omega-6 intake.
- **Read Labels**: Become a savvy shopper by reading nutrition labels to identify and limit foods high in saturated and trans fats.

**Practical Tips for Everyday Eating:**
- When dining out, ask for dishes to be prepared with little or no added fat.

- Swap out butter for olive oil or avocado spread on your toast.
- Savor naturally low-fat snacks like whole-grain crackers, fruits, and veggies.
- Instead of frying, try baking, grilling, or steaming your foods to minimize added fats.

Navigating the world of fruits and vegetables can sometimes feel like walking through a minefield, especially for individuals managing type 2 diabetes. While these natural foods are often lauded for their health benefits, including high fiber, vitamins, and minerals, it's crucial to understand that not all fruits and vegetables are created equal when it comes to their impact on blood sugar levels. This distinction is largely determined by the glycemic index (GI), a measure of how quickly foods cause increases in blood glucose levels. High-GI fruits and vegetables can cause rapid spikes in blood sugar, which can be detrimental for individuals striving to manage their diabetes effectively. Understanding which foods fall into this category and how to balance them within your diet is essential for maintaining optimal health and well-being.

### High-Glycemic Fruits

Fruits, while nutritious and an integral part of a balanced diet, can vary significantly in their GI values. High-GI fruits are typically those that contain more simple sugars and less fiber, which can lead to quicker absorption and, consequently, faster rises in blood sugar. Here are some examples of high-GI fruits that should be consumed with caution:

- **Watermelon**: With a GI score that can reach as high as 76, watermelon is on the higher end of the glycemic index, primarily due to its low fiber content and high fructose level.
- **Pineapple**: Another tropical fruit, pineapple has a GI score of around 59. While it's packed with vitamins, its sugar content can cause blood sugar levels to rise quickly.
- **Bananas**: Especially ripe bananas have a higher GI score (around 51) compared to their less ripe counterparts. The ripening process breaks down the fruit's starches into sugars, increasing its glycemic load.

### Managing High-GI Fruits in Your Diet

- **Portion Control**: Enjoying these fruits in small amounts can help mitigate their impact on your blood sugar.
- **Pairing with Protein or Healthy Fats**: Eating high-GI fruits along with foods high in protein or healthy fats can slow the absorption of sugar into the bloodstream.
- **Opting for Whole Fruit**: Consuming whole fruits, as opposed to juices, ensures you're getting the fruit's full fiber content, which can help slow down sugar absorption.

### High-Glycemic Vegetables

While most vegetables are low in calories and high in fiber, making them excellent choices for diabetes management, there are a few exceptions. Certain starchy vegetables can have a higher GI and should be eaten in moderation:

- **Potatoes**: Depending on the type and cooking method, potatoes can have a GI score ranging from moderate to very high. For example, a baked potato can have a GI score as high as 85.
- **Parsnips**: This root vegetable has a GI score of around 97, one of the highest among vegetables, due to its starch content.
- **Pumpkin**: With a GI score of 75, pumpkin is another vegetable that's higher on the glycemic index, primarily when cooked.

### Balancing High-GI Vegetables in Your Meal Plan

- **Incorporate with Low-GI Foods**: Balancing your meal with more low-GI vegetables can help moderate your overall glycemic load.
- **Mind the Cooking Method**: Cooking methods that involve boiling or steaming are generally preferable, as they have a lesser impact on the vegetable's GI than baking or frying.
- **Portion Sizes Matter**: Just like with fruits, being mindful of portion sizes can help control the impact of these vegetables on your blood sugar levels.

**Understanding the Glycemic Index and Glycemic Load**

- **Glycemic Index**: Foods containing carbohydrates are ranked on a GI scale ranging from 0 to 100 based on how much their blood glucose-raising power increases when compared to a reference food.
- **Glycemic Load**: This calculates the true effect of a food on blood sugar levels by accounting for both the GI rating and the quantity of carbs in a serving. To better control blood sugar levels, a reduced glycemic load is ideal.

**Embracing a Balanced Approach**

The key to incorporating high-GI fruits and vegetables into a diabetes management plan lies in moderation and balance. By understanding the effects these foods can have on your blood sugar and making informed choices, you can enjoy a wide variety of fruits and vegetables without compromising your health goals. Always remember to:

- Combine high-GI foods with low-GI counterparts to balance the meal.
- Focus on whole, unprocessed foods for maximum nutritional benefit.
- Monitor your blood sugar levels to understand how different foods affect you personally.

## Treats and Sweets: A Guided Approach

In managing type 2 diabetes, the approach to treats and sweets necessitates a delicate balance. It's a journey not of complete abstinence but of moderation and informed choices. Understanding how treats and sweets fit into a diabetes-friendly diet allows for occasional indulgence without compromising blood sugar control. Here, we explore a guided approach to navigating treats and sweets, emphasizing choices that minimize negative impacts on blood sugar levels while still satisfying the sweet tooth.

Treats and sweets, often high in simple sugars and refined carbohydrates, can cause rapid spikes in blood glucose levels. These foods are typically devoid of the fiber, proteins, and healthy fats that help mediate blood sugar responses. However, completely eliminating these foods is not always realistic or necessary for maintaining a healthy relationship with food. The key is understanding how to incorporate them judiciously.

**Choosing Wisely**

When it comes to sweets and treats, the choice of what and how much you consume can make a significant difference. Opting for options that are lower in sugar and higher in nutritional value can mitigate blood sugar spikes. Here are some strategies:

- **Fruit-Based Desserts**: Opt for desserts that use fruits as their primary sweetener. Fruits like berries, apples, and pears come with natural sugars but also contain fiber, which helps slow the absorption of sugar into the bloodstream.
- **Dark Chocolate**: Choose dark chocolate with a cocoa content of 70% or higher. Dark chocolate contains less sugar than milk chocolate and offers antioxidants.
- **Homemade Treats**: Making your own treats allows you to control the ingredients. Use alternative sweeteners like stevia or monk fruit, which do not impact blood sugar levels the same way traditional sugar does. Experiment with almond flour or coconut flour instead of refined white flour for added fiber and nutrients.

**Portion Control**

The amount of sweet food you consume at once is critical. Small, controlled portions help prevent the large blood sugar spikes associated with larger servings. Practice these portion control tips:

- **Share Desserts**: When dining out or at a gathering, consider sharing a dessert to automatically halve the portion size.
- **Use Smaller Dishes**: Serve sweets on small plates or bowls. Visually, a smaller portion appears more substantial on a smaller dish, which can help satisfy cravings without overindulging.
- **Mindful Eating**: Eat slowly and savor each bite. It takes time for the brain to register fullness, so eating slowly can help prevent overeating.

**Timing Matters**

The timing of when you enjoy treats and sweets can also influence your blood sugar control:

- **After Meals**: Enjoying a small sweet treat after a balanced meal can help mitigate blood sugar spikes. The presence of other nutrients like fiber, protein, and fat from the meal slows the absorption of sugar.
- **Active Days**: On days when you are more physically active, your body uses sugar more efficiently as energy. A small treat on these days might have less impact on your overall blood sugar levels.

**Healthy Alternatives**

Finding alternatives to traditional sweets can satisfy cravings without the same blood sugar impact. Consider these substitutions:

- **Greek Yogurt with Berries**: A rich source of protein, Greek yogurt can be sweetened with fresh berries for a dessert that feels indulgent but is blood sugar-friendly.
- **Nuts and Dark Chocolate**: A small handful of nuts with a few pieces of dark chocolate offers a satisfying crunch with the sweetness of chocolate, plus the healthy fats in nuts help slow sugar absorption.
- **Frozen Grapes**: Frozen grapes offer a sweet, sorbet-like treat without added sugar.

It's important to know how diet affects your blood sugar. Frequent observation before and after eating sweets can provide you with individualized knowledge about how your body reacts to various foods and serving sizes. Make adjustments to your plans in light of these findings.

# MASTERING DINING OUT

Dining out can often feel like navigating a minefield for those managing type 2 diabetes. The array of choices, the hidden ingredients, and the temptation of high-sugar, high-carbohydrate dishes can make it challenging to stick to a diabetes-friendly diet. However, with some knowledge and planning, you can enjoy eating out without compromising your health goals. This section will guide you through selecting diabetic-friendly dishes and navigating menus at popular restaurants and fast-food chains, ensuring you can make informed choices while enjoying a meal out.

When dining out, the first step is to understand that not all menu items are created equal, especially concerning their impact on blood sugar levels. The goal is to find meals that are high in fiber, protein, and healthy fats while low in processed sugars and unhealthy fats. Here are some general tips to keep in mind:

1. **Start with a Salad**: Beginning your meal with a salad (dressing on the side) can help fill you up with fiber, making you less likely to overeat on higher-carbohydrate dishes later. Opt for salads with lots of non-starchy vegetables and a source of protein like grilled chicken or fish.
2. **Choose Grilled Over Fried**: Foods that are grilled, baked, or steamed are generally less likely to be loaded with unhealthy fats and calories compared to their fried counterparts. This simple choice can help you manage your fat intake and make it easier to control blood sugar levels.
3. **Look for Whole Grains**: When choosing dishes that include grains, go for whole-grain options whenever possible. Whole grains like brown rice, quinoa, and whole wheat pasta have a lower glycemic index than white rice or regular pasta, meaning they have a less significant impact on blood sugar levels.
4. **Be Mindful of Portions**: Restaurant portions can be significantly larger than standard serving sizes. Consider sharing a dish with someone else at the table, or ask for half of your meal to be boxed up before it even arrives at your table to avoid overeating.
5. **Special Requests are Okay**: Don't be afraid to ask for substitutions or modifications to your meal. Most restaurants are willing to accommodate requests like dressing on the side, no cheese, or extra vegetables instead of fries.

## Selecting Diabetic-Friendly Dishes

When scanning the menu, here are some specific dishes to look for and some to avoid:

**Good Choices:**

- Grilled fish or seafood with a side of vegetables.
- Chicken or turkey breast, grilled or baked, with a side salad.
- Vegetable stir-fry with tofu or chicken, ask if it can be made with less oil.
- Bean or lentil soups, which are high in fiber and protein.

**Dishes to Avoid:**

- Anything described as crispy, fried, or battered.
- White pasta dishes with creamy sauces.
- High-carb sides like fries, mashed potatoes, or white rice.
- Desserts, especially those that are high in sugar and fat.

## Navigating Menus at Popular Restaurants and Fast-Food Chains

Eating at fast-food chains can be particularly challenging, but it's not impossible to find options that fit within a diabetic-friendly diet. Here are some strategies:

- **Fast-Food Chains**: Look for salads with grilled protein, wraps with whole grains and lean protein, and grilled chicken sandwiches. Avoid sugary drinks by opting for water, unsweetened iced tea, or diet sodas.
- **Italian Restaurants**: Choose dishes with tomato-based sauces rather than cream-based ones. Opt for whole-grain pasta if available, or ask for a half portion of regular pasta with extra vegetables on the side.
- **Mexican Restaurants**: Fajitas are a great option because you can control the fillings — opt for grilled vegetables, chicken, or beef, and use lettuce wraps instead of flour tortillas. Avoid dishes with a lot of cheese, sour cream, or refried beans.
- **Asian Cuisine**: Look for stir-fry dishes with lots of vegetables and lean protein. Be cautious of dishes with sweet sauces, as they can be high in sugar. Sushi can be a good option, but choose rolls made with brown rice and avoid tempura rolls or those with creamy sauces.

Remember, managing type 2 diabetes doesn't mean you have to miss out on eating out; it just means becoming more mindful of your choices and planning ahead.

# BUILDING A BALANCED PLATE

Creating a balanced plate is fundamental for managing type 2 diabetes and promoting overall health. This section delves into practical strategies to achieve this, including the Plate Method for meal planning, employing healthy cooking techniques, using salt wisely, and understanding the benefits of organic foods. These elements work in concert to provide a comprehensive approach to eating well for diabetes management.

## The Plate Method: A Visual Guide to Meal Planning

The Plate Method serves as an intuitive, visual framework for meal planning, particularly beneficial for individuals managing type 2 diabetes. It's grounded in the concept of portion control and balanced nutrition, aiming to streamline dietary choices without compromising on variety or flavor. Here, we'll delve deeper into how to effectively implement the Plate Method, ensuring each meal is a step toward better blood sugar control and overall well-being.

## Understanding the Plate Division

- **Half the Plate: Non-Starchy Vegetables:**
  - The emphasis on filling half your plate with non-starchy vegetables is pivotal. These vegetables, including leafy greens like spinach and kale, cruciferous vegetables like broccoli and cauliflower, and other colorful options such as bell peppers and eggplants, are nutrient powerhouses. They're packed with vitamins, minerals, antioxidants, and fiber, contributing to satiety, aiding digestion, and providing essential nutrients with minimal impact on blood sugar levels.
  - To incorporate variety, experiment with different cooking methods such as roasting, sautéing, or raw preparations. Season with herbs and spices rather than relying heavily on salt or fatty dressings.
- **One-Quarter of the Plate: Lean Protein Sources:**
  - Protein is essential for building and repairing tissues, producing hormones and enzymes, and supporting immune function. By allocating a quarter of your plate to lean protein sources, you ensure adequate protein intake without excessive saturated fat, which can be detrimental to heart health.
  - Opt for grilled or baked poultry, fish rich in omega-3 fatty acids like salmon or mackerel, plant-based proteins such as tofu, tempeh, or legumes. These proteins support muscle health and keep you feeling fuller for longer, curbing the urge for snacking between meals.
- **One-Quarter of the Plate: Whole Grains or Starchy Vegetables:**
  - Carbohydrates are a primary energy source, but choosing the right type and quantity is crucial, especially for those managing diabetes. Whole grains and starchy vegetables provide fiber, which helps slow down glucose absorption, moderating blood sugar spikes.
  - Favor whole grains like quinoa, barley, and brown rice, or starchy vegetables like sweet potatoes and squash. These options offer complex carbohydrates for sustained energy release, alongside vital nutrients and fiber for digestive health.

## The Benefits of the Plate Method

- **Simplifies Meal Planning**: The visual nature of the Plate Method demystifies healthy eating, making it accessible to everyone, regardless of nutritional expertise. It eliminates the need for meticulous calorie counting by focusing on proportions and food quality.
- **Promotes Nutrient Diversity**: By encouraging a variety of food groups, the Plate Method ensures a well-rounded intake of essential nutrients, supporting overall physical and metabolic health.
- **Flexible and Adaptable**: This approach can be adapted to any cuisine and dietary preference, from vegan to paleo, making it universally applicable. It also accommodates eating out, as you can visually estimate plate divisions even when dining at restaurants.

## Implementing the Plate Method

- **Start Small**: If the Plate Method represents a significant shift from your current eating habits, start by adjusting one meal a day and gradually expand to all meals.
- **Plan Ahead**: Think about your plate composition when grocery shopping, ensuring you have a variety of non-starchy vegetables, lean proteins, and whole grains at home.
- **Mind the Details**: Pay attention to cooking methods and seasonings to keep your meals within the healthful spectrum of the Plate Method.

## *Healthy Cooking Techniques and Substitutions*

Understanding the impact of cooking techniques and ingredient substitutions on the nutritional quality of meals is crucial, especially for individuals managing type 2 diabetes. The way we prepare food can either enhance its nutritional value or diminish it. Choosing healthier cooking methods and ingredients can significantly improve your diet's overall quality, making it easier to control blood sugar levels while enjoying delicious meals. Let's dive deeper into how to implement these strategies effectively.

### Healthy Cooking Techniques

**Grilling:** Grilling is a fantastic way to cook meats, vegetables, and even fruits, imparting a smoky flavor that enhances the food's natural taste without the need for extra fats or oils. However, it's important to monitor the grilling process closely to prevent charring, which can produce harmful compounds. Opt for lean cuts of meat and marinate them in vinegar or lemon juice-based marinades to reduce these risks.

**Baking:** Baking allows for the slow cooking of foods at relatively low temperatures, making it ideal for tenderizing meat and roasting vegetables. To keep baked goods on the healthier side, focus on recipes that call for whole grain flours, minimal added sugars, and healthy fats like olive oil or avocado oil. Consider swapping out white flour for whole wheat, almond, or oat flour to increase fiber content, which is beneficial for blood sugar control.

**Steaming:** This method is perhaps one of the best ways to preserve the nutritional integrity of vegetables. Steaming softens the food while retaining its vitamins and minerals, which can be lost during boiling. Investing in a simple steamer basket can transform your vegetable intake, making it easy to prepare vibrant, nutrient-packed sides.

**Stir-frying:** Stir-frying in a wok or large skillet allows for quick cooking at high temperatures, using minimal oil. The key is to use heart-healthy oils like olive or canola oil and to keep the food moving constantly to prevent overcooking. This method is perfect for making vegetable-heavy dishes that are both flavorful and filling.

### Substitutions for Healthier Meals

**Fats and Oils:** Replacing saturated fats with unsaturated fats is a straightforward way to make meals healthier. Use olive oil for cooking and salad dressings instead of butter or margarine. Avocado oil is another excellent option for high-heat cooking due to its high smoke point.

**Salt:** Reducing sodium intake can help manage blood pressure, a common concern in diabetes. Enhance flavors with herbs, spices, garlic, onion, and citrus juices instead of relying on salt. These natural flavor boosters add depth to dishes without the health risks associated with high sodium consumption.

**Sugar:** Refined sugars can spike blood sugar levels, making management more challenging. Natural sweeteners like stevia, monk fruit, or erythritol can sweeten foods without the adverse effects on glucose levels. When baking, consider using fruit purees, such as unsweetened applesauce or mashed bananas, to add sweetness along with additional nutrients and fiber.

**Whole Foods:** Incorporating whole foods into your cooking is a powerful way to boost the nutritional content of your meals. For example, add grated vegetables to meatballs or meatloaf to increase their moisture, flavor, and nutritional value. Use whole grains like quinoa, bulgur, or farro as bases for salads or sides to add fiber and protein, which can help stabilize blood sugar levels.

## *The Role of Salt and How to Use It Wisely*

Salt, composed mainly of sodium chloride, plays a crucial role in our diet, impacting flavor, food preservation, and essential bodily functions. Sodium, a component of salt, is necessary for nerve function, muscle contraction, and maintaining fluid balance within the body. However, the relationship between salt intake and health, especially for those with diabetes, is a balancing act. While salt is indispensable for its roles, excessive consumption is a well-documented risk factor for hypertension (high blood pressure), a condition that significantly compounds the risk of heart disease, particularly in individuals with diabetes.

The American Heart Association recommends no more than 2,300 milligrams of sodium per day, moving toward an ideal limit of about 1,500 mg per day for most adults. This is because high sodium intake is associated with increased blood pressure, which can lead to cardiovascular diseases, stroke, and kidney damage – conditions that individuals with diabetes are already at higher risk for.

**Using Salt Wisely**

1. **Enhancing Flavors Naturally:** To mitigate the health risks without compromising taste, it's advisable to use salt sparingly and lean on natural flavor enhancers. Herbs and spices, whether fresh or dried, can introduce complex flavors to dishes without the need for excessive salt. For instance, rosemary and thyme can add depth to meats, while cilantro and lime can brighten up a dish. Lemon juice and vinegar can provide the acidity that balances a dish's flavors, reducing the need for additional salt.

2. **Salt Additions:** When cooking, adding salt in increments and tasting regularly can prevent over-salting. It's easier to add more salt to a dish than to correct an overly salty one. Incorporating salt towards the end of the cooking process can also help, as it preserves its potency and reduces the overall quantity required.

3. **Understanding Hidden Sodium:** A significant proportion of dietary sodium comes from processed and packaged foods, not just the salt shaker. Foods that might not even taste salty, like bread, packaged snacks, and even some breakfast cereals, can contain high levels of sodium. Reading nutrition labels is essential for managing sodium intake. Opting for products labeled "low sodium," "reduced sodium," or "no added salt" can make a substantial difference. For example, choosing a low-sodium version of canned vegetables or soups can drastically reduce sodium intake without sacrificing convenience.

4. **Rinse to Reduce:** For canned products, even those not labeled as low sodium, rinsing the contents under cold water can wash away a significant amount of the added sodium, making them a healthier addition to meals.

5. **Be Cautious with Condiments:** Condiments, although used in small quantities, can be surprisingly high in sodium. For instance, soy sauce, ketchup, and prepared salad dressings can pack a lot of sodium in just a few tablespoons. Opting for lower-sodium versions or making homemade alternatives can provide control over the amount of sodium added to your food.

6. **Balance with Potassium:** Potassium can help mitigate the effects of sodium on blood pressure. Including foods high in potassium, such as bananas, potatoes, spinach, and beans, in your diet can help counterbalance sodium intake and support healthy blood pressure levels.

## *The Benefits of Organic Foods*

The conversation around organic foods is becoming increasingly relevant, not just for those focused on environmental sustainability but also for individuals managing chronic health conditions, such as diabetes. The benefits of organic foods stem from the methods used in their production, which are designed to work with natural systems rather than dominating them. Here, we delve into the nutritional and environmental advantages of organic foods, emphasizing their importance for people with diabetes and others seeking a healthier lifestyle.

**Benefits to Nutrition** When comparing organic foods to their conventionally cultivated equivalents, it is common knowledge that organic foods have more nutrients. Studies have indicated that some elements, such as vitamins, minerals, and antioxidants, may be present in higher concentrations in organic vegetables.Antioxidants, for example, play a critical role in fighting inflammation—a key concern for individuals with diabetes, as chronic inflammation can exacerbate insulin resistance. The enhanced nutritional profile of organic foods can be attributed to the healthier, more naturally balanced soil in which they are grown. Without synthetic fertilizers, organic plants tend to grow more slowly but in the process, they can accumulate more nutrients.

**Reduced Chemical Exposure** One of the most compelling reasons to choose organic foods is the reduced exposure to synthetic pesticides and fertilizers. These chemicals can remain as residues on (and in) the foods we eat, and their long-term health effects are still being studied. For people with diabetes, who often have to be more mindful of their health, reducing exposure to potential toxins is crucial. Pesticides have been linked to a range of health issues, including hormonal imbalances and immune system effects. By choosing organic, individuals can lower their risk of pesticide exposure, potentially reducing the likelihood of these adverse effects.

**Sustainable Practices** Organic farming is inherently more sustainable than conventional agriculture. It promotes biodiversity, conserves water, and enhances soil health. By avoiding synthetic chemicals, organic farms support the ecosystems they occupy, including pollinators, soil microorganisms, and local wildlife. These practices lead to healthier soil, which in turn supports plant health and contributes to the sequestration of carbon, reducing the impact of farming on climate change. For consumers concerned about their ecological footprint, choosing organic is a step towards supporting agricultural practices that are in harmony with nature.

**Choosing Organic Foods** While organic foods can be more expensive, their benefits often justify the higher price tag. For those on a budget, prioritizing organic purchases can be strategic. The Environmental Working Group's "Dirty Dozen" list identifies fruits and vegetables that typically carry higher pesticide residues; opting for organic versions of these items can be a good starting point. Leafy greens and berries are often highlighted for their pesticide loads, making them prime candidates for organic selection. Furthermore, organic whole grains, legumes, and lean meats offer cleaner sources of essential nutrients, free from the additives and preservatives common in conventional products.

# Part IV
# Living Well with Type 2 Diabetes , Practical Steps for Change and Prevention

## TEN DIETARY HACKS FOR DIABETES

## *Detailing Ten Fundamental Principles*

Managing type 2 diabetes requires thoughtful dietary choices that sustain balanced blood sugar levels and promote overall health. In this context, implementing simple, effective dietary hacks can significantly impact your well-being.

**1. Embrace Whole Foods**: Opt for foods in their most natural state. Whole foods like vegetables, fruits, nuts, seeds, lean meats, and fish are rich in nutrients and fiber, which help regulate blood sugar levels. For instance, swap processed snacks for a handful of almonds or a piece of fruit.

**2. Prioritize Low-Glycemic Index Foods**: Foods with a low glycemic index (GI) have a lesser impact on blood sugar levels. Incorporate more non-starchy vegetables, such as leafy greens, and whole grains, like quinoa and barley, into your meals. Berries are an excellent low-GI fruit option.

**3. Incorporate Healthy Fats**: Healthy fats can slow the absorption of sugar into the bloodstream, reducing blood sugar spikes. Avocados, olive oil, nuts, and seeds are excellent sources. Drizzling olive oil on salads or adding avocado slices to your meals can be beneficial.

**4. Lean on Lean Proteins**: Protein can increase satiety and has little effect on blood sugar levels. Lean protein options include fish, tofu, chicken breast, turkey, and lentils. A grilled salmon fillet or a stir-fry with tofu and vegetables are diabetic-friendly meal choices.

**5. Favor Fiber-Rich Foods**: Because fiber slows the absorption of glucose, it helps control blood sugar levels. Beans, lentils, whole grains, and vegetables are high in fiber. Starting your day with oatmeal topped with berries or adding lentils to your soups are simple ways to increase your fiber intake.

**6. Hydrate Healthily**: Replace sugary drinks with water, herbal teas, or unsweetened sparkling water. Proper hydration is key to managing diabetes, and making water your primary beverage choice can make a significant difference.

**7. Plan Your Portions**: Being mindful of portion sizes helps control blood sugar and weight. Use measuring cups or scales to familiarize yourself with standard serving sizes, and consider using smaller plates to naturally reduce portion sizes.

**8. Time Your Meals**: Blood sugar levels can be kept stable by eating at regular intervals. Aim for three to five hours of well-balanced meals and snacks. A handful of walnuts and a little apple could make a satisfying midmorning snack.

**9. Simplify Carb Counting**: Instead of eliminating carbs entirely, focus on the type and quantity. Limit high-carb and processed foods, and when you do consume carbs, pair them with protein or healthy fats to mitigate blood sugar spikes.

**10. Cook at Home**: You have control over the ingredients and quantity sizes when you prepare your own food. Experiment with diabetic-friendly recipes that emphasize fresh, whole ingredients. Homemade vegetable stir-fry with brown rice or a turkey and vegetable soup can be both satisfying and healthy.

## *Simple Changes for Maximum Impact*

Incorporating the ten dietary hacks for managing type 2 diabetes is the first step. The next phase involves implementing these strategies to ensure they yield maximum impact with minimal disruption to your lifestyle. These adjustments are designed to fit seamlessly into your lifestyle, making it easier to maintain healthy blood sugar levels without feeling deprived or overwhelmed. Remember, the goal is progress, not perfection; every small change contributes to a larger impact on your health. Here are simple yet effective changes that can significantly improve your dietary habits and, consequently, your blood sugar management:

**Maximize Vegetable Intake**: Start by filling half of your plate with non-starchy vegetables at every meal. This simple change increases fiber intake, which aids in blood sugar control and promotes satiety, reducing the temptation to overeat. For example, a dinner plate could include grilled chicken, a small serving of quinoa, and a large portion of steamed broccoli and carrots.

**Choose Whole Grains Wisely**: Swap refined grains for their whole-grain counterparts. For example, swap out white bread for whole-grain bread or white rice for brown rice. These substitutions help lower the meal's glycemic impact, providing a steadier source of energy without the sharp spikes in blood sugar.

**Smart Snacking**: Replace high-carb or sugary snacks with healthier alternatives. Snack on a small handful of nuts, a piece of cheese with some slices of cucumber, or a hard-boiled egg. These snacks are low in carbs and high in protein and healthy fats, helping to keep blood sugar levels stable between meals.

**Cooking Methods Matter**: Opt for cooking methods that preserve the nutritional integrity of food and require less added fat. Grilling, baking, steaming, and sautéing are excellent choices. For instance, instead of frying fish, try baking it with herbs and a splash of lemon for flavor.

**Herbs and Spices are Your Friends**: Enhance the flavor of your meals with herbs and spices instead of salt or sugar. Not only do they add a burst of flavor without extra calories, but many herbs and spices, such as cinnamon and turmeric, have been shown to have blood sugar-lowering properties.

**Mindful Eating**: Eating mindfully involves observing your meal and taking it gently. By developing this habit, you can identify hunger and fullness cues more accurately and avoid overindulging. It's a small adjustment that can help with weight management and blood sugar regulation.

**Hydration Hacks**: For a refreshing twist, add pieces of fruit or herbs, such as basil or mint, to your water. It makes drinking water more enjoyable, encouraging you to stay well-hydrated without reaching for sugary drinks.

**Portion Control Tools**: Use measuring tools or visual cues for portion control. For instance, a serving of meat should be about the size of a deck of cards, and a serving of cooked rice or pasta about the size of a tennis ball. This visual approach simplifies portion control without the need for constant measuring.

**Meal Prep Mastery**: Dedicate a few hours each week to meal prep. Preparing meals and snacks ahead of time ensures you have healthy options readily available, reducing the likelihood of making less nutritious choices when you're hungry.

**Adaptable Recipes**: Modify your favorite recipes to make them more diabetes-friendly. For example, reduce the amount of sugar called for in recipes or use mashed bananas or applesauce as a natural sweetener. Experiment with replacing some of the flour in baked goods with almond or coconut flour for lower-carb alternatives.

# LIFESTYLE MODIFICATIONS FOR DIABETES MANAGEMENT

Physical activity stands as a pivotal ally in the management and prevention of type 2 diabetes, highlighting the essential role of daily movement in maintaining optimal health. In today's increasingly sedentary world, where prolonged sitting has become the norm for many, incorporating regular physical activity into our routines has never been more crucial. This section will delve into the importance of daily movement and provide simple strategies to enhance physical activity, tailored to fit the lifestyle of the average American with minimal background knowledge on the subject.

The link between physical activity and diabetes management is well-documented and supported by numerous studies. Regular exercise helps control blood sugar levels, improves insulin sensitivity, and can lead to weight loss, reducing the risk of developing type 2 diabetes or managing the condition more effectively for those already diagnosed. Here are the key benefits and strategies to increase physical activity:

## *The Importance of Daily Movement*

- **Blood Sugar Control**: Exercise helps muscles absorb blood sugar, decreasing the body's reliance on insulin. This absorption process aids in stabilizing blood glucose levels, crucial for managing diabetes.
- **Weight Management**: Engaging in physical activity burns calories, which is essential for weight loss and maintaining a healthy weight. Since obesity is a significant risk factor for type 2 diabetes, regular exercise is beneficial in preventing and managing the disease.
- **Enhanced Insulin Sensitivity**: Physical activity improves the body's sensitivity to insulin, allowing it to use this hormone more effectively. Improved insulin sensitivity means that the body requires less insulin to control blood sugar levels.

## Simple Strategies to Increase Physical Activity

Implementing regular physical activity into one's daily routine does not necessitate drastic changes or a gym membership. Here are practical tips to seamlessly integrate more movement into everyday life:

1. **Incorporate Walking into Your Routine:**
   - Take a brisk walk for at least 30 minutes a day. Consider walking to work, taking a stroll during lunch breaks, or walking the dog in the evening.
   - Use stairs instead of elevators whenever possible. This simple switch can significantly increase your daily calorie burn and strengthen your leg muscles.

2. **Deskercise for Office Workers:**
   - Stand up and stretch every hour. Set a timer to remind yourself to take short breaks from sitting.
   - Try desk exercises, such as seated leg lifts or chair squats, to keep the blood flowing even while at work.

3. **Engage in Fun Activities:**
   - Choose physical activities that you enjoy. Whether it's dancing, swimming, cycling, or playing a sport, engaging in enjoyable activities increases the likelihood of sticking with an exercise routine.
   - Involve friends or family. Group activities not only make exercising more fun but also provide motivation and support.

4. **Embrace Household Chores:**
   - View household chores as an opportunity for movement. Gardening, vacuuming, and even washing dishes can contribute to your daily physical activity quota.
   - Turn chores into mini-workouts by incorporating lunges while vacuuming or doing squats while loading the dishwasher.

5. **Use Technology to Your Advantage:**
   - Wear a fitness tracker to monitor your steps, heart rate, and calories burned. Setting daily goals can motivate you to move more.
   - Download fitness apps that provide guided workouts you can do at home, requiring minimal or no equipment.

6. **Start Small and Gradually Increase Activity:**
   - Begin with short, manageable sessions of physical activity and gradually increase the duration and intensity. Starting too ambitiously can lead to burnout or injury.
   - Remember, consistency is key. Aim for at least 160 minutes of moderate aerobic activity or 80 minutes of vigorous activity each week, as recommended by health guidelines.

## Stress Management Techniques

Managing stress is an essential, yet often overlooked, component of diabetes management. Chronic stress can have a profound impact on blood glucose levels, making it crucial for individuals with type 2 diabetes to develop effective stress management techniques. Understanding the relationship between stress and blood glucose levels and implementing strategies to mitigate stress can significantly contribute to better overall health and diabetes control. This section will delve into the mechanisms by which stress affects diabetes and provide practical, science-backed methods for reducing stress.

Stress, whether it's physical or emotional, triggers the release of various hormones like adrenaline and cortisol. These hormones can cause an increase in blood glucose levels by stimulating glucose production in the liver and reducing the effectiveness of insulin. For individuals with type 2 diabetes, where the body's ability to use insulin efficiently is already compromised, stress can exacerbate blood sugar control issues. Therefore, incorporating stress management techniques into one's lifestyle is as vital as dietary changes and physical activity for managing diabetes.

Effective Stress Management Techniques

**1. Mindfulness and Meditation**: Mindfulness meditation involves paying attention to the present moment without judgment. Studies have shown that regular mindfulness practice can reduce stress levels, improve focus, and even lower blood glucose levels. Starting with as little as five minutes a day can make a difference.

**2. Deep Breathing Exercises**: Deep, diaphragmatic breathing is a simple yet effective way to trigger the body's relaxation response. Stress can be reduced and the mind calmed by using techniques like the 4-7-8 method, which involves inhaling for 4 seconds, holding your breath for 7 seconds, and then gently exhaling for 8 seconds.

**3. Regular Physical Activity**: A great way to reduce stress is to exercise. It can be as easy as taking a daily stroll, doing yoga, or engaging in any other consistent and enjoyable exercise. The body's natural mood enhancers, endorphins, are released more frequently when people exercise, which also helps reduce stress chemicals.

**4. Adequate Sleep**: Stress can make it more difficult to get a good night's sleep, which can lead to a vicious cycle where stress exacerbates poor sleep. Improved sleep quality can be achieved by making a pleasant sleeping environment, avoiding gadgets and caffeine right before bed, and establishing a regular sleep pattern.

**5. Healthy Social Connections**: Having social interactions with friends and family can ease stress, lessen feelings of loneliness, and offer emotional support. Virtual meetings or phone conversations can provide substantial emotional support even in situations where face-to-face interactions are not feasible.

**6. Time Management**: Feeling overwhelmed by tasks and responsibilities can increase stress. Effective time management, including prioritizing tasks, breaking them into smaller steps, and setting aside time for relaxation and self-care, can help reduce this stress.

**7. Engage in Hobbies**: Activities that you find enjoyable and fulfilling can serve as an excellent stress outlet. Whether it's gardening, painting, playing a musical instrument, or cooking, hobbies can provide a sense of accomplishment and relaxation.

**8. Seek Professional Help**: Sometimes, stress can be overwhelming, affecting not just diabetes management but overall health and well-being. In such cases, seeking help from a psychologist or counselor can provide strategies to cope with stress more effectively.

**Incorporating Stress Management into Daily Life**

Implementing stress management techniques requires practice and consistency. Here are some practical steps to integrate these strategies into your daily routine:

- **Create a Routine**: Dedicate specific times of the day for stress-reducing activities like exercise or meditation. Having a routine can make it easier to stick to these practices.
- **Set Realistic Goals**: Begin with manageable objectives, like going for a ten-minute walk or five minutes of meditation each day. As you get more comfortable, gradually increase the time and frequency.
- **Monitor Your Progress**: Keeping a journal of your stress levels and blood glucose readings can help you see the correlation between stress management and diabetes control, providing motivation to continue these practices.
- **Be Patient with Yourself**: Forming new routines requires time. If you miss a day or find it hard to follow your regimen at first, treat yourself with kindness. Recall that long-term health and wellbeing are the main objectives.

## *The Importance of Regular Health Check-Ups*

Regular health check-ups are a cornerstone of effective diabetes management and prevention. They provide a structured approach to monitoring your condition, offer a platform for education and adjustment, and most importantly, they empower you to take an active role in your health journey. Remember, the goal of managing type 2 diabetes is not just to keep blood sugar levels in check but to maintain overall health and prevent the onset of complications. Regular health check-ups are your best ally in achieving this goal.

**The Foundation of Health Management**

Regular health check-ups serve multiple purposes, primarily acting as a preventive measure. They allow for early detection of changes in health status, particularly concerning blood sugar levels, which, if unmonitored, could lead to severe complications. Here's why they are indispensable:

- **Monitoring Blood Sugar Levels**: Regular testing of blood sugar levels is paramount. It helps in adjusting diets, medication, and exercise plans to better manage diabetes. The A1C test, which measures your average blood sugar level over the past two to three months, is particularly insightful for long-term monitoring.

- **Identifying Complications Early**: Diabetes can affect various parts of the body, including the heart, kidneys, eyes, and nerves. Regular check-ups can catch the early signs of such complications, enabling prompt treatment to prevent progression.
- **Adjusting Treatment Plans**: As your lifestyle changes, so too might your diabetes management needs. Regular appointments provide the opportunity to review and adjust your treatment plan, ensuring it remains effective.
- **Educational Opportunity**: Each visit is a chance to learn more about managing diabetes. Whether it's nutritional advice, exercise tips, or understanding medication side effects, these sessions are invaluable for education and empowerment.

### Key Aspects of Health Check-Ups

During a health check-up, your healthcare provider will focus on several key areas, including:

- **Blood Pressure Monitoring**: High blood pressure is a common issue among those with diabetes, increasing the risk of heart disease and stroke. Regular monitoring can detect any changes early on.
- **Foot Examinations**: Diabetes can lead to nerve damage and reduced blood flow to the feet, increasing the risk of infections and ulcers. Annual foot exams are crucial for detecting such issues early.
- **Eye Examinations**: Diabetic retinopathy, a condition that can lead to blindness, is a significant risk. Regular eye exams help catch and treat these problems early.
- **Kidney Function Tests**: Over time, renal function may be impacted by diabetes. The functioning of your kidneys is determined by tests such as the estimated glomerular filtration rate (eGFR) test and the urine albumin test.
- **Lipid Profile Testing**: Checking cholesterol levels is important since diabetes increases the risk of heart disease. A lipid profile test can help your healthcare provider recommend dietary or medication changes if needed.

### Making the Most of Your Health Check-Ups

To benefit fully from your health check-ups, preparation and active participation are key. Here's how to ensure each visit is as productive as possible:

- **Come Prepared**: Before your appointment, make a list of any questions or concerns you have, including any changes in your health, new symptoms, or effects of medication.
- **Be Open and Honest**: Share all relevant information with your healthcare provider, including your eating habits, physical activity levels, and any challenges you're facing in managing diabetes.
- **Follow Through**: After your check-up, make sure to follow your healthcare provider's recommendations, whether it's adjusting your diet, changing your medication, or undergoing further testing.

# CHALLENGES AND SETBACKS

Navigating the path of managing or preventing type 2 diabetes is akin to embarking on a journey with its own set of challenges and setbacks. This journey demands resilience, adaptability, and an unwavering commitment to your health. Managing diabetes or working towards its prevention is not a linear process; it involves navigating ups and downs. Remember, every step taken on this journey, no matter how small, is a step towards a healthier, more fulfilling life.

## Coping with Food Cravings

Coping with food cravings, especially for sugary or high-carb foods, is a nuanced challenge in the management of diabetes. These cravings are not merely about self-control or discipline; they stem from a complex web of physiological, psychological, and environmental factors, including stress, hormonal changes, and established eating habits.

Understanding and addressing these cravings with practical strategies can significantly impact diabetes management positively.

**Understanding Your Triggers**

The initial step towards managing food cravings effectively is to identify and understand your personal triggers. Cravings can be triggered by a variety of factors:

- **Emotional Responses**: Stress, anxiety, and even happiness can trigger cravings. Emotional eating is a common response to dealing with feelings, both positive and negative.
- **Boredom**: Sometimes, eating becomes an activity to pass the time rather than a response to actual hunger.
- **Social Settings**: Being in environments where high-carb or sugary foods are readily available, such as parties or dinners out, can ignite cravings.
- **Habitual Eating**: Eating sweets or snacks at a certain time of day can become a hard habit to break.

Recognizing these triggers is crucial because it allows you to prepare and develop specific strategies to counteract them, rather than succumbing to the cravings blindly.

**Healthy Substitutes**

One of the most effective tactics to deal with cravings is to have a list of healthier alternatives ready. This doesn't mean you have to give up on flavor or satisfaction. For instance:

- If you're craving something sweet, instead of reaching for candy or sugary snacks, consider a piece of fruit like berries, which are lower in sugar and high in fiber, or a small piece of dark chocolate with a high cocoa content, which is lower in sugar and contains antioxidants.
- For savory cravings, opt for nuts or seeds, which offer a satisfying crunch and are packed with healthy fats and protein, rather than chips or other processed snacks.

The key is to find substitutes that you enjoy and are readily accessible, making the healthier choice the easier choice.

**Stay Hydrated**

Many times, cravings for food or hunger are mistaken for thirst. Wait a few minutes and sip on a glass of water before giving in to a temptation. It's possible that the craving goes away. Keeping hydrated has numerous benefits for overall health and can help manage hunger and satiety signals more effectively.

**Mindful Eating**

Mindful eating is about being fully present during meals, focusing on the experience of eating, and listening to your body's hunger and fullness signals. This approach can help you enjoy food more and feel satisfied with smaller portions. Here are a few mindful eating practices:

- **Eat Slowly**: Between bites, take your time chewing your food fully and set down your utensils. This promotes improved digestion and allows your body more time to detect fullness.
- **Eliminate Distractions**: Aim to eat without using your phone, TV, or computer. When you eat in silence, you may concentrate on the tastes and textures of your meal as well as your feelings at the moment.
- **Check-in with Your Feelings**: Before you eat, consider if you're actually hungry or whether you're just filling up on food to deal with emotions or boredom.
- **Savor Each Bite**: Take note of your food's flavor, texture, and scent. Making more fulfilling decisions and appreciating the food you eat can result from this.

## *Handling Social Situations and Holidays*

Handling social situations and holidays requires a strategic approach, especially when managing or preventing type 2 diabetes. The abundance of food, often rich and indulgent, can pose significant challenges. However, with a thoughtful plan, you can fully enjoy these gatherings without compromising your health goals. Here's an expanded explanation on how to navigate these situations effectively:

**Plan Ahead**

Foreknowledge of the menu can significantly impact your ability to stick to your dietary plan. Before attending any event, inquire about the menu. This allows you to psychologically get ready for the decisions you'll be making. If you expect to find few healthful options, think about having a modest, well-balanced meal before you leave. This may lessen the need to overindulge and curb hunger.

Offering to bring a dish not only ensures there's something you can comfortably eat, but it also introduces others to healthy, delicious alternatives. Choose recipes that are both nutritious and flavorful. Dishes rich in fibers, like salads with leafy greens, quinoa dishes, or vegetable-based casseroles, can be great choices. They're not only suitable for you but can also offer a healthful option for all guests, subtly promoting a healthier eating culture.

**Portion Control**

Portion control is an invaluable tool in any dietary plan, more so in social settings where food is plentiful. Use smaller plates to naturally limit portion sizes. Fill half your plate with vegetables and the other half with equal parts of protein and whole grains or legumes. This method helps ensure a balanced intake without feeling deprived.

When faced with buffet-style dining, scan all the options before filling your plate. Prioritize dishes that align with your dietary needs, and allow yourself a small portion of a "treat" food if you feel it's too hard to pass up entirely. Enjoy each bite slowly, savoring the flavors, which can help you feel satisfied with less.

**Communicate Your Needs**

Open communication about your dietary needs can ease the stress of dining in social settings. When invited to a gathering, don't shy away from discussing your dietary restrictions with the host. Most hosts appreciate knowing in advance and can often accommodate your needs without inconvenience.

Offer suggestions for simple modifications to dishes that can make them more suitable for your dietary requirements. For example, suggesting olive oil and vinegar as a salad dressing instead of a cream-based option is a small change that can make a big difference in managing your blood sugar levels.

**Focus on Non-Food Enjoyments**

While food is often a central aspect of gatherings, shifting your focus to non-food joys can enrich your experience. Engage deeply in conversations, savoring the connections with friends and family. Participate in games, dancing, or any group activities available. These moments contribute significantly to the enjoyment of social gatherings and can make food seem like just one of many pleasures.

## *Strategies for Maintaining Motivation*

Maintaining motivation in the long-term management or prevention of type 2 diabetes is both a challenge and a necessity. Without sustained motivation, it becomes difficult to adhere to healthy lifestyle choices that are critical in managing this condition. Below, we delve deeper into strategies for keeping motivation high, ensuring that individuals remain committed to their health goals over time.

**Setting Realistic Goals**

Creating achievable goals is fundamental in maintaining motivation. Goals that are too ambitious may lead to disappointment and a loss of motivation if they are not met. It is crucial to set goals that are:

- **Specific**: Clearly define what you want to achieve. For instance, rather than saying "I want to be healthier," specify "I want to reduce my A1C levels by 1% in the next six months."
- **Measurable**: Ensure that you can track your progress. This could mean monitoring your blood sugar levels, keeping a food diary, or logging exercise sessions.
- **Time-bound**: Assign a deadline to your objective. This keeps you focused and instills a sense of urgency.

**Celebrating Small Wins**

The journey to managing diabetes is made up of small steps. Each healthy meal, each day you exercise, and every time you choose water over a sugary drink is a step in the right direction. Celebrating these small victories can provide a significant boost to your motivation. It serves as a gentle reminder that you are improving. Creating a system of rewards for accomplishing these small objectives might also work well as a motivator.

## Seeking Support

You don't have to walk the path of diabetes management alone, even though it can occasionally feel lonely. Looking for assistance from:

- **Support Groups**: Getting involved in a diabetes support group can help people feel like they belong and part of the community. Exchanges of advice and experiences can be very encouraging.
- **Friends and Family**: Engaging your family members can provide a network of support and empathy. They may assist in keeping you responsible for your health objectives.
- **Healthcare Professionals**: Regular check-ins with your healthcare team not only monitor your progress but also provide professional guidance tailored to your specific needs.

## Educating Yourself

Particularly when it comes to treating a medical condition, knowledge truly is power. You can take control of your health and make wise decisions if you keep up your education on diabetes. This can involve:

- **Reading up on the Latest Research**: Stay informed about new treatments, management strategies, and nutritional guidelines.
- **Attending Workshops or Seminars**: These can provide valuable information and introduce you to others on the same journey.
- **Understanding Food and Activity Impacts**: You can make better decisions every day if you understand how various diets and physical activity affect your blood sugar levels.

## Reflecting on Your 'Why'

Remembering why you started this journey is perhaps the most potent motivator. Whether it's wanting to live a healthier life, being there for your family, or reducing the risk of diabetes-related complications, your 'why' is your anchor. During moments of temptation or frustration, reflecting on your reasons for embarking on this journey can provide a renewed sense of purpose and motivation.

## *Finding Support Groups and Communities*

Navigating the journey of managing or reversing type 2 diabetes is not a path one should walk alone. The support of family and friends is invaluable, yet there's another layer of support that can make a significant difference: support groups and communities. These groups offer a unique form of camaraderie, understanding, and shared experience that can provide comfort, motivation, and practical advice for those living with type 2 diabetes. In this section, we'll explore the importance of finding and joining support groups and communities, the benefits they offer, and how they can be a pivotal part of your diabetes management strategy.

### The Role of Support Groups

Support groups, whether online or in-person, serve as a gathering of individuals who share the common goal of managing their diabetes more effectively. Here's why they are essential:

- **Shared Experiences**: There's a sense of relief that comes from knowing you're not alone in your struggles. Having sympathetic ears to listen to your struggles, triumphs, and experiences can be immensely comforting.
- **Practical Advice**: Members often share tips and strategies that have worked for them, from navigating dining out to finding diabetic-friendly recipes and effective exercise routines. This practical advice can be a valuable supplement to the guidance you receive from your healthcare provider.

- **Emotional Support**: Managing diabetes can be emotionally taxing. Support groups offer a safe space to express frustrations, fears, and concerns, helping to alleviate the emotional burden of the disease.
- **Motivation and Accountability**: Seeing the progress of others can be highly motivating. Moreover, some groups set collective goals or challenges, fostering a sense of accountability that can drive you to adhere more closely to your management plan.

## Finding the Right Group

The key to benefiting from a support group is finding the right fit. Here's how to start your search:

- **Ask Your Healthcare Provider**: Many healthcare providers are aware of local or online support groups and can recommend ones that might be a good fit for you.
- **Research Online**: The internet is a treasure trove of forums, social media groups, and websites dedicated to diabetes management. Look for groups with active participation and positive, supportive interactions.
- **Check Local Community Centers**: Some community or religious centers host support groups for individuals with chronic illnesses, including diabetes.
- **Consider National Organizations**: Organizations such as the American Diabetes Association offer resources for finding support groups and even host their own.

## Engaging with Your Chosen Community

Once you've found a support group that feels like a good match, here are some tips to engage effectively:

- **Be an Active Participant**: Whether it's asking questions, sharing your experiences, or responding to others, active participation will help you get the most out of the group.
- **Respect Privacy**: Remember that support groups are built on trust.By keeping shared information private, you may show respect for other people's privacy.
- **Keep an Open Mind**: You'll likely encounter a wide range of perspectives and experiences. Keep an open mind and consider new ideas, but always consult with your healthcare provider before making any significant changes to your management plan.
- **Offer Support**: Just as you're looking for support, be there to offer encouragement and understanding to others. The mutual give-and-take is what makes these groups so beneficial.

## The Benefits Beyond

While the primary focus of diabetes support groups is managing the condition, the benefits often extend beyond:

- **Broader Health and Wellness Tips**: Many groups also focus on overall health and well-being, sharing advice on stress management, sleep improvement, and more.
- **Social Connections**: Regular interactions can lead to lasting friendships, providing a social outlet and reducing feelings of isolation.
- **Increased Knowledge**: Discussions often touch on the latest research, treatments, and technologies in diabetes care, helping you stay informed.

# Part V
# Diabetic Friendly Recipes

# BREAKFASTS

## *Oatmeal with Almonds and Berries*

**Instructions:**
1. In a medium saucepan, bring the water or almond milk to a boil. Add the rolled oats and reduce the heat to simmer. Cook, stirring occasionally, until the oats are soft, about 5 minutes.
2. Stir in the ground flaxseed and cinnamon.
3. Serve the oatmeal topped with fresh berries and chopped almonds.

**Time:** 10 minutes
**Servings:** 1
**Nutritional Information (approx.):** Calories: 280 | Carbohydrates: 45g | Fiber: 9g | Sugar: 5g | Protein: 10g | Fat: 9g | (Glycemic Index: Low)

**Ingredients:**
- ½ cup rolled oats
- 1 cup water or unsweetened almond milk
- ¼ cup fresh berries (blueberries, raspberries)
- 10 almonds, chopped
- 1 tablespoon flaxseed, ground
- Cinnamon to taste

## *Spinach and Feta Egg Muffins*

**Instructions:**
1. Preheat the oven to 375°F (190°C). Grease a muffin tin or line with muffin cups.
2. In a bowl, whisk the eggs. Stir in the chopped spinach, crumbled feta, diced bell peppers, salt, and pepper.
3. Pour the mixture into the muffin tin, filling each cup about ¾ full.
4. Bake for 20 minutes, or until the muffins are set and slightly golden on top.

**Time:** 25 minutes
**Servings:** 6 muffins (3 servings)

**Nutritional Information (approx.):** Calories: 200 per 2 muffins | Carbohydrates: 3g | Fiber: 1g | Sugar: 2g | Protein: 14g | Fat: 15g | (Glycemic Index: Low)

**Ingredients:**
- 4 large eggs
- 1 cup spinach, chopped
- ¼ cup feta cheese, crumbled
- ¼ cup bell peppers, diced
- Salt and pepper to taste

## *Chia Seed Pudding with Coconut Milk*

**Ingredients:**
- ¼ cup chia seeds
- 1 cup unsweetened coconut milk
- ½ teaspoon vanilla extract
- 1 tablespoon monk fruit sweetener (or adjust to taste)
- Fresh berries for topping

**Instructions:**
1. In a bowl, combine the chia seeds, coconut milk, vanilla extract, and monk fruit sweetener. Stir until well mixed.
2. Cover and refrigerate overnight, or for at least 6 hours, until the pudding achieves a thick and creamy texture.
3. Serve topped with fresh berries.

**Time:** 8 hours (mostly refrigeration time)
**Servings:** 2
**Nutritional Information (approx.):** Calories: 250 per serving | Carbohydrates: 15g | Fiber: 10g | Sugar: 1g | Protein: 5g | Fat: 19g | (Glycemic Index: Low)

## *Whole Grain Avocado Toast*

### Ingredients:
- 1 slice whole grain bread
- ½ ripe avocado
- Salt and pepper to taste
- Red pepper flakes (optional)
- A sprinkle of chia seeds

### Instructions:
1. Toast the whole grain bread to your preference.
2. Mash the avocado in a bowl and season with salt, pepper, and optional red pepper flakes for a little heat.
3. Over the toast, equally distribute the mashed avocado.
4. For an additional dose of fiber and omega-3 fatty acids, sprinkle some chia seeds on top.

**Time:** 5 minutes
**Servings:** 1

**Nutritional Information (approx.):** Calories: 250 | Carbohydrates: 30g | Fiber: 9g | Sugar: 3g | Protein: 7g | Fat: 14g)

## *Greek Yogurt with Walnut and Apple*

### Instructions:
1. Place the Greek yogurt in a bowl.
2. Top with diced apple and chopped walnuts.
3. Sprinkle cinnamon over the top for flavor without added sugar.

**Time:** 5 minutes
**Servings:** 1

**Nutritional Information (approx.):** Calories: 200 | Carbohydrates: 18g | Fiber: 4g | Sugar: 10g (natural sugars from apple) | Protein: 12g |Fat: 10g

### Ingredients:
- ½ cup plain Greek yogurt (unsweetened)
- 1 small apple, diced
- A handful of walnuts, chopped
- Cinnamon to taste

## *Quinoa Breakfast Bowl with Mixed Berries*

### Ingredients:
- ½ cup quinoa (rinsed)
- 1 cup water
- ½ cup mixed berries (blueberries, strawberries, raspberries)
- 1 tablespoon flaxseed meal
- A drizzle of almond milk (unsweetened)
- A sprinkle of cinnamon (optional)

### Instructions:
1. In a saucepan, combine quinoa and water. Bring to a boil, then cover and simmer for 15 minutes, or until water is absorbed.
2. Fluff the cooked quinoa with a fork and divide between two bowls.
3. Top with mixed berries and sprinkle flaxseed meal over each bowl.
4. Add a drizzle of almond milk and a sprinkle of cinnamon for extra flavor.

**Time:** 20 minutes
**Servings:** 2

**Nutritional Information (approx.):** Calories: 220 per serving | Carbohydrates: 39g | Fiber: 6g | Sugar: 5g (natural sugars from berries) | Protein: 8g | Fat: 4g

## *Egg White Omelet with Mixed Vegetables*

**Ingredients:**

- 4 egg whites
- ½ cup mixed vegetables (spinach, bell peppers, onions, diced)
- ¼ cup low-fat shredded cheese (optional)
- Salt and pepper to taste
- 1 tsp olive oil

**Instructions:**

1. Heat olive oil in a non-stick skillet over medium heat. Sauté the mixed vegetables until they are just tender, about 5 minutes.
2. In a bowl, whisk the egg whites with salt and pepper. Pour over the sautéed vegetables in the skillet.
3. Cook until the egg whites are set, about 3-4 minutes. Sprinkle with cheese if using, fold the omelet in half, and cook for another minute.
4. Serve hot.

**Time:** 15 minutes
**Servings:** 1

**Nutritional Information (approx.):** Calories: 180 (with cheese) | Carbohydrates: 5g | Fiber: 2g | Sugar: 3g | Protein: 18g | Fat: 8g | (Glycemic Index: Low)

## *Low-GI Berry Smoothie*

**Instructions:**

1. Combine all ingredients in a blender.
2. Blend on high until smooth.
3. Serve immediately.

**Time:** 5 minutes
**Servings:** 1

**Nutritional Information (approx.):** Calories: 150 (without protein powder) | Carbohydrates: 15g | Fiber: 6g | Sugar: 7g | Protein: 8g (without protein powder) | Fat: 4.5g | (Glycemic Index: Low)

**Ingredients:**

- ½ cup frozen mixed berries (blueberries, strawberries, raspberries)
- 1 cup unsweetened almond milk
- 1 tablespoon chia seeds
- 1 scoop protein powder (optional)
- A few ice cubes

## *Cottage Cheese with Sliced Peaches*

**Instructions:**

1. Place the cottage cheese in a bowl.
2. Top with fresh peach slices.
3. Sprinkle with cinnamon if desired. Serve.

**Time:** 5 minutes
**Servings:** 1

**Nutritional Information (approx.):** Calories: 150 | Carbohydrates: 20g | Fiber: 2g | Sugar: 18g | Protein: 14g | Fat: 2g (Glycemic Index: Medium due to the natural sugars in peaches, but balanced by the protein in the cottage cheese)

**Ingredients:**

- ½ cup low-fat cottage cheese
- 1 medium peach, sliced
- A sprinkle of cinnamon (optional)

## Almond Butter and Banana Whole Grain Pancakes

**Ingredients:**
- 1 cup whole wheat flour
- 1 teaspoon baking powder
- ½ teaspoon cinnamon
- 1 ripe banana, mashed
- 1 egg
- ¾ cup unsweetened almond milk
- 2 tablespoons almond butter
- 1 teaspoon vanilla extract
- Cooking spray or 1 tsp olive oil for the pan

**Instructions:**
1. In a large bowl, mix together the flour, baking powder, and cinnamon.
2. In another bowl, whisk the egg, almond milk, mashed banana, almond butter, and vanilla extract until smooth.
3. Combine the wet ingredients with the dry ingredients, stirring until just mixed.
4. Heat a non-stick skillet over medium heat and lightly coat with cooking spray or olive oil.
5. Pour ¼ cup of batter for each pancake. Cook until bubbles form on the surface, then flip and cook until golden brown.
6. Serve warm.

**Time:** 20 minutes
**Servings:** 2
**Nutritional Information (approx.):** Calories: 350 per serving | Carbohydrates: 45g | Fiber: 8g | Sugar: 10g | Protein: 13g | Fat: 16g | (Glycemic Index: Medium-Low, thanks to whole grains and almond butter)

## Buckwheat Porridge with Almonds

**Instructions:**
1. Rinse the buckwheat groats under cold water.
2. In a medium saucepan, bring water to a boil. Add buckwheat and cinnamon, reduce heat to low, and simmer, covered, for 10-12 minutes, or until tender.
3. Stir in almond milk to reach your desired consistency.
4. Serve topped with chopped almonds and a drizzle of honey or maple syrup if using.

**Time:** 15 minutes
**Servings:** 2
**Nutritional Information (approx.):** Calories: 280 per serving | Carbohydrates: 50g | Fiber: 7g | Sugar: 5g (without honey/maple syrup) | Protein: 9g | Fat: 7g | (Glycemic Index: Low, buckwheat is a good option for blood sugar control)

**Ingredients:**
- 1 cup buckwheat groats
- 2 cups water
- ½ teaspoon cinnamon
- ¼ cup almonds, chopped
- 1 tablespoon honey or maple syrup (optional)
- ¼ cup unsweetened almond milk

## Savory Mashed Cauliflower with Poached Egg

**Ingredients:**
- 1 large head cauliflower, cut into florets
- 2 tablespoons olive oil
- Salt and pepper to taste
- 4 eggs
- 2 tablespoons vinegar (for poaching eggs)
- Chopped chives for garnish (optional)

**Instructions:**
1. Steam the cauliflower florets until very tender, about 15 minutes.
2. Transfer to a bowl, add olive oil, salt, and pepper, and mash until smooth.
3. Bring a pot of water to a simmer and add vinegar. Carefully crack eggs into the water. Poach for 3-4 minutes or until the whites are set but yolks are still runny.
4. Serve the mashed cauliflower topped with poached eggs and sprinkle with chives if desired.

**Time:** 25 minutes
**Servings:** 2
**Nutritional Information (approx.):** Calories: 300 per serving | Carbohydrates: 15g | Fiber: 7g | Sugar: 5g | Protein: 14g | Fat: 22g | (Glycemic Index: Low, cauliflower is an excellent low-carb substitute for starchier sides)

**Ingredients:**
- 4 eggs, beaten
- 1 cup kale, chopped
- ½ cup mushrooms, sliced
- ¼ cup onions, diced
- 1 tbsp olive oil
- Salt and pepper to taste
- ¼ cup low-fat feta cheese (optional)

**Instructions:**
1. Preheat the oven to 375°F (190°C).
2. In a skillet, heat olive oil over medium heat. Sauté onions, mushrooms, and kale until soft, about 5 minutes.
3. In a bowl, whisk eggs with salt and pepper. Add the sautéed vegetables and mix well.
4. Pour the mixture into a greased baking dish. Sprinkle with feta cheese if using.
5. Bake for 15-20 minutes or until the eggs are set.
6. Serve warm.

**Time:** 25 minutes
**Servings:** 2

**Nutritional Information (approx.):** Calories: 220 | Carbohydrates: 6g | Fiber: 1g | Sugar: 3g | Protein: 14g | Fat: 16g (Glycemic Index: Low)

## *Steel-Cut Oats with Cinnamon and Flaxseed*

**Instructions:**
1. In a pot, bring water to a boil. Add steel-cut oats and reduce heat to simmer.
2. Cook uncovered, stirring occasionally, for about 15-20 minutes or until oats are tender.
3. Stir in cinnamon, flaxseed, and apple sauce or sweetener.
4. Serve warm.

**Time:** 20 minutes
**Servings:** 2

**Nutritional Information (approx.):** Calories: 150 | Carbohydrates: 27g | Fiber: 5g | Sugar: 0g (not including sweetener) | Protein: 5g | Fat: 3g (Glycemic Index: Low)

**Ingredients:**
- ½ cup steel-cut oats
- 2 cups water
- 1 tsp cinnamon
- 1 tbsp flaxseed, ground
- 1 tbsp no-sugar-added apple sauce or a sweetener of choice

## *Scrambled Tofu with Spinach and Tomatoes*

**Ingredients:**
- 1 cup firm tofu, crumbled
- 1 cup spinach, fresh
- ½ cup tomatoes, diced
- 1 tbsp olive oil
- ½ tsp turmeric
- Salt and pepper to taste

**Instructions:**
1. Heat olive oil in a skillet over medium heat.
2. Add crumbled tofu and turmeric, cook for 5 minutes, stirring frequently.
3. Add spinach and tomatoes, cook until spinach is wilted, about 3 minutes.
4. Season with salt and pepper. Serve hot.

**Time:** 15 minutes
**Servings:** 2

**Nutritional Information (approx.):** Calories: 180 | Carbohydrates: 6g | Fiber: 2g | Sugar: 2g | Protein: 12g | Fat: 12g (Glycemic Index: Low)

## Broccoli and Cheese Mini Quiches

**Ingredients:**

- 1 cup finely chopped broccoli
- 4 large eggs
- ½ cup low-fat milk
- ½ cup shredded low-fat cheese
- Salt and pepper to taste
- Non-stick cooking spray

**Instructions:**

1. Preheat the oven to 375°F (190°C). Spray a mini muffin tin with non-stick cooking spray.
2. Steam the broccoli until just tender, about 3-4 minutes, then evenly distribute it among the muffin cups.
3. In a bowl, whisk together the eggs, milk, salt, and pepper. Stir in the cheese.
4. Pour the egg mixture over the broccoli, filling each muffin cup.
5. Bake for 15-18 minutes, or until the quiches are set and lightly golden.
6. Let cool for a few minutes before serving.

**Time:** 25 minutes
**Servings:** 4

**Nutritional Information (approx.):** Calories: 130 | Carbohydrates: 5g | Fiber: 1g | Sugar: 3g | Protein: 12g | Fat: 7g | (Glycemic Index: Low)

## Low-GI Mango and Chia Seed Smoothie

**Instructions:**

1. Combine all ingredients in a blender.
2. Blend on high until smooth.
3. Serve immediately for a refreshing treat.

**Time:** 5 minutes
**Servings:** 1

**Nutritional Information (approx.):** Calories: 200 | Carbohydrates: 25g | Fiber: 8g | Sugar: 15g | Protein: 5g | Fat: 9g | (Glycemic Index: Medium, balanced by fiber from chia seeds and healthy fats))

**Ingredients:**

- ½ cup frozen mango chunks
- 1 cup unsweetened almond milk
- 2 tablespoons chia seeds
- 1 tablespoon lime juice
- A few ice cubes

## Whole Wheat Vegetable Upma

**Ingredients:**

- 1 cup whole wheat semolina
- 2 cups water
- 1 cup mixed vegetables (carrots, peas, bell peppers), finely chopped
- 1 teaspoon mustard seeds
- 1 tablespoon olive oil
- Salt to taste
- 2 tablespoons chopped cilantro for garnish

**Instructions:**

1. Heat the olive oil in a pan over medium heat. Add mustard seeds and wait till they splutter.
2. Add the mixed vegetables and sauté for 2-3 minutes.
3. Add the semolina and toast for about 2 minutes, stirring constantly.
4. Slowly add the water and salt, stirring continuously to avoid lumps.
5. Cook until the water is absorbed and the upma has a fluffy texture, about 5-7 minutes.
6. Garnish with cilantro before serving.

**Time:** 20 minutes
**Servings:** 4

**Nutritional Information (approx.):** Calories: 200 | Carbohydrates: 35g | Fiber: 6g | Sugar: 3g | Protein: 7g | Fat: 4g | (Glycemic Index: Medium, with high fiber content for better blood sugar management)

## Zucchini and Carrot Breakfast Muffins

**Ingredients:**

- 1 cup whole wheat flour
- ½ cup almond flour
- ¼ cup rolled oats
- 2 tsp baking powder
- ½ tsp cinnamon
- ¼ tsp salt

**Time:** 12 muffins
**Servings:** 4

- 2 eggs, beaten
- ¼ cup olive oil
- ½ cup unsweetened applesauce
- ¼ cup almond milk
- 1 cup grated zucchini, excess water squeezed out
- 1 cup grated carrot
- ¼ cup walnuts, chopped (optional)

**Instructions:**

1. Preheat oven to 350°F (175°C) and line a muffin tin with paper liners.
2. In a large bowl, mix together the whole wheat flour, almond flour, oats, baking powder, cinnamon, and salt.
3. In another bowl, combine the eggs, olive oil, applesauce, and almond milk.
4. Add the wet ingredients to the dry ingredients, stirring until just combined. Fold in the zucchini, carrot, and walnuts.
5. Divide the batter evenly among the muffin cups.
6. Bake for 20-25 minutes, or until a toothpick inserted into the center comes out clean.
7. Let cool before serving.

**Nutritional Information (approx.):** Calories: 180 | Carbohydrates: 20g | Fiber: 3g | Sugar: 4g | Protein: 5g | Fat: 10g | (Glycemic Index: Low)

---

## Protein-Packed Lentil Pancakes

**Instructions:**

1. Blend soaked lentils with water until smooth to make the batter.
2. Stir in cumin and salt.
3. Heat olive oil in a non-stick pan over medium heat. Pour a quarter of the batter into the pan, spreading to form a pancake.
4. Cook until the edges turn golden, about 2-3 minutes, then flip and cook the other side.
5. Serve hot, garnished with fresh herbs if desired.

**Time:** 20 minutes
**Servings:** 4 pancakes

**Nutritional Information (approx.):** Calories: 150 | Carbohydrates: 18g | Fiber: 9g | Sugar: 1g | Protein: 9g | Fat: 4g | (Glycemic Index: Low)

**Ingredients:**

- 1 cup red lentils, soaked for 4 hours and drained
- ½ cup water
- 1 tsp ground cumin
- Salt to taste
- 1 tbsp olive oil
- Fresh herbs for garnish (optional)

---

## Egg and Avocado Breakfast Wrap

**Ingredients:**

- 2 whole wheat tortillas
- 4 eggs, beaten
- Salt and pepper to taste
- 1 avocado, sliced
- ½ cup fresh spinach
- ¼ cup salsa
- 1 tbsp olive oil

**Instructions:**

1. Heat olive oil in a skillet over medium heat. Add the beaten eggs, season with salt and pepper, and scramble until cooked through.
2. Warm the tortillas in a separate pan or in the microwave.
3. Lay out the tortillas and divide the scrambled eggs between them.
4. Top with avocado slices, fresh spinach, and salsa.
5. Roll up the tortillas, securing the contents inside.
6. Serve immediately.

**Time:** 15 minutes
**Servings:** 2 wraps

**Nutritional Information (approx.):** Calories: 400 | Carbohydrates: 30g | Fiber: 8g | Sugar: 4g | Protein: 20g | Fat: 22g | (Glycemic Index: Medium))

## Tomato and Basil Breakfast Bruschetta

**Ingredients:**

- 4 slices whole-grain bread
- 2 tomatoes, finely chopped
- ¼ cup fresh basil leaves, chopped
- 1 garlic clove, minced
- 2 tsp extra virgin olive oil
- Salt and pepper to taste

**Instructions:**

1. Toast the whole-grain bread slices until golden brown.
2. In a bowl, mix the chopped tomatoes, basil, garlic, olive oil, salt, and pepper.
3. Spoon the tomato mixture evenly onto the toasted bread slices. Serve immediately.

**Time:** 10 minutes
**Servings:** 2

**Nutritional Information (approx.):** Calories: 180 per serving | Carbohydrates: 25g | Fiber: 5g | Sugar: 4g | Protein: 7g | Fat: 7g | (Glycemic Index: Medium)

## Overnight Oats with Pumpkin Seeds

**Instructions:**

1. In a mason jar or airtight container, combine the rolled oats, almond milk, chia seeds, cinnamon, and sugar-free maple syrup.
2. Stir well, cover, and refrigerate overnight.
3. Before serving, stir again and top with pumpkin seeds.

**Time:** 8 hours (overnight soaking)
**Servings:** 1

**Nutritional Information (approx.):** Calories: 300 | Carbohydrates: 35g | Fiber: 9g | Sugar: 1g | Protein: 12g | Fat: 14g | (Glycemic Index: Low)

**Ingredients:**

- ½ cup rolled oats
- ¾ cup unsweetened almond milk
- 1 tablespoon chia seeds
- 2 tablespoons pumpkin seeds
- ¼ teaspoon cinnamon
- 1 tablespoon sugar-free maple syrup or to taste

## Spinach and Quinoa Breakfast Bars

**Ingredients:**

- 1 cup cooked quinoa
- 2 eggs
- 1 cup fresh spinach, chopped
- ¼ cup onions, finely chopped
- ½ cup low-fat cheese, shredded
- ¼ teaspoon salt
- Pepper to taste

**Instructions:**

1. Preheat the oven to 375°F (190°C). Line a baking dish with parchment paper.
2. In a large bowl, mix the cooked quinoa, eggs, spinach, onions, cheese, salt, and pepper until well combined.
3. Spread the mixture evenly in the prepared baking dish.
4. Bake for 25-30 minutes, or until the edges are golden and the center is set.
5. Let cool before cutting into bars.

**Time:** 40 minutes
**Servings:** 8 bars

**Nutritional Information (approx.):** Calories: 100 per bar | Carbohydrates: 10g | Fiber: 2g | Sugar: 1g | Protein: 6g | Fat: 4g | (Glycemic Index: Low)

## Baked Sweet Potato and Greens Bowl

**Ingredients:**

- 2 medium sweet potatoes, washed and pierced
- 2 cups mixed greens (spinach, kale, arugula)
- ¼ cup red onion, thinly sliced
- ½ avocado, sliced
- 2 tbsp balsamic vinegar
- 1 tbsp olive oil
- Salt and pepper to taste
- 2 tbsp pumpkin seeds (optional)

**Instructions:**

1. Preheat the oven to 400°F (200°C). Place sweet potatoes on a baking sheet and bake for 25-30 minutes, or until tender.
2. In a large bowl, toss the mixed greens and red onion with balsamic vinegar, olive oil, salt, and pepper.
3. Split the baked sweet potatoes open and fill each with the salad mixture. Top with avocado slices and sprinkle with pumpkin seeds if desired.

**Time:** 30 minutes
**Servings:** 2

**Nutritional Information (approx.):** Calories: 320 | Carbohydrates: 45g | Fiber: 9g | Sugar: 13g | Protein: 6g | Fat: 14g | (Glycemic Index: Medium, balanced with fiber and healthy fats)

## Smoked Salmon and Cream Cheese Bagel

**Instructions:**

1. Spread each half of the toasted bagel with cream cheese.
2. Top with smoked salmon, capers, and red onion slices.
3. Garnish with fresh dill.
4. Serve immediately.

**Time:** 10 minutes
**Servings:** 1

**Nutritional Information (approx.):** Calories: 400 | Carbohydrates: 55g |Fiber: 8g |Sugar: 7g |Protein: 22g |Fat: 12g | (Glycemic Index: Medium, whole grain bagel for slower glucose absorption)

**Ingredients:**

- 1 whole grain bagel, halved and toasted
- 2 oz smoked salmon
- 2 tbsp low-fat cream cheese
- 1 tbsp capers
- 2 slices red onion
- Fresh dill for garnish

## Almond Flour Blueberry Muffin

**Ingredients:**

- 2 cups almond flour
- 3 large eggs
- ¼ cup unsweetened almond milk
- ¼ cup coconut oil, melted
- ⅓ cup erythritol (or another low-GI sweetener)
- 1 tsp vanilla extract
- 1 tsp baking powder
- ½ cup blueberries

**Instructions:**

1. Preheat the oven to 350°F (175°C). Line a muffin tin with paper liners.
2. In a bowl, mix almond flour, eggs, almond milk, coconut oil, erythritol, vanilla extract, and baking powder until well combined.
3. Gently fold in the blueberries. Divide the batter evenly among the muffin cups.
4. Bake for 18-20 minutes, or until a toothpick inserted into the center comes out clean. Cool before serving.

**Time:** 25 minutes
**Servings:** 12 muffins

**Nutritional Information (approx.):** Calories: 190 | Carbohydrates: 8g | Fiber: 3g | Sugar: 2g | Protein: 6g | Fat: 16g | (Glycemic Index: Low, made with almond flour and low-GI sweetener)

## Turkey Sausage and Veggie Scramble

**Ingredients:**
- 4 oz turkey sausage, casing removed
- ½ cup diced bell peppers
- ½ cup chopped spinach
- 4 large eggs
- Salt and pepper to taste
- 1 tsp olive oil

**Instructions:**
1. Heat olive oil in a skillet over medium heat. Add the turkey sausage, breaking it apart with a spatula, and cook until browned.
2. Add the diced bell peppers and cook until slightly soft, about 3 minutes.
3. Stir in the chopped spinach and cook until wilted, about 2 minutes.
4. Beat the eggs with salt and pepper, then pour into the skillet. Stir gently until the eggs are fully cooked and scrambled with the sausage and veggies.
5. Serve warm.

**Time:** 20 minutes
**Servings:** 2
**Nutritional Information (approx.):** Calories: 250 | Carbohydrates: 4g | Fiber: 1g | Sugar: 2g | Protein: 22g | Fat: 16g | (Glycemic Index: Low)

## Low-Carb Cauliflower Hash Browns

**Instructions:**
1. Preheat your oven to 400°F (200°C) and line a baking sheet with parchment paper.
2. In a bowl, mix the grated cauliflower, egg, almond flour, salt, and pepper until well combined.
3. Form the mixture into small patties and place them on the prepared baking sheet.
4. Brush the tops with olive oil and bake for 15-20 minutes, flipping halfway through, until golden and crispy.
5. Serve hot.

**Time:** 25 minutes
**Servings:** 2
**Nutritional Information (approx.):** Calories: 130 | Carbohydrates: 10g | Fiber: 4g | Sugar: 4g | Protein: 7g | Fat: 7g | (Glycemic Index: Low)

**Ingredients:**
- 2 cups grated cauliflower (about 1 medium head)
- 1 large egg
- ¼ cup almond flour
- Salt and pepper to taste
- 1 tsp olive oil

## Greek Yogurt Parfait with Nuts and Cinnamon

**Ingredients:**
- 1 cup unsweetened Greek yogurt
- 2 tbsp mixed nuts (almonds, walnuts, pecans), chopped
- 1 tsp cinnamon
- 1 tbsp flaxseeds

**Instructions:**
1. In a serving bowl or glass, layer the Greek yogurt at the bottom.
2. Sprinkle the mixed nuts and flaxseeds over the yogurt.
3. Dust the top with cinnamon.
4. Serve immediately or chill for a few minutes before serving for flavors to meld.

**Time:** 5 minutes
**Servings:** 1

**Nutritional Information (approx.):** Calories: 250 | Carbohydrates: 12g | Fiber: 3g | Sugar: 7g (naturally occurring in yogurt) | Protein: 20g | Fat: 15g | (Glycemic Index: Low)

# Vegetable and Bean Breakfast Tacos

**Ingredients:**

- 4 small whole grain tortillas
- ½ cup black beans, rinsed and drained
- 1 cup mixed vegetables (bell peppers, onions, spinach), chopped
- 2 eggs (or egg substitute)
- ¼ cup low-fat shredded cheese (optional)
- 1 tbsp olive oil
- Salt and pepper to taste
- ¼ avocado, sliced
- Salsa, for serving

**Instructions:**

1. Heat olive oil in a pan over medium heat. Sauté mixed vegetables until softened, about 5-7 minutes.
2. Add black beans to the pan and heat through.
3. In another pan, scramble the eggs and season with salt and pepper.
4. Warm tortillas in a dry pan or in the microwave.
5. Assemble the tacos: spoon the vegetable and bean mixture onto each tortilla, top with scrambled eggs, avocado slices, and cheese if using.
6. Serve with salsa on the side.

**Time:** 20 minutes
**Servings:** 2

**Nutritional Information (approx.):** Calories: 320 | Carbohydrates: 35g | Fiber: 9g | Sugar: 5g | Protein: 18g | Fat: 12g | (Glycemic Index: Low to Medium)

# Protein Smoothie with Spinach and Avocado

**Instructions:**

1. Combine all ingredients in a blender.
2. Blend until smooth and creamy.
3. Serve immediately.

**Time:** 5 minutes
**Servings:** 1

**Nutritional Information (approx.):** Calories: 280 | Carbohydrates: 14g | Fiber: 7g | Sugar: 1g | Protein: 25g | Fat: 16g | (Glycemic Index: Low)

**Ingredients:**

- 1 cup unsweetened almond milk
- 1 handful fresh spinach
- ½ avocado
- 1 scoop vanilla or unflavored protein powder
- A few ice cubes

# Raspberry and Almond Butter Toast

**Ingredients:**
- 1 slice whole grain bread, toasted
- 2 tbsp almond butter
- ¼ cup fresh raspberries
- A sprinkle of chia seeds (optional)

**Instructions:**

1. Spread almond butter over the toasted whole grain bread.
2. Top with fresh raspberries.
3. Sprinkle with chia seeds for added fiber and nutrients.

**Time:** 5 minutes
**Servings:** 1

**Nutritional Information (approx.):** Calories: 280 | Carbohydrates: 30g | Fiber: 9g | Sugar: 10g | Protein: 10g | Fat: 14g | (Glycemic Index: Low to Medium)

## Mushroom and Spinach Breakfast Skillet

**Ingredients:**

- 1 tablespoon olive oil
- 2 cups fresh spinach
- 1 cup sliced mushrooms
- 4 large eggs
- Salt and pepper to taste
- ¼ teaspoon garlic powder

**Instructions:**

1. Heat olive oil in a skillet over medium heat. Add mushrooms, cooking until softened, about 5 minutes.
2. Stir in spinach until wilted, approximately 2 minutes.
3. Make four wells in the vegetable mixture. Crack an egg into each well. Season with salt, pepper, and garlic powder.
4. Cover and cook until eggs are set to your liking, about 5-7 minutes for soft yolks.
5. Serve hot directly from the skillet.

**Time:** 20 minutes
**Servings:** 2

**Nutritional Information (approx.):** Calories: 220 per serving | Carbohydrates: 3g | Fiber: 1g | Sugar: 1g | Protein: 14g | Fat: 17g | (Glycemic Index: Low)

## Baked Eggs in Avocado

**Instructions:**

1. Preheat oven to 425°F (220°C).
2. Scoop out a bit more avocado from each half to create space for the egg.
3. Place avocado halves in a baking dish to prevent tipping. Crack an egg into each avocado half. Season with salt and pepper.
4. Bake for 15 minutes, or until the eggs are cooked to your preference.
5. Garnish with chives before serving.

**Time:** 15 minutes
**Servings:** 2

**Nutritional Information (approx.):** Calories: 300 per serving | Carbohydrates: 9g | Fiber: 7g | Sugar: 1g | Protein: 10g | Fat: 25g | (Glycemic Index: Low)

**Ingredients:**

- 1 ripe avocado, halved and pitted
- 2 eggs
- Salt and pepper to taste
- 1 tablespoon chopped chives

## Quinoa and Berry Porridge

**Ingredients:**

- ½ cup quinoa, rinsed
- 1 cup unsweetened almond milk
- ½ teaspoon cinnamon
- 1 cup mixed berries (blueberries, raspberries, strawberries)
- Optional: A drizzle of honey or a sprinkle of stevia for sweetness

**Instructions:**

1. In a small pot, combine quinoa, almond milk, and cinnamon. Bring to a boil.
2. Reduce heat to low, cover, and simmer for 15 minutes, or until most of the liquid is absorbed and quinoa is tender.
3. Remove from heat. Stir in mixed berries, allowing the residual heat to warm them.
4. Serve in bowls with an optional drizzle of honey or sprinkle of stevia for added sweetness if desired.

**Time:** 20 minutes
**Servings:** 2

**Nutritional Information (approx.):** Calories: 210 per serving | Carbohydrates: 35g | Fiber: 5g | Sugar: 8g (natural sugars from berries, adjust if adding honey or stevia) | Protein: 8g | Fat: 4g | (Glycemic Index: Medium-Low, balanced with fiber and protein)

## *Spicy Tofu and Kale Breakfast Stir-Fry*

**Instructions:**

1. Heat olive oil in a skillet over medium heat. Add onion, bell pepper, and garlic, sautéing until soft.

2. Add the crumbled tofu and kale. Cook until the tofu is lightly browned and kale is wilted.

3. Stir in soy sauce and red pepper flakes. Cook for another 2 minutes. Serve hot.

**Time:** 20 minutes
**Servings:** 2

**Nutritional Information (approx.):** Calories: 150 | Carbohydrates: 10g | Fiber: 3g | Sugar: 4g | Protein: 12g | Fat: 7g | (Glycemic Index: Low)

**Ingredients:**

- ½ block firm tofu, drained and crumbled
- 2 cups kale, chopped
- 1 small onion, diced
- 1 bell pepper, diced
- 2 cloves garlic, minced
- 1 tbsp low-sodium soy sauce
- ½ tsp red pepper flakes (adjust to taste)
- 1 tsp olive oil

## *Chickpea Flour Pancakes*

**Instructions:**

1. Whisk together chickpea flour, water, olive oil, salt, and pepper until smooth. Let the batter sit for 5 minutes.

2. Heat a non-stick pan over medium heat. Pour batter to form pancakes. Cook until edges are dry, then flip and cook the other side.

3. Serve with optional toppings as desired.

**Time:** 15 minutes
**Servings:** 2

**Nutritional Information (approx.):** Calories: 200 | Carbohydrates: 22g | Fiber: 5g | Sugar: 4g | Protein: 10g | Fat: 8g | (Glycemic Index: Medium)

**Ingredients:**

- 1 cup chickpea flour
- 1 ¼ cups water
- 1 tbsp olive oil
- ½ tsp salt
- ¼ tsp black pepper
- Optional toppings: chopped herbs, diced vegetables

## Stuffed Bell Peppers with Eggs and Spinach

**Ingredients:**

- 2 bell peppers, halved and seeded
- 4 eggs
- 1 cup spinach, chopped
- ¼ cup shredded low-fat cheese
- Salt and pepper to taste
- 1 tsp olive oil

**Instructions:**

1. Preheat the oven to 350°F (175°C). Brush the inside of bell pepper halves with olive oil. Place in a baking dish.
2. Divide the spinach among the bell pepper halves. Crack an egg into each half. Season with salt and pepper.
3. Bake for 15-20 minutes, or until the eggs are set. Sprinkle with cheese in the last 5 minutes.
4. Serve warm.

**Time:** 25 minutes
**Servings:** 2

**Nutritional Information (approx.):** Calories: 250 | Carbohydrates: 12g | Fiber: 3g | Sugar: 6g | Protein: 18g | Fat: 15g | (Glycemic Index: Low)

## Zucchini Bread Oatmeal

**Ingredients:**

- 1 cup rolled oats
- 2 cups water or unsweetened almond milk
- 1 cup grated zucchini
- 1 tsp cinnamon
- ½ tsp nutmeg
- 2 tbsp chopped walnuts
- 1 tbsp flaxseeds
- Optional: Stevia or monk fruit sweetener to taste

**Instructions:**

1. In a pot, bring water or almond milk to a boil. Add oats, stirring occasionally, until they begin to thicken.
2. Stir in grated zucchini, cinnamon, and nutmeg. Cook for another 5 minutes, until oats are soft and creamy.
3. Serve hot, topped with walnuts, flaxseeds, and optional sweetener.

**Time:** 10 minutes
**Servings:** 2

**Nutritional Information (approx.):** Calories: 220 | Carbohydrates: 27g | Fiber: 6g | Sugar: 2g (natural sugars from zucchini; adjust if adding sweetener) | Protein: 8g | Fat: 10g | (Glycemic Index: Low)

# LUNCHES

## *Mixed Bean Salad with a Lemon-Tahini Dressing*

**Ingredients:**
- 1 cup mixed beans (canned, rinsed and drained - black beans, kidney beans, chickpeas)
- ½ cucumber, diced
- 1 red bell pepper, diced
- ¼ red onion, finely chopped
- 2 tablespoons tahini
- Juice of 1 lemon
- 1 garlic clove, minced
- Salt and pepper to taste
- 2 tablespoons chopped parsley

**Instructions:**
1. In a large bowl, combine the mixed beans, cucumber, bell pepper, and red onion.
2. In a small bowl, whisk together tahini, lemon juice, garlic, salt, and pepper until smooth. If the dressing is too thick, add a tablespoon of water to reach the desired consistency.
3. Pour the dressing over the bean mixture and toss to coat evenly.
4. Garnish with chopped parsley before serving.

**Time:** 20 minutes
**Servings:** 2
**Nutritional Information (approx.):** Calories: 250 | Carbohydrates: 35g | Fiber: 10g | Sugar: 5g | Protein: 12g | Fat: 8g | (Glycemic Index: Low)

## *Quinoa Tabbouleh with Chickpeas*

**Ingredients:**
- ½ cup quinoa, cooked and cooled
- 1 cup canned chickpeas, rinsed and drained
- 1 large tomato, diced
- 1 cucumber, diced
- ¼ cup chopped fresh parsley
- ¼ cup chopped fresh mint
- Juice of 1 lemon
- 2 tablespoons olive oil
- Salt and pepper to taste

**Instructions:**
1. In a large bowl, combine cooked quinoa, chickpeas, tomato, cucumber, parsley, and mint.
2. In a small bowl, whisk together lemon juice, olive oil, salt, and pepper.
3. Pour the dressing over the quinoa mixture and toss to combine thoroughly.
4. Chill in the refrigerator for at least 15 minutes before serving to allow flavors to meld

**Time:** 30 minutes
**Servings:** 2
**Nutritional Information (approx.):** Calories: 300 | Carbohydrates: 45g | Fiber: 8g | Sugar: 6g | Protein: 10g | Fat: 10g | (Glycemic Index: Low)

## Grilled Chicken Caesar Salad with Kale

**Ingredients:**

- 2 boneless, skinless chicken breasts
- 4 cups chopped kale, stems removed
- 2 tablespoons low-fat Caesar dressing
- 2 tablespoons grated Parmesan cheese
- 1 whole wheat pita bread, toasted and cut into strips
- Salt and pepper to taste
- Lemon wedges for serving

**Instructions:**

1. Season chicken breasts with salt and pepper. Grill over medium heat until cooked through, about 6-7 minutes per side. Let rest for 5 minutes, then slice thinly.
2. In a large bowl, massage kale with Caesar dressing until leaves begin to soften.
3. Add the grilled chicken slices and Parmesan cheese to the kale. Toss to combine.
4. Serve the salad topped with whole wheat pita strips and lemon wedges on the side.

**Time:** 25 minutes
**Servings:** 2
**Nutritional Information (approx.):** Calories: 350 | Carbohydrates: 18g | Fiber: 3g | Sugar: 2g | Protein: 38g | Fat: 14g | (Glycemic Index: Low)

## Lentil Soup with Spinach and Carrots

**Ingredients:**

- 1 cup lentils, rinsed
- 4 cups vegetable broth
- 1 cup spinach, chopped
- 1 cup carrots, diced
- 1 onion, diced
- 2 cloves garlic, minced
- 1 teaspoon olive oil
- Salt and pepper to taste

**Instructions:**

1. Heat olive oil in a large pot over medium heat. Add onion and garlic, sautéing until translucent.
2. Add carrots and lentils, stirring to combine.
3. Pour in vegetable broth and bring to a boil. Reduce heat and simmer until lentils are tender, about 30 minutes.
4. Stir in spinach and cook until wilted, about 5 minutes.
5. Season with salt and pepper. Serve hot.

**Time:** 45 minutes
**Servings:** 4
**Nutritional Information (approx.):** Calories: 220 | Carbohydrates: 38g | Fiber: 15g | Sugar: 4g | Protein: 14g | Fat: 2g | (Glycemic Index: Low)

## Vegetable Stir-Fry with Tofu and Brown Rice

**Ingredients:**

- 1 cup brown rice
- 200g firm tofu, cubed
- 2 cups mixed vegetables (bell peppers, broccoli, snap peas)
- 2 tablespoons low-sodium soy sauce
- 1 tablespoon sesame oil
- 1 garlic clove, minced
- 1 teaspoon grated ginger

**Instructions:**

1. Cook the brown rice according to package instructions.
2. Heat sesame oil in a large pan over medium heat. Add garlic and ginger, sautéing until fragrant.
3. Add tofu cubes, sautéing until golden on all sides.
4. Add mixed vegetables and stir-fry until just tender.
5. Stir in soy sauce and cook for an additional minute.
6. Serve the stir-fry over the cooked brown rice.

**Time:** 30 minutes
**Servings:** 2

**Nutritional Information (approx.):** Calories: 350 | Carbohydrates: 45g | Fiber: 6g | Sugar: 5g | Protein: 18g | Fat: 12g | (Glycemic Index: Medium)

## Turkey and Avocado Wrap

**Ingredients:**
- 2 whole wheat tortillas
- 4 slices turkey breast
- 1 ripe avocado, sliced
- 1 cup mixed salad greens
- 1 tablespoon mustard
- Salt and pepper to taste

**Instructions:**
1. Spread mustard evenly over each tortilla.
2. Lay turkey slices on top of the mustard.
3. Add avocado slices and mixed salad greens.
4. Season with salt and pepper.
Roll up the tortillas tightly and cut in half. Serve.

**Time:** 10 minutes
**Servings:** 2
**Nutritional Information (approx.):**
Calories: 300 | Carbohydrates: 35g | Fiber: 7g | Sugar: 2g | Protein: 20g | Fat: 12g | (Glycemic Index: Low)

## Vegetable and Hummus Whole Wheat Pita

**Instructions:**
1. Cut the pita bread in half to open the pockets.
2. Spread hummus inside each pita half.
3. Stuff with mixed vegetables. Drizzle with olive oil, and season with salt and pepper.
4. Sprinkle feta cheese if using. Serve immediately.

**Time:** 10 minutes
**Servings:** 1

**Nutritional Information (approx.):** Calories: 260 | Carbohydrates: 35g | Fiber: 6g | Sugar: 4g | Protein: 12g | Fat: 10g | (Glycemic Index: Medium due to whole wheat pita, balanced with fiber and protein)

**Ingredients:**
- 1 whole wheat pita bread
- ¼ cup hummus
- ½ cup mixed vegetables (cucumber, tomatoes, spinach, sliced)
- 1 tablespoon feta cheese, crumbled (optional)
- 1 tsp olive oil
- Salt and pepper to taste

## Salmon Nicoise Salad

**Ingredients:**
- 2 salmon fillets (4 oz each)
- 4 small new potatoes, boiled and sliced
- 1 cup green beans, steamed
- 2 hard-boiled eggs, quartered
- ½ cup cherry tomatoes, halved
- Mixed salad greens
- 2 tablespoons olive oil
- 1 tablespoon lemon juice
- Salt and pepper to taste

**Instructions:**
1. Grill or bake salmon until cooked through, about 10-12 minutes.
2. Arrange mixed salad greens on plates. Top with potatoes, green beans, eggs, and cherry tomatoes.
3. Place a salmon fillet on each salad. Drizzle with olive oil and lemon juice. Season with salt and pepper.
4. Serve immediately.

**Time:** 20 minutes
**Servings:** 2
**Nutritional Information (approx.):**
Calories: 400 | Carbohydrates: 20g | Fiber: 4g | Sugar: 3g | Protein: 30g | Fat: 22g | (Glycemic Index: Low, balanced meal with healthy fats, protein, and low GI vegetables)

# Spicy Black Bean and Quinoa Bowl

**Time:** 30 minutes
**Servings:** 2
**Nutritional Information (approx.):**
Calories: 450 | Carbohydrates: 60g | Fiber: 15g | Sugar: 5g | Protein: 15g | Fat: 20g | (Glycemic Index: Medium due to quinoa, but high in fiber for balanced blood sugar levels)

**Ingredients:**
- 1 cup quinoa, cooked
- 1 cup black beans, rinsed and drained
- ½ cup corn, fresh or frozen
- 1 avocado, sliced
- ½ cup cherry tomatoes, halved
- 1 small red onion, finely chopped
- 1 jalapeño, diced (optional)
- 2 tablespoons lime juice
- 1 tablespoon olive oil
- Salt and pepper to taste
- Cilantro for garnish

**Instructions:**

1. Combine cooked quinoa, black beans, corn, cherry tomatoes, red onion, and jalapeño in a bowl.

2. Top with sliced avocado.

3. Whisk together lime juice, olive oil, salt, and pepper. Drizzle over the bowl.

4. Garnish with cilantro. Serve immediately.

# Mediterranean Chickpea and Feta Salad

**Time:** 15 minutes
**Servings:** 2
**Nutritional Information (approx.):**
Calories: 260 | Carbohydrates: 24g | Fiber: 6g | Sugar: 5g |Protein: 9g | Fat: 16g | (Glycemic Index: Low)

**Ingredients:**
- 1 cup canned chickpeas, rinsed and drained
- ½ cup diced cucumber
- ½ cup cherry tomatoes, halved
- ¼ cup red onion, finely chopped
- ¼ cup feta cheese, crumbled
- 2 tablespoons olive oil
- 1 tablespoon lemon juice
- Salt and pepper to taste
- 1 teaspoon dried oregano

**Instructions:**
1. In a large bowl, combine chickpeas, cucumber, cherry tomatoes, and red onion.
2. In a small bowl, whisk together olive oil, lemon juice, salt, pepper, and oregano.
3. Pour the dressing over the salad and toss to combine.
4. Sprinkle feta cheese on top before serving.

# Balsamic Grilled Vegetable Plate

**Ingredients:**
- 1 bell pepper, sliced
- 1 zucchini, sliced lengthwise
- 1 eggplant, sliced into rounds
- 1 red onion, cut into wedges
- 2 tablespoons olive oil
- 2 tablespoons balsamic vinegar
- Salt and pepper to taste
- Fresh herbs for garnish (optional)

**Instructions:**
1. Preheat the grill to medium-high heat.
2. Toss the vegetables in olive oil, balsamic vinegar, salt, and pepper.
3. Grill the vegetables until tender and slightly charred, about 5-7 minutes per side.
4. Serve garnished with fresh herbs if desired.

**Time:** 20 minutes
**Servings:** 2
**Nutritional Information (approx.):**
Calories: 180 | Carbohydrates: 23g | Fiber: 8g | Sugar: 13g | Protein: 3g | Fat: 10g | (Glycemic Index: Low)

## *Chicken, Apple, and Walnut Salad*

**Ingredients:**

- 2 cups mixed salad greens
- 1 cooked chicken breast, sliced
- 1 apple, cored and sliced
- ¼ cup walnuts, chopped
- 2 tablespoons crumbled blue cheese (optional)

**For the dressing:**

o 2 tablespoons olive oil
o 1 tablespoon apple cider vinegar
o 1 teaspoon honey
o Salt and pepper to taste

**Time:** 20 minutes
**Servings:** 2

**Nutritional Information (approx.):** Calories: 350 | Carbohydrates: 18g | Fiber: 3g | Sugar: 12g | Protein: 26g | Fat: 20g | (Glycemic Index: Medium due to the apple, but balanced with protein and healthy fats)

**Instructions:**

1. In a large bowl, combine salad greens, sliced chicken, apple slices, and chopped walnuts.
2. In a small bowl, whisk together olive oil, apple cider vinegar, honey, salt, and pepper to create the dressing.
3. Drizzle the dressing over the salad and toss to combine.
4. Sprinkle with blue cheese if using before serving.

## *Stuffed Acorn Squash with Quinoa and Kale*

**Time:** 45 minutes
**Servings:** 2
**Nutritional Information (approx.):** Calories: 315 | Carbohydrates: 55g | Fiber: 9g | Sugar: 9g | Protein: 8g | Fat: 8g | (Glycemic Index: Low)

**Ingredients:**

- 1 acorn squash, halved and seeds removed
- ½ cup quinoa, rinsed
- 1 cup vegetable broth
- 1 tablespoon olive oil
- 1 small onion, chopped
- 2 cloves garlic, minced
- 2 cups kale, chopped
- ¼ cup dried cranberries
- Salt and pepper to taste

**Instructions:**

1. Preheat the oven to 375°F (190°C). Place squash halves cut-side down on a baking sheet and bake for 25 minutes, or until tender.
2. Meanwhile, cook quinoa in vegetable broth according to package instructions; set aside.
3. Heat olive oil in a pan over medium heat. Sauté onion and garlic until translucent. Add kale and cook until wilted. Stir in cooked quinoa and dried cranberries. Season with salt and pepper.
4. Fill the roasted squash halves with the quinoa and kale mixture. Return to the oven and bake for an additional 10 minutes.
5. Serve warm.

# Asian Lettuce Wraps with Ground Turkey

**Ingredients:**

- ½ pound ground turkey
- 1 tablespoon sesame oil
- 2 cloves garlic, minced
- 1 tablespoon ginger, minced
- 1 bell pepper, finely diced
- 2 green onions, chopped
- 1 tablespoon soy sauce (low sodium)
- 1 teaspoon rice vinegar
- 1 head of lettuce (e.g., butter lettuce or iceberg), leaves separated
- Optional: sesame seeds for garnish

**Instructions:**

1. Heat sesame oil in a skillet over medium heat. Add garlic, ginger, and ground turkey, cooking until the turkey is browned.
2. Stir in bell pepper, green onions, soy sauce, and rice vinegar. Cook for an additional 3-5 minutes until the vegetables are just tender.
3. Spoon the turkey mixture into lettuce leaves. Garnish with sesame seeds if desired.
4. Serve immediately.

**Time:** 20 minutes
**Servings:** 2
**Nutritional Information (approx.):** Calories: 235 | Carbohydrates: 8g | Fiber: 2g | Sugar: 4g | Protein: 27g | Fat: 12g | (Glycemic Index: Low)

## Broccoli and Almond Soup

**Instructions:**

1. In a large pot, heat olive oil over medium heat. Add onion and garlic, sautéing until softened.
2. Add broccoli and vegetable broth. Bring to a boil, then reduce heat and simmer until broccoli is tender, about 15 minutes.
3. Transfer the soup to a blender, add almonds, and blend until smooth. Return to the pot and heat through. Season with salt and pepper.
4. Serve hot, garnished with chopped almonds.

**Time:** 30 minutes
**Servings:** 2

**Nutritional Information (approx.):** Calories: 220 | Carbohydrates: 18g | Fiber: 6g | Sugar: 6g | Protein: 8g | Fat: 15g | (Glycemic Index: Low)

**Ingredients:**

- 2 cups broccoli florets
- 1 tablespoon olive oil
- 1 small onion, chopped
- 2 cloves garlic, minced
- 3 cups vegetable broth
- ¼ cup almonds, plus more for garnish
- Salt and pepper to taste

## Grilled Shrimp and Mango Salad

**Ingredients:**

- 8 oz shrimp, peeled and deveined
- 1 ripe mango, peeled and sliced
- 2 cups mixed salad greens
- ½ red bell pepper, thinly sliced
- ¼ red onion, thinly sliced
- 2 tbsp lime juice
- 1 tbsp olive oil
- Salt and pepper to taste
- A pinch of chili flakes (optional)

**Instructions:**

1. Preheat grill to medium-high heat. Toss shrimp with half the lime juice, olive oil, salt, pepper, and chili flakes if using.
2. Grill shrimp until opaque and cooked through, about 2-3 minutes per side.
3. In a large bowl, combine the salad greens, mango slices, red bell pepper, and red onion.
4. Top the salad with grilled shrimp. Drizzle with the remaining lime juice and olive oil. Toss gently to combine.
5. Serve immediately.

**Time:** 20 minutes
**Servings:** 2

**Nutritional Information (approx.):** Calories: 250 | Carbohydrates: 22g | Fiber: 3g | Sugar: 15g | Protein: 25g | Fat: 8g | (Glycemic Index: Low)

**Ingredients:**

- 1 can (5 oz) tuna in water, drained
- 2 ripe avocados, halved and pitted
- ¼ cup diced celery
- ¼ cup diced red onion
- 2 tbsp Greek yogurt
- 1 tbsp lemon juice
- Salt and pepper to taste
- Fresh parsley for garnish

**Instructions:**

1. In a bowl, mix together the tuna, celery, red onion, Greek yogurt, lemon juice, salt, and pepper.

2. Scoop out some of the avocado flesh to create more space, and chop it into small pieces. Stir into the tuna mixture.

3. Fill avocado halves with the tuna salad mixture.

4. Garnish with fresh parsley. Serve immediately.

**Time:** 10 minutes
**Servings:** 2
**Nutritional Information (approx.):** Calories: 350 | Carbohydrates: 17g | Fiber: 7g | Sugar: 3g | Protein: 23g | Fat: 22g | (Glycemic Index: Low)

## *Zucchini Noodles with Pesto and Cherry Tomatoes*

**Time:** 15 minutes
**Servings:** 2
**Nutritional Information (approx.):** Calories: 200 | Carbohydrates: 10g | Fiber: 3g | Sugar: 5g | Protein: 6g | Fat: 16g | (Glycemic Index: Low)

**Ingredients:**

- 2 large zucchinis, spiralized
- 1 cup cherry tomatoes, halved
- ¼ cup pesto (homemade or store-bought, check for low sugar content)
- 2 tbsp pine nuts, toasted
- Salt and pepper to taste
- Grated Parmesan cheese for garnish (optional)

**Instructions:**

1. Place spiralized zucchini noodles in a large bowl. If desired, lightly salt the noodles and let sit for 5 minutes to draw out moisture. Drain any excess liquid.

2. Add cherry tomatoes and pesto to the zucchini noodles. Toss until well coated.

3. Season with salt and pepper to taste. Garnish with toasted pine nuts and grated Parmesan if using.

4. Serve immediately or chill for a refreshing cold salad.

## *Vegetarian Chili with Sweet Potatoes*

**Time:** 40 minutes
**Servings:** 4
**Nutritional Information (approx.):** Calories: 250 | Carbohydrates: 45g | Fiber: 10g | Sugar: 12g | Protein: 8g | Fat: 5g | (Glycemic Index: Medium; the fiber from the beans and sweet potatoes helps moderate blood sugar response.)

**Ingredients:**

- 1 large sweet potato, peeled and diced
- 1 can black beans, rinsed and drained
- 1 can diced tomatoes (with juice)
- 1 bell pepper, chopped
- 1 onion, chopped
- 2 cloves garlic, minced
- 1 tablespoon chili powder
- 1 teaspoon cumin
- ½ teaspoon paprika
- Salt and pepper to taste
- 2 cups vegetable broth
- 1 tablespoon olive oil

**Instructions:**

1. In a large pot, heat the olive oil over medium heat. Add the onion, bell pepper, and garlic, sautéing until soft.
2. Add the sweet potato, beans, tomatoes (with their juice), chili powder, cumin, paprika, salt, and pepper. Stir to combine.
3. Pour in the vegetable broth and bring the mixture to a boil. Reduce the heat to low and simmer, covered, for about 30 minutes, or until the sweet potatoes are tender.
4. Serve warm.

# Curried Lentil and Carrot Soup

**Ingredients:**
- 1 cup red lentils, rinsed
- 4 large carrots, peeled and diced
- 1 onion, chopped
- 2 cloves garlic, minced
- 1 tablespoon curry powder
- 4 cups vegetable broth
- 1 can coconut milk
- Salt and pepper to taste
- 1 tablespoon olive oil

**Instructions:**
1. In a large pot, heat the olive oil over medium heat. Add the onion and garlic, sautéing until translucent.
2. Stir in the carrots and curry powder, cooking for another 2 minutes.
3. Add the lentils and vegetable broth. Bring to a boil, then reduce heat and simmer for 20 minutes.
4. Stir in coconut milk, and continue to cook until the soup is heated through and carrots are tender, about 10 more minutes.
5. Season with salt and pepper. Serve hot.

**Time:** 45 minutes
**Servings:** 4
**Nutritional Information (approx.):** Calories: 350 | Carbohydrates: 40g | Fiber: 15g | Sugar: 6g | Protein: 14g | Fat: 16g | (Glycemic Index: Low; lentils provide a slow, steady source of glucose.)

## Sardine and Arugula Sandwich

**Ingredients:**
- 2 slices whole-grain bread
- 1 can sardines in olive oil, drained
- 1 cup arugula
- 1 tablespoon mayonnaise (optional)
- 1 teaspoon lemon juice
- Salt and pepper to taste

**Instructions:**
1. Toast the whole-grain bread to your liking.
2. In a small bowl, mix the sardines with mayonnaise (if using) and lemon juice. Season with salt and pepper.
3. Spread the sardine mixture on one slice of toast. Top with arugula, then cover with the second slice of toast.
4. Serve immediately.

**Time:** 10 minutes
**Servings:** 1
**Nutritional Information (approx.):** Calories: 310 | Carbohydrates: 30g | Fiber: 6g | Sugar: 4g | Protein: 20g | Fat: 15g | (Glycemic Index: Low; whole-grain bread and protein-rich sardines make this a balanced, diabetic-friendly option.)

## Caprese Salad with a Balsamic Reduction

**Instructions:**
1. In a small saucepan, bring balsamic vinegar to a boil, then reduce heat to simmer. Cook until the vinegar has reduced by half and is syrupy, about 15 minutes. Allow to cool.
2. Arrange tomato and mozzarella slices on a plate, alternating them and adding a basil leaf between each.
3. Drizzle with olive oil and the balsamic reduction. Season with salt and pepper.
4. Serve immediately.

**Ingredients:**
- 2 large ripe tomatoes, sliced
- 4 ounces fresh mozzarella cheese, sliced
- Fresh basil leaves
- ½ cup balsamic vinegar
- 1 tablespoon olive oil
- Salt and pepper to taste

**Time:** 20 minutes
**Servings:** 2

**Nutritional Information (approx.):** Calories: 250 | Carbohydrates: 14g | Fiber: 2g | Sugar: 10g | Protein: 14g | Fat: 17g | (Glycemic Index: Low)

## Spinach and Goat Cheese Stuffed Chicken Breast

**Ingredients:**
- 4 boneless, skinless chicken breasts
- 1 cup fresh spinach, chopped
- 4 ounces goat cheese
- 2 tablespoons olive oil
- Salt and pepper to taste
- 1 teaspoon dried herbs (thyme, oregano)

**Instructions:**
1. Preheat oven to 375°F (190°C).
2. Make a pocket in each chicken breast by cutting along the side. Mix spinach and goat cheese, then stuff into the chicken.
3. Season chicken with salt, pepper, and herbs. Heat olive oil in a skillet over medium-high heat and sear chicken on both sides until golden.
4. Transfer chicken to a baking dish and bake for 20 minutes, or until cooked through.
5. Serve hot.

**Time:** 30 minutes
**Servings:** 4
**Nutritional Information (approx.):** Calories: 290 | Carbohydrates: 2g | Fiber: 1g | Sugar: 1g | Protein: 38g | Fat: 14g | (Glycemic Index: Low)

## Eggplant and Chickpea Stew

**Time:** 45 minutes
**Servings:** 4
**Nutritional Information (approx.):** Calories: 210 | Carbohydrates: 31g | Fiber: 10g | Sugar: 11g | Protein: 7g | Fat: 7g | (Glycemic Index: Low)

**Ingredients:**
- 1 large eggplant, diced
- 1 can (15 oz) chickpeas, drained and rinsed
- 1 can (14.5 oz) diced tomatoes
- 1 onion, diced
- 2 cloves garlic, minced
- 2 tablespoons olive oil
- 1 teaspoon ground cumin
- 1 teaspoon smoked paprika
- Salt and pepper to taste
- Fresh cilantro for garnish

**Instructions:**
1. Heat olive oil in a large pot over medium heat. Add onion and garlic, cooking until softened.
2. Add eggplant, chickpeas, diced tomatoes (with juice), cumin, and paprika. Season with salt and pepper.
3. Bring to a boil, then reduce heat to simmer. Cover and cook for 30 minutes, or until eggplant is tender.
4. Garnish with fresh cilantro before serving.

## Beef and Broccoli Stir-Fry with Brown Rice

**Ingredients:**
- ½ pound lean beef, thinly sliced
- 2 cups broccoli florets
- 1 tablespoon olive oil
- 2 cloves garlic, minced
- 1 tablespoon low-sodium soy sauce
- 1 teaspoon sesame oil
- ½ cup brown rice (uncooked)

**Instructions:**
1. Cook brown rice according to package instructions; set aside.
2. Heat olive oil in a skillet over medium heat. Add garlic and beef. Cook until beef is nearly cooked through.
3. Add broccoli and stir-fry until vegetables are tender and beef is fully cooked, about 5-7 minutes.
4. Stir in soy sauce and sesame oil, cooking for an additional minute.
5. Serve the stir-fry over cooked brown rice.

**Time:** 30 minutes
**Servings:** 2

**Nutritional Information (approx.):** Calories: 350 | Carbohydrates: 45g | Fiber: 4g | Protein: 25g | Fat: 10g | (Glycemic Index: Low for brown rice; Medium overall)

## Cucumber, Tomato, and Feta Cheese Salad

**Ingredients:**
- 1 large cucumber, diced
- 2 medium tomatoes, diced
- ¼ cup feta cheese, crumbled
- 2 tablespoons olive oil
- 1 tablespoon balsamic vinegar
- Salt and pepper to taste
- Fresh herbs (optional, such as basil or dill)

**Instructions:**
1. In a large bowl, combine cucumber, tomatoes, and feta cheese.
2. Drizzle with olive oil and balsamic vinegar. Toss to combine.
3. Season with salt and pepper to taste. Add fresh herbs if using.
4. Serve chilled.

**Time:** 10 minutes
**Servings:** 2
**Nutritional Information (approx.):** Calories: 180 | Carbohydrates: 10g | Fiber: 2g | Protein: 5g | Fat: 14g | (Glycemic Index: Low)

## Pumpkin and Chicken Salad with Spinach

**Time:** 20 minutes
**Servings:** 2
**Nutritional Information (approx.):** Calories: 300 | Carbohydrates: 20g | Fiber: 5g | Protein: 30g | Fat: 12g | (Glycemic Index: Low)

**Ingredients:**
- 2 cups diced pumpkin
- ½ pound chicken breast, cooked and shredded
- 4 cups baby spinach
- 1 tablespoon olive oil
- 1 tablespoon apple cider vinegar
- Salt and pepper to taste
- ¼ cup toasted pumpkin seeds

**Instructions:**
1. Preheat oven to 400°F (200°C). Toss pumpkin in olive oil, salt, and pepper, and roast until tender, about 15 minutes.
2. In a large salad bowl, combine roasted pumpkin, shredded chicken, and baby spinach.
3. Drizzle with apple cider vinegar and toss to combine.
4. Sprinkle toasted pumpkin seeds on top before serving.

## Roasted Vegetable and Quinoa Salad

**Time:** 30 minutes
**Servings:** 2
**Nutritional Information (approx.):** Calories: 350 (with feta) | Carbohydrates: 45g | Fiber: 8g | Sugar: 5g | Protein: 12g | Fat: 15g | (Glycemic Index: Low)

**Ingredients:**
- 1 cup quinoa, cooked
- 2 cups mixed vegetables (zucchini, bell peppers, cherry tomatoes), chopped
- 2 tbsp olive oil
- 1 tbsp balsamic vinegar
- Salt and pepper to taste
- ¼ cup feta cheese, crumbled (optional)
- Fresh parsley for garnish

**Instructions:**
1. Preheat the oven to 425°F (220°C). Toss the chopped vegetables with 1 tablespoon olive oil, salt, and pepper. Spread on a baking sheet and roast for 20 minutes, or until tender and slightly charred.
2. In a large bowl, mix the roasted vegetables with cooked quinoa. Add the remaining olive oil and balsamic vinegar. Toss to combine.
3. Serve topped with crumbled feta and fresh parsley.

## Spiced Lentil Tacos with Avocado Cream

**Ingredients:**
- 1 cup cooked lentils
- 1 tbsp olive oil
- 1 tsp chili powder
- ½ tsp cumin
- Salt and pepper to taste
- 4 small whole-grain or corn tortillas
- ½ avocado
- 2 tbsp Greek yogurt
- 1 tbsp lime juice
- 1 small tomato, diced
- ¼ cup shredded lettuce

**Instructions:**
1. Heat olive oil in a pan over medium heat. Add cooked lentils, chili powder, cumin, salt, and pepper. Cook for 5-7 minutes, stirring occasionally.
2. Mash the avocado and mix with Greek yogurt and lime juice to make the avocado cream.
3. Warm the tortillas in a pan or microwave.
4. Assemble the tacos: spread a spoonful of avocado cream on each tortilla, top with spiced lentils, diced tomato, and shredded lettuce.

**Time:** 25 minutes
**Servings:** 2
**Nutritional Information (approx.):** Calories: 400 | Carbohydrates: 60g | Fiber: 15g | Sugar: 5g | Protein: 20g | Fat: 12g | (Glycemic Index: Medium-Low)

## Asian Cabbage Salad with Grilled Chicken

**Ingredients:**
- 2 chicken breasts, grilled and sliced
- 2 cups red cabbage, shredded
- 1 cup carrots, julienned
- ½ cup cucumbers, thinly sliced
- 2 tbsp almonds, slivered
- 2 tbsp soy sauce (low sodium)
- 1 tbsp rice vinegar
- 1 tsp honey
- 1 tsp sesame oil
- Sesame seeds for garnish

**Instructions:**
1. In a large bowl, combine the shredded cabbage, julienned carrots, and sliced cucumbers.
2. In a small bowl, whisk together soy sauce, rice vinegar, honey, and sesame oil for the dressing.
3. Toss the salad with the dressing and top with grilled chicken slices and slivered almonds.
4. Garnish with sesame seeds before serving.

**Time:** 20 minutes
**Servings:** 2

**Nutritional Information (approx.):** Calories: 350 | Carbohydrates: 20g | Fiber: 5g | Sugar: 10g | Protein: 38g | Fat: 14g | (Glycemic Index: Low)

## Roasted Butternut Squash and Black Bean Salad

**Ingredients:**
- 1 cup butternut squash, cubed
- ½ cup black beans, drained and rinsed
- 2 cups mixed salad greens
- ¼ red onion, thinly sliced
- 2 tbsp olive oil
- 1 tbsp balsamic vinegar
- Salt and pepper to taste
- 1 tsp ground cumin
- 2 tbsp feta cheese, crumbled (optional)

**Instructions:**
1. Preheat the oven to 400°F (200°C). Toss the butternut squash cubes with 1 tablespoon of olive oil, salt, pepper, and cumin. Spread on a baking sheet and roast for 20 minutes, until tender.
2. In a large bowl, mix the roasted butternut squash, black beans, salad greens, and red onion.
3. Drizzle with the remaining olive oil and balsamic vinegar. Toss to combine.
4. Serve sprinkled with feta cheese if desired.

**Time:** 30 minutes
**Servings:** 2

**Nutritional Information (approx.):** Calories: 230 | Carbohydrates: 30g | Fiber: 8g | Sugar: 4g | Protein: 7g | Fat: 11g | (Glycemic Index: Low)

**Ingredients:**
- 2 medium zucchinis, spiralized into zoodles
- 1 chicken breast, grilled and sliced
- 1 cup cherry tomatoes, halved
- ½ cup snap peas, trimmed
- 1 garlic clove, minced
- 2 tbsp olive oil
- Salt and pepper to taste
- 1 tbsp grated Parmesan cheese (optional)
- 1 tsp lemon zest

**Instructions:**
1. Heat 1 tablespoon of olive oil in a large skillet over medium heat. Add the garlic and sauté for 1 minute.
2. Add the cherry tomatoes and snap peas, cooking until just tender, about 3 minutes.
3. Toss in the zoodles, cooking for an additional 2 minutes. Season with salt and pepper.
4. Top with sliced grilled chicken, a sprinkle of Parmesan cheese, and lemon zest before serving.

**Time:** 20 minutes
**Servings:** 2
**Nutritional Information (approx.):** Calories: 290 | Carbohydrates: 15g | Fiber: 4g | Sugar: 6g | Protein: 27g | Fat: 15g | (Glycemic Index: Low)

## *Turkey and Vegetable Skewers*

**Time:** 25 minutes
**Servings:** 2
**Nutritional Information (approx.):** Calories: 250 | Carbohydrates: 10g | Fiber: 2g | Sugar: 5g | Protein: 26g | Fat: 12g | (Glycemic Index: Low)

**Ingredients:**
- 8 oz turkey breast, cut into cubes
- 1 bell pepper, cut into pieces
- 1 zucchini, sliced
- 1 red onion, cut into wedges
- 2 tbsp olive oil
- 1 tbsp lemon juice
- Salt and pepper to taste
- 1 tsp dried oregano

**Instructions:**
1. Preheat the grill to medium-high heat.
2. Thread the turkey, bell pepper, zucchini, and red onion onto skewers.
3. Whisk together olive oil, lemon juice, salt, pepper, and oregano. Brush the mixture over the skewers.
4. Grill for 10-12 minutes, turning occasionally, until the turkey is cooked through.
5. Serve hot.

## *Cold Quinoa Salad with Edamame and Carrots*

**Time:** 20 minutes
**Servings:** 2
**Nutritional Information (approx.):** Calories: 220 | Carbohydrates: 30g | Fiber: 5g | Protein: 9g | Fat: 8g | (Glycemic Index: Low)

**Ingredients:**
- 1 cup cooked quinoa (cooled)
- ½ cup shelled edamame (cooked and cooled)
- ½ cup shredded carrots
- 2 tablespoons chopped fresh cilantro
- 1 tablespoon olive oil
- 1 tablespoon lemon juice
- Salt and pepper to taste

**Instructions:**
1. In a large bowl, combine the quinoa, edamame, carrots, and cilantro.
2. In a small bowl, whisk together the olive oil, lemon juice, salt, and pepper.
3. Pour the dressing over the quinoa mixture and toss to combine.
4. Chill in the refrigerator for at least 15 minutes before serving.

**Instructions:**

1. Preheat grill to medium-high heat. Brush salmon and asparagus with olive oil and season with salt and pepper.
2. Grill salmon for about 4-5 minutes per side or until cooked through. Grill asparagus for about 3-4 minutes, turning occasionally, until tender and charred.
3. Serve the grilled salmon and asparagus over a bed of quinoa. Squeeze lemon over the top before serving.

**Time:** 30 minutes
**Servings:** 2

**Nutritional Information (approx.):** Calories: 310 | Carbohydrates: 23g | Fiber: 4g | Protein: 25g | Fat: 13g | (Glycemic Index: Low)

**Ingredients:**

- 2 salmon fillets (about 4 oz each)
- 1 cup asparagus, trimmed
- 1 cup cooked quinoa
- 1 tablespoon olive oil
- Salt and pepper to taste
- Lemon wedges for serving

## *Kale and White Bean Soup*

**Ingredients:**
- 1 tablespoon olive oil
- 1 onion, diced
- 2 garlic cloves, minced
- 4 cups chopped kale
- 1 can (15 oz) white beans, rinsed and drained
- 4 cups low-sodium vegetable broth
- Salt and pepper to taste
- 1 teaspoon dried thyme

**Instructions:**

1. In a large pot, heat the olive oil over medium heat. Add the onion and garlic, sautéing until soft, about 5 minutes.
2. Add the kale and sauté until wilted, about 5 minutes.
3. Add the white beans, vegetable broth, salt, pepper, and thyme. Bring to a boil, then reduce heat and simmer for 20-25 minutes.
4. Adjust seasoning as needed and serve hot.

**Time:** 40 minutes
**Servings:** 4

**Nutritional Information (approx.):** Calories: 180 | Carbohydrates: 27g | Fiber: 6g | Protein: 10g | Fat: 4g | (Glycemic Index: Low)

## *Kale and White Bean Soup*

**Time:** 40 minutes
**Servings:** 4
**Nutritional Information (approx.):** Calories: 180 | Carbohydrates: 27g | Fiber: 6g | Protein: 10g | Fat: 4g | (Glycemic Index: Low)

**Ingredients:**
- 1 tablespoon olive oil
- 1 onion, diced
- 2 garlic cloves, minced
- 4 cups chopped kale
- 1 can (15 oz) white beans, rinsed and drained
- 4 cups low-sodium vegetable broth
- Salt and pepper to taste
- 1 teaspoon dried thyme

**Instructions:**

1. In a large pot, heat the olive oil over medium heat. Add the onion and garlic, sautéing until soft, about 5 minutes.
2. Add the kale and sauté until wilted, about 5 minutes.
3. Add the white beans, vegetable broth, salt, pepper, and thyme. Bring to a boil, then reduce heat and simmer for 20-25 minutes.
4. Adjust seasoning as needed and serve hot.

## Stuffed Bell Peppers with Ground Turkey and Quinoa

**Ingredients:**
- 4 large bell peppers, halved and seeds removed
- 1 lb ground turkey
- 1 cup cooked quinoa
- 1 cup chopped tomatoes
- 1 small onion, diced
- 2 cloves garlic, minced
- 1 tsp olive oil
- ½ tsp each salt and pepper
- 1 tsp smoked paprika
- ¼ cup low-sodium chicken broth
- ¼ cup shredded low-fat cheese (optional)

**Instructions:**
1. Preheat oven to 375°F (190°C). Place bell peppers on a baking sheet, cut-side up.
2. In a skillet, heat olive oil over medium heat. Add onion and garlic, sauté until translucent.
3. Add ground turkey, cook until browned. Stir in tomatoes, cooked quinoa, paprika, salt, and pepper. Cook for an additional 5 minutes.
4. Spoon the mixture into each bell pepper half. Pour chicken broth on the baking sheet to help peppers steam.
5. Bake for 25-30 minutes until peppers are tender. Top with cheese and bake for another 5 minutes until melted (optional).
6. Serve warm.

**Time:** 45 minutes
**Servings:** 4
**Nutritional Information (approx.):** Calories: 320 | Carbohydrates: 22g | Fiber: 5g | Sugar: 6g | Protein: 28g | Fat: 12g | (Glycemic Index: Low)

## Vegetarian Lettuce Wraps with Tofu and Mushrooms

**Ingredients:**
- 8 large lettuce leaves
- 1 lb firm tofu, crumbled
- 1 cup diced mushrooms
- 1 small carrot, julienned
- 2 green onions, sliced
- 2 tbsp low-sodium soy sauce
- 1 tbsp sesame oil
- 1 clove garlic, minced
- 1 tsp grated ginger
- 1 tsp rice vinegar

**Instructions:**
1. Heat sesame oil in a pan over medium heat. Add garlic and ginger; sauté for 1 minute.
2. Add crumbled tofu and mushrooms. Cook for 7-10 minutes until browned.
3. Stir in soy sauce, rice vinegar, and cook for an additional 2 minutes.
4. Remove from heat. Mix in green onions and carrots.
5. Spoon the mixture into lettuce leaves. Serve immediately.

**Time:** 20 minutes
**Servings:** 4

**Nutritional Information (approx.):** Calories: 150 | Carbohydrates: 8g | Fiber: 3g | Sugar: 3g | Protein: 12g | Fat: 9g | (Glycemic Index: Low)

## Spaghetti Squash with Tomato Sauce and Meatballs

**Time:** 1 hour
**Servings:** 4
**Nutritional Information (approx.):** Calories: 390 | Carbohydrates: 30g | Fiber: 6g | Sugar: 8g | Protein: 26g | Fat: 18g | (Glycemic Index: Medium)

**Ingredients:**
- 1 large spaghetti squash, halved and seeds removed
- 1 lb lean ground beef
- 1 cup breadcrumbs
- 1 egg
- 2 cups low-sugar tomato sauce
- 1 tsp olive oil
- Salt and pepper to taste
- 1 tsp Italian seasoning

**Instructions:**
1. Preheat oven to 400°F (200°C). Place squash cut-side down on a baking sheet. Bake for 40 minutes until tender.
2. Mix ground beef, breadcrumbs, egg, salt, pepper, and Italian seasoning. Form into meatballs.
3. Heat olive oil in a pan. Brown meatballs on all sides. Add tomato sauce and simmer for 20 minutes.
4. Use a fork to scrape the spaghetti squash into strands. Serve topped with meatballs and sauce.

### Ingredients:

- 1 large head cauliflower, riced
- 1 lb chicken breast, cooked and shredded
- 1 cup black beans, rinsed and drained
- 1 avocado, sliced
- 1 cup cherry tomatoes, halved
- 1 lime, juiced
- 1 tsp cumin
- Salt and pepper to taste
- Fresh cilantro for garnish

### Instructions:

1. In a skillet over medium heat, cook riced cauliflower with lime juice, cumin, salt, and pepper for 5-7 minutes until tender.
2. Divide cauliflower rice among bowls. Top with shredded chicken, black beans, avocado slices, and cherry tomatoes.
3. Garnish with fresh cilantro. Serve immediately.

**Time:** 30 minutes
**Servings:** 4
**Nutritional Information (approx.):**
Calories: 320 | Carbohydrates: 20g | Fiber: 9g | Sugar: 4g | Protein: 28g | Fat: 14g | (Glycemic Index: Low)

# DINNERS

## *Grilled Lemon-Garlic Salmon with Asparagus*

**Time:** 25 minutes
**Servings:** 2
**Nutritional Information (approx.):**
Calories: 300 | Carbohydrates: 5g | Fiber: 2g | Sugar: 2g | Protein: 34g | Fat: 16g | (Glycemic Index: Low)

**Ingredients:**
- 2 salmon fillets (6 oz each)
- 1 tablespoon olive oil
- 2 cloves garlic, minced
- 1 lemon, half juiced and half sliced
- Salt and pepper to taste
- 1 bunch asparagus, trimmed

**Instructions:**
1. Preheat the grill to medium-high heat. In a small bowl, mix olive oil, garlic, lemon juice, salt, and pepper.
2. Brush the salmon fillets and asparagus with the garlic-lemon mixture.
3. Grill the salmon and asparagus, turning once, until the salmon is cooked through and asparagus is tender, about 6-8 minutes for the salmon and 5 minutes for the asparagus.
4. Serve the salmon with asparagus and garnish with lemon slices.

## *Stir-Fried Chicken and Broccoli with Brown Rice*

**Ingredients:**
- 1 cup brown rice
- 2 chicken breasts, thinly sliced
- 2 cups broccoli florets
- 1 tablespoon olive oil
- 2 cloves garlic, minced
- 2 tablespoons low-sodium soy sauce
- 1 teaspoon sesame oil

**Instructions:**
1. Cook brown rice according to package instructions.
2. Heat olive oil in a pan over medium heat. Add garlic and chicken slices, stir-fry until chicken is nearly cooked through.
3. Add broccoli, soy sauce, and sesame oil, continue to stir-fry until the chicken is cooked and broccoli is tender-crisp, about 5-7 minutes.
4. Serve the chicken and broccoli over cooked brown rice.

**Time:** 30 minutes
**Servings:** 2
**Nutritional Information (approx.):**
Calories: 450 | Carbohydrates: 45g | Fiber: 5g | Sugar: 3g | Protein: 38g | Fat: 14g | (Glycemic Index: Medium)

## *Eggplant Parmesan with Whole Wheat Pasta*

**Time:** 45 minutes
**Servings:** 2
**Nutritional Information (approx.):**
Calories: 420 | Carbohydrates: 62g | Fiber: 11g | Sugar: 8g | Protein: 20g | Fat: 12g | (Glycemic Index: Medium)

**Ingredients:**
- 1 large eggplant, sliced into ½-inch rounds
- 2 cups whole wheat pasta
- 1 cup low-sodium marinara sauce
- ½ cup low-fat mozzarella cheese, shredded
- 2 tablespoons grated Parmesan cheese
- 1 teaspoon olive oil
- Salt and pepper to taste
- 1 teaspoon dried oregano

**Instructions:**
1. Preheat the oven to 375°F (190°C). Brush eggplant slices with olive oil, season with salt, pepper, and oregano.
2. Bake eggplant in a single layer on a baking sheet until tender, about 20 minutes, flipping halfway through.
3. Cook whole wheat pasta according to package instructions, drain.
4. In a baking dish, layer marinara sauce, baked eggplant slices, and sprinkle with mozzarella and Parmesan cheese. Bake until cheese is melted and bubbly, about 15 minutes.
5. Serve hot over whole wheat pasta.

## *Baked Cod with Roasted Vegetables*

**Ingredients:**
- 2 cod fillets (6 oz each)
- 1 cup cherry tomatoes, halved
- 1 medium zucchini, sliced
- 1 bell pepper, sliced
- 2 tablespoons olive oil
- 1 teaspoon dried oregano
- Salt and pepper to taste

**Instructions:**
1. Preheat the oven to 400°F (200°C). Toss the vegetables with 1 tablespoon of olive oil, oregano, salt, and pepper. Spread on a baking sheet and roast for 20 minutes.
2. Brush the cod fillets with the remaining olive oil, season with salt and pepper, and place them on the baking sheet with the vegetables during the last 10 minutes of cooking time.
3. Bake until the fish is flaky and vegetables are tender. Serve immediately.

**Time:** 30 minutes
**Servings:** 2

**Nutritional Information (approx.):** Calories: 250 | Carbohydrates: 10g | Fiber: 3g | Sugar: 6g | Protein: 30g | Fat: 10g | (Glycemic Index: Low)

## *Vegetable and Bean Casserole*

**Ingredients:**
- 1 can (15 oz) low-sodium black beans, drained and rinsed
- 1 can (15 oz) low-sodium kidney beans, drained and rinsed
- 2 cups diced butternut squash
- 1 cup frozen corn
- 1 bell pepper, diced
- 1 onion, diced
- 2 cloves garlic, minced
- 1 can (15 oz) low-sodium diced tomatoes
- 1 teaspoon cumin
- 1 teaspoon chili powder
- Salt and pepper to taste
- ¼ cup shredded low-fat cheese (optional)

**Instructions:**
1. Preheat the oven to 375°F (190°C). In a large bowl, combine all ingredients except cheese, mixing well.
2. Transfer the mixture to a casserole dish. Bake covered for 35 minutes.
3. Uncover, sprinkle with cheese if using, and bake for an additional 10 minutes or until the cheese is melted and vegetables are tender.
4. Serve hot.

**Time:** 45 minutes
**Servings:** 4

**Nutritional Information (approx.):** Calories: 280 | Carbohydrates: 45g | Fiber: 12g | Sugar: 8g | Protein: 16g | Fat: 3g | (Glycemic Index: Medium)

## *Spaghetti Squash and Meatballs*

**Ingredients:**
- 1 large spaghetti squash
- 1 lb ground turkey
- 1 egg, beaten
- ¼ cup almond flour
- 1 teaspoon Italian seasoning
- Salt and pepper to taste
- 2 cups low-sodium marinara sauce

**Instructions:**
1. Preheat the oven to 400°F (200°C). Halve the spaghetti squash and remove the seeds. Place cut side down on a baking sheet and bake for 40 minutes or until tender.
2. In a bowl, mix ground turkey, egg, almond flour, Italian seasoning, salt, and pepper. Form into meatballs.
3. In a large skillet, cook meatballs over medium heat until browned on all sides, then add marinara sauce. Simmer for 20 minutes.
4. Use a fork to scrape the spaghetti squash into strands. Serve topped with meatballs and sauce.

**Time:** 60 minutes
**Servings:** 4
**Nutritional Information (approx.):** Calories: 350 | Carbohydrates: 18g | Fiber: 4g | Sugar: 8g | Protein: 28g | Fat: 18g | (Glycemic Index: Low)

## Zucchini Lasagna with Ground Turkey

**Time:** 60 minutes
**Servings:** 4
**Nutritional Information (approx.):** Calories: 350 | Carbohydrates: 12g | Fiber: 3g | Sugar: 5g | Protein: 38g | Fat: 18g | (Glycemic Index: Low)

### Ingredients:
- 2 large zucchinis, sliced lengthwise
- 1 lb ground turkey
- 1 cup low-sodium tomato sauce
- 1 cup low-fat ricotta cheese
- ¼ cup grated Parmesan cheese
- 1 egg
- 1 tsp olive oil
- 1 tsp garlic powder
- 1 tsp Italian seasoning
- Salt and pepper to taste

### Instructions:
1. Preheat the oven to 375°F (190°C). Grease a baking dish with olive oil.
2. In a skillet, cook ground turkey over medium heat until browned. Drain excess fat.
3. Stir in tomato sauce, garlic powder, Italian seasoning, salt, and pepper. Simmer for 5 minutes.
4. In a bowl, mix ricotta cheese, Parmesan cheese, and egg.
5. Layer the bottom of the baking dish with sliced zucchini. Top with a layer of the turkey mixture, then the cheese mixture. Repeat layers.
6. Cover with foil and bake for 45 minutes. Uncover and bake for an additional 15 minutes until the top is golden.
7. Let it cool for 10 minutes before serving.

## Grilled Tofu with Quinoa and Green Beans

**Time:** 30 minutes
**Servings:** 4
**Nutritional Information (approx.):** Calories: 280 | Carbohydrates: 33g | Fiber: 6g | Sugar: 3g | Protein: 18g | Fat: 9g | (Glycemic Index: Low)

### Ingredients:
- 1 block (14 oz) firm tofu, pressed and sliced
- 1 cup quinoa
- 2 cups green beans, trimmed
- 2 tbsp soy sauce (low sodium)
- 1 tbsp olive oil
- 1 tsp garlic, minced
- Salt and pepper to taste

### Instructions:
1. Cook quinoa according to package instructions. Set aside.
2. In a bowl, mix soy sauce, olive oil, and garlic. Marinate tofu slices for 15 minutes.
3. Heat a grill pan over medium heat. Grill tofu until golden brown on each side, about 4 minutes per side.
4. In the same pan, quickly sauté green beans until tender-crisp, about 3 minutes.
5. Serve grilled tofu over a bed of quinoa with green beans on the side.

## Roasted Chicken with Sweet Potatoes and Brussels Sprouts

### Ingredients:
- 4 chicken breasts (boneless, skinless)
- 2 sweet potatoes, cubed
- 2 cups Brussels sprouts, halved
- 2 tbsp olive oil
- 1 tsp paprika
- 1 tsp rosemary
- Salt and pepper to taste

### Instructions:
1. Preheat the oven to 400°F (200°C). Line a baking sheet with parchment paper.
2. Toss sweet potatoes and Brussels sprouts with 1 tablespoon olive oil, paprika, rosemary, salt, and pepper. Spread on the baking sheet.
3. Rub the remaining olive oil on chicken breasts and season with salt and pepper. Place among the vegetables on the baking sheet.
4. Roast for 30-35 minutes, or until the chicken is cooked through and vegetables are tender.
5. Serve hot.

**Time:** 45 minutes
**Servings:** 4
**Nutritional Information (approx.):** Calories: 320 | Carbohydrates: 22g | Fiber: 5g | Sugar: 6g | Protein: 35g | Fat: 10g | (Glycemic Index: Medium for sweet potatoes, but balanced with protein and fiber)

## Vegetable Curry with Brown Basmati Rice

**Time:** 30 minutes
**Servings:** 2
**Nutritional Information (approx.):**
Calories: 450 | Carbohydrates: 65g | Fiber: 8g | Sugar: 8g | Protein: 9g | Fat: 18g | (Glycemic Index: Medium for rice, Low for curry)

**Ingredients:**
- 1 cup brown basmati rice
- 2 cups water
- 1 tbsp olive oil
- 1 small onion, chopped
- 2 cloves garlic, minced
- 1 carrot, diced
- 1 bell pepper, diced
- 1 small zucchini, diced
- 1 cup cauliflower florets
- 1 cup canned diced tomatoes
- 1 cup coconut milk
- 2 tsp curry powder
- Salt and pepper to taste

**Instructions:**
1. Rinse the rice under cold water. Bring water to a boil in a saucepan, add rice, reduce heat, cover, and simmer for 25 minutes until water is absorbed.
2. Heat olive oil in a large pan over medium heat. Sauté onion and garlic until translucent.
3. Add carrot, bell pepper, zucchini, and cauliflower. Cook until vegetables are slightly soft, about 5 minutes.
4. Stir in diced tomatoes, coconut milk, and curry powder. Season with salt and pepper. Simmer for 15 minutes.
5. Serve the curry over the cooked brown basmati rice.

## Turkey Chili with Beans and Vegetables

**Ingredients:**
- 1 tbsp olive oil
- 1 lb ground turkey
- 1 onion, chopped
- 2 cloves garlic, minced
- 1 bell pepper, chopped
- 1 zucchini, diced
- 1 cup kidney beans, drained and rinsed
- 1 cup black beans, drained and rinsed
- 2 cups canned diced tomatoes
- 1 tsp cumin
- 1 tsp chili powder
- Salt and pepper to taste

**Instructions:**
1. Heat olive oil in a large pot over medium heat. Add ground turkey, onion, and garlic. Cook until turkey is browned.
2. Add bell pepper and zucchini, cooking until vegetables are tender.
3. Stir in kidney beans, black beans, diced tomatoes, cumin, and chili powder. Season with salt and pepper.
4. Simmer for 25-30 minutes, stirring occasionally.
5. Serve hot.

**Time:** 40 minutes
**Servings:** 4
**Nutritional Information (approx.):**
Calories: 350 | Carbohydrates: 30g | Fiber: 10g | Sugar: 5g | Protein: 28g | Fat: 12g | (Glycemic Index: Low)

## Stuffed Portobello Mushrooms with Quinoa

**Time:** 30 minutes
**Servings:** 2
**Nutritional Information (approx.):** Calories: 250 | Carbohydrates: 27g | Fiber: 5g | Sugar: 4g | Protein: 12g | Fat: 12g | (Glycemic Index: Low)

**Ingredients:**
- 4 large portobello mushroom caps, stems removed
- 1 cup cooked quinoa
- 1 tbsp olive oil, plus more for brushing
- 1 small onion, finely chopped
- 1 clove garlic, minced
- 1 tomato, diced
- ½ cup spinach, chopped
- ¼ cup feta cheese, crumbled
- Salt and pepper to taste

**Instructions:**
1. Preheat oven to 375°F (190°C). Brush mushroom caps with olive oil and place on a baking sheet.
2. Heat 1 tbsp olive oil in a skillet over medium heat. Sauté onion and garlic until translucent.
3. Add cooked quinoa, tomato, and spinach to the skillet. Cook until spinach is wilted.
4. Remove from heat, stir in feta cheese, and season with salt and pepper.
5. Stuff each mushroom cap with the quinoa mixture. Bake for 15-20 minutes until mushrooms are tender.
6. Serve immediately.

## Pan-Seared Tilapia with Lemon and Capers

**Ingredients:**
- 2 tilapia fillets (about 6 ounces each)
- 2 tablespoons olive oil
- Juice of 1 lemon
- 1 tablespoon capers, drained
- Salt and pepper to taste
- Fresh parsley for garnish

**Instructions:**
1. Season the tilapia fillets with salt and pepper.
2. Heat the olive oil in a skillet over medium-high heat. Add the tilapia and cook for 3-4 minutes on each side or until golden brown and fish flakes easily with a fork.
3. Transfer the tilapia to a serving plate. Add the lemon juice and capers to the skillet, swirling to combine. Cook for 1 minute, then pour over the tilapia.
4. Garnish with fresh parsley and serve immediately.

**Time:** 20 minutes
**Servings:** 2

**Nutritional Information (approx.):** Calories: 230 | Carbohydrates: 1g | Fiber: 0g | Sugar: 0g | Protein: 34g | Fat: 10g | (Glycemic Index: Low)

## Vegetarian Stuffed Peppers

**Ingredients:**
- 4 large bell peppers, tops removed, seeded
- 1 cup quinoa, cooked
- 1 can (15 oz) black beans, rinsed and drained
- 1 cup corn kernels
- 1 cup tomato sauce
- ½ cup shredded low-fat cheese
- 1 teaspoon cumin
- Salt and pepper to taste
- Fresh cilantro for garnish

**Instructions:**
1. Preheat the oven to 350°F (175°C).
2. In a bowl, mix the cooked quinoa, black beans, corn, tomato sauce, cumin, salt, and pepper.
3. Stuff the mixture into the bell peppers, place in a baking dish, and cover with foil.
4. Bake for 30 minutes, then remove foil, top each pepper with cheese, and bake for an additional 10 minutes, or until the cheese is melted.
5. Garnish with fresh cilantro and serve.

**Time:** 45 minutes
**Servings:** 4
**Nutritional Information (approx.):** Calories: 280 | Carbohydrates: 45g | Fiber: 10g | Sugar: 8g | Protein: 15g | Fat: 5g | (Glycemic Index: Medium)

## Beef Stir-Fry with Broccoli and Bell Peppers

**Ingredients:**
- 1 pound lean beef, thinly sliced
- 2 cups broccoli florets
- 1 red bell pepper, sliced
- 1 tablespoon olive oil
- 2 tablespoons low-sodium soy sauce
- 1 tablespoon ginger, minced
- 2 cloves garlic, minced
- Salt and pepper to taste

**Instructions:**
1. Heat the olive oil in a large skillet over high heat. Add the beef and cook until browned, about 3-4 minutes. Remove beef and set aside.
2. In the same skillet, add the broccoli and bell pepper. Cook for 5 minutes, or until vegetables are tender but still crisp.
3. Add the garlic and ginger to the skillet and cook for 1 minute. Return the beef to the skillet, add soy sauce, and stir to combine. Cook for an additional 2 minutes.
4. Season with salt and pepper to taste and serve immediately.

**Time:** 25 minutes
**Servings:** 4

**Nutritional Information (approx.):** Calories: 250 | Carbohydrates: 10g | Fiber: 3g | Sugar: 4g | Protein: 26g | Fat: 11g | (Glycemic Index: Low)

## Baked Trout with Walnut Crust

**Ingredients:**
- 2 trout fillets (about 6 ounces each)
- ¼ cup crushed walnuts
- 1 tablespoon Dijon mustard
- 1 tablespoon olive oil
- Salt and pepper to taste
- Fresh lemon wedges for serving

**Instructions:**
1. Preheat the oven to 375°F (190°C). Line a baking sheet with parchment paper.
2. Brush each trout fillet with Dijon mustard and olive oil. Season with salt and pepper.
3. Press the crushed walnuts onto the mustard-coated side of each fillet.
4. Place the fillets, walnut side up, on the prepared baking sheet.
5. Bake for 15-20 minutes or until the trout is flaky.
6. Serve with fresh lemon wedges.

**Time:** 25 minutes
**Servings:** 2

**Nutritional Information (approx.):** Calories: 310 | Carbohydrates: 2g | Fiber: 1g | Sugar: 0g | Protein: 34g | Fat: 18g | (Glycemic Index: Low)

## Pork Tenderloin with Roasted Apples and Onions

**Ingredients:**
- 1 pork tenderloin (about 1 lb or 450g)
- 2 medium apples, cored and sliced
- 1 large onion, sliced
- 2 tablespoons olive oil
- 1 teaspoon dried thyme
- Salt and pepper to taste

**Instructions:**
1. Preheat the oven to 425°F (220°C).
2. Season the pork tenderloin with salt, pepper, and thyme.
3. In a roasting pan, toss the apple and onion slices with olive oil, and spread them around the pork.
4. Roast for 25-30 minutes, or until the pork reaches an internal temperature of 145°F (63°C).
5. Let the pork rest for 5 minutes before slicing. Serve with the roasted apples and onions.

**Time:** 45 minutes
**Servings:** 4
**Nutritional Information (approx.):** Calories: 220 | Carbohydrates: 15g | Fiber: 3g | Sugar: 10g | Protein: 24g | Fat: 8g | (Glycemic Index: Medium, balanced by the protein and fiber content)

## Cauliflower Steak with Chimichurri Sauce

**Time:** 30 minutes
**Servings:** 2

**Nutritional Information (approx.):** Calories: 320 | Carbohydrates: 11g | Fiber: 5g | Sugar: 5g | Protein: 4g | Fat: 29g | (Glycemic Index: Low)

**Ingredients:**
- 1 large head of cauliflower
- 2 tablespoons olive oil
- Salt and pepper to taste

**For the Chimichurri Sauce:**
- ½ cup fresh parsley, chopped
- ¼ cup fresh cilantro, chopped
- 2 garlic cloves, minced
- 3 tablespoons red wine vinegar
- ½ cup olive oil
- Salt and chili flakes to taste

**Instructions:**
1. Preheat the oven to 400°F (200°C).
2. Cut the cauliflower into two 1-inch thick steaks. Brush both sides with olive oil and season with salt and pepper.
3. Roast on a baking sheet for 20-25 minutes, flipping halfway through, until tender and golden.
4. For the chimichurri, mix parsley, cilantro, garlic, vinegar, and olive oil in a bowl. Season with salt and chili flakes.
5. Serve the cauliflower steaks topped with chimichurri sauce.

## Lamb Chops with Mint Pesto

**Time:** 25 minutes
**Servings:** 2
**Nutritional Information (approx.):**
Calories: 350 | Carbohydrates: 2g | Fiber: 1g | Sugar: 0g | Protein: 24g | Fat: 28g | (Glycemic Index: Low)

**Ingredients:**
- 4 lamb chops
- Salt and pepper to taste
- 1 tbsp olive oil

**For the Mint Pesto:**
- 1 cup fresh mint leaves
- 2 tbsp almonds, toasted
- 2 cloves garlic
- 3 tbsp olive oil
- Salt to taste

**Instructions:**
1. Season the lamb chops with salt and pepper. Heat olive oil in a grill pan over medium-high heat and cook the chops to your preferred doneness, about 3-4 minutes per side for medium-rare.
2. For the pesto, blend mint leaves, almonds, garlic, olive oil, and salt until smooth.
3. Serve the lamb chops topped with mint pesto.

## Grilled Vegetable Platter with Herb Yogurt Dressing

**Ingredients:**
- 1 zucchini, sliced
- 1 bell pepper, cut into pieces
- 1 small eggplant, sliced
- 1 red onion, cut into wedges
- 1 tbsp olive oil
- Salt and pepper to taste

**For the Dressing:**
- ½ cup Greek yogurt
- 1 tbsp lemon juice
- 1 tbsp chopped fresh herbs (dill, parsley, mint)
- Salt to taste

**Instructions:**
1. Preheat the grill to medium-high. Toss vegetables with olive oil, salt, and pepper.

2. Grill vegetables until tender and charred, about 5-7 minutes per side.

3. For the dressing, mix Greek yogurt, lemon juice, fresh herbs, and salt.

4. Serve grilled vegetables with herb yogurt dressing on the side.

**Time:** 20 minutes
**Servings:** 2
**Nutritional Information (approx.):**
Calories: 200 | Carbohydrates: 18g | Fiber: 6g | Sugar: 10g | Protein: 6g | Fat: 12g | (Glycemic Index: Low)

## Chicken and Vegetable Kebabs

**Ingredients:**
- 2 chicken breasts, cut into chunks
- 1 zucchini, cut into rounds
- 1 bell pepper, cut into chunks
- 1 red onion, cut into wedges
- 2 tbsp olive oil
- 1 tsp each: paprika, ground cumin, garlic powder
- Salt and pepper to taste

**Instructions:**
1. In a bowl, combine chicken, vegetables, olive oil, paprika, cumin, garlic powder, salt, and pepper. Marinate for at least 30 minutes.
2. Thread chicken and vegetables onto skewers.
3. Grill over medium-high heat, turning occasionally, until the chicken is cooked through and vegetables are tender, about 10-12 minutes.
4. Serve hot.

**Time:** 30 minutes (plus marinating)
**Servings:** 2

**Nutritional Information (approx.):** Calories: 320 | Carbohydrates: 12g | Fiber: 3g | Sugar: 5g | Protein: 36g | Fat: 14g | (Glycemic Index: Low)

## Salmon with Avocado Salsa

**Ingredients:**
- 2 salmon fillets (6 ounces each)
- 1 ripe avocado, diced
- ½ cup cherry tomatoes, halved
- ¼ cup red onion, finely chopped
- Juice of 1 lime
- Salt and pepper to taste
- 1 tbsp olive oil

**Instructions:**
1. Preheat the oven to 375°F (190°C). Season the salmon with salt and pepper, and drizzle with olive oil. Place on a baking sheet.
2. Bake for 12-15 minutes or until salmon flakes easily with a fork.
3. In a bowl, combine avocado, cherry tomatoes, red onion, lime juice, and salt. Mix gently.
4. Serve the salmon topped with avocado salsa.

**Time:** 20 minutes
**Servings:** 2

**Nutritional Information (approx.):** Calories: 400 | Carbohydrates: 9g | Fiber: 5g | Sugar: 2g | Protein: 34g | Fat: 27g | (Glycemic Index: Low)

## Roasted Duck Breast with Orange Sauce

**Instructions:**
1. Preheat the oven to 400°F (200°C). Score the duck skin in a crosshatch pattern; season with salt and pepper.
2. Heat a skillet over medium heat. Place duck, skin-side down, and cook until golden brown, about 6-7 minutes. Flip and cook for an additional minute.
3. Transfer duck to a roasting pan, skin-side up, and roast for 6-8 minutes for medium-rare. Let rest for 5 minutes.
4. For the sauce, combine orange juice and zest, honey, vinegar, and broth in a saucepan. Simmer until reduced by half.
5. Slice duck and serve with orange sauce.

**Time:** 30 minutes
**Servings:** 2
**Nutritional Information (approx.):** Calories: 410 | Carbohydrates: 15g | Fiber: 1g | Sugar: 12g | Protein: 30g | Fat: 24g | (Glycemic Index: Medium, due to honey but balanced with protein and fat)

**Ingredients:**
- 2 duck breasts (6 ounces each)
- Salt and pepper to taste
- 1 orange, juiced and zest grated
- 1 tbsp honey
- 1 tsp apple cider vinegar
- ½ cup low-sodium chicken broth

## Spicy Tofu with Cashews

**Time:** 25 minutes
**Servings:** 2
**Nutritional Information (approx.):** Calories: 380 | Carbohydrates: 18g | Fiber: 3g | Sugar: 5g | Protein: 24g | Fat: 26g | (Glycemic Index: Low)

**Ingredients:**
- 1 block (14 oz) firm tofu, pressed and cubed
- ½ cup cashews, unsalted
- 1 red bell pepper, diced
- 2 green onions, sliced
- 2 tbsp low-sodium soy sauce
- 1 tbsp chili paste
- 1 tsp sesame oil
- 1 garlic clove, minced

**Instructions:**
1. Heat sesame oil in a pan over medium heat. Add garlic and sauté until fragrant, about 1 minute.
2. Add tofu and cook until golden on all sides, about 7-8 minutes. Remove and set aside.
3. In the same pan, add bell pepper and green onions. Sauté for 2-3 minutes.
4. Return tofu to the pan, add cashews, soy sauce, and chili paste. Stir well and cook for another 5 minutes.
5. Serve hot.

# Beef and Vegetable Kabobs

**Ingredients:**

- 8 oz beef sirloin, cut into 1-inch cubes
- 1 bell pepper, cut into 1-inch pieces
- 1 zucchini, sliced
- 8 cherry tomatoes
- 1 tablespoon olive oil
- Salt and pepper to taste
- 1 teaspoon dried oregano

**Instructions:**

1. Preheat grill to medium-high heat.
2. Thread beef, bell pepper, zucchini, and cherry tomatoes onto skewers. Brush with olive oil and season with salt, pepper, and oregano.
3. Grill for 10-15 minutes, turning occasionally, until beef reaches desired doneness and vegetables are tender.
4. Serve hot.

**Time:** 25 minutes
**Servings:** 2

**Nutritional Information (approx.):** Calories: 250 per serving | Carbohydrates: 9g | Fiber: 2g | Sugar: 5g | Protein: 26g | Fat: 12g | (Glycemic Index: Low)

# Pesto Chicken with Roasted Tomatoes

**Ingredients:**

- 2 boneless, skinless chicken breasts
- ½ cup cherry tomatoes, halved
- 2 tablespoons pesto sauce
- 1 tablespoon olive oil
- Salt and pepper to taste

**Instructions:**

1. Preheat oven to 400°F (200°C).
2. Place chicken breasts in a baking dish. Spread pesto sauce over the chicken.
3. Toss cherry tomatoes in olive oil, salt, and pepper, and scatter around the chicken.
4. Bake for 20-25 minutes, or until the chicken is cooked through and tomatoes are roasted.
5. Serve hot.

**Time:** 30 minutes
**Servings:** 2
**Nutritional Information (approx.):** Calories: 290 per serving | Carbohydrates: 4g | Fiber: 1g | Sugar: 2g | Protein: 30g | Fat: 16g | (Glycemic Index: Low)

# Shrimp and Asparagus Stir-Fry

**Ingredients:**

- 8 oz shrimp, peeled and deveined
- 1 bunch asparagus, trimmed and cut into 1-inch pieces
- 2 cloves garlic, minced
- 1 tablespoon soy sauce (low sodium)
- 1 teaspoon sesame oil
- 1 tablespoon olive oil

**Instructions:**

1. Heat olive oil in a large skillet over medium-high heat. Add garlic and asparagus, stir-frying for 3-4 minutes.
2. Add shrimp and continue to stir-fry until the shrimp are pink and opaque, about 3-5 minutes.
3. Drizzle with soy sauce and sesame oil, stir to combine, and cook for an additional minute.
4. Serve immediately.

**Time:** 20 minutes
**Servings:** 2

**Nutritional Information (approx.):** Calories: 220 per serving | Carbohydrates: 6g | Fiber: 2g | Sugar: 2g | Protein: 24g | Fat: 11g | (Glycemic Index: Low)

## Lemon-Roasted Chicken with Garlic and Herbs

**Time:** 1 hour
**Servings:** 4

**Nutritional Information (approx.):**
Calories: 220 | Carbohydrates: 5g | Fiber: 1g | Sugar: 1g | Protein: 35g | Fat: 7g | (Glycemic Index: Low)

**Ingredients:**
- 4 boneless, skinless chicken breasts
- 2 lemons, sliced
- 4 garlic cloves, minced
- 1 tbsp olive oil
- 1 tsp dried rosemary
- 1 tsp dried thyme
- Salt and pepper to taste

**Instructions:**
1. Preheat your oven to 375°F (190°C).
2. Arrange chicken breasts in a baking dish. Drizzle with olive oil.
3. Sprinkle minced garlic, rosemary, thyme, salt, and pepper over the chicken.
4. Place lemon slices on and around the chicken.
5. Bake for 45-50 minutes, or until the chicken is cooked through.
6. Serve with a side of steamed vegetables.

## Vegetable Paella with Brown Rice

**Ingredients:**
- 1 cup brown rice
- 2 cups vegetable broth
- 1 small onion, chopped
- 1 red bell pepper, chopped
- 1 cup frozen peas
- 2 tomatoes, diced
- 3 garlic cloves, minced
- 1 tsp smoked paprika
- ½ tsp saffron threads
- 2 tbsp olive oil
- Salt and pepper to taste

**Instructions:**
1. Heat olive oil in a large skillet over medium heat. Sauté onion and bell pepper until softened.
2. Add garlic, tomatoes, smoked paprika, and saffron. Cook for 2-3 minutes.
3. Stir in brown rice until well coated with the tomato mixture.
4. Pour in vegetable broth. Bring to a boil, then reduce heat to low. Cover and simmer for 35 minutes.
5. Add peas, cover, and cook for an additional 10 minutes.
6. Season with salt and pepper to taste. Serve hot.

**Time:** 45 minutes
**Servings:** 4
**Nutritional Information (approx.):**
Calories: 260 | Carbohydrates: 45g | Fiber: 5g | Sugar: 5g | Protein: 6g | Fat: 7g | (Glycemic Index: Medium, balanced by high fiber content)

## Mushroom and Spinach Frittata

**Ingredients:**
- 8 eggs
- 2 cups fresh spinach, chopped
- 1 cup mushrooms, sliced
- ½ cup low-fat milk
- ¼ cup grated Parmesan cheese
- 1 tbsp olive oil
- Salt and pepper to taste

**Instructions:**
1. Preheat the oven to 400°F (200°C).
2. Heat olive oil in an oven-safe skillet over medium heat. Add mushrooms; cook until tender.
3. Add spinach and cook until wilted.
4. In a bowl, whisk together eggs, milk, Parmesan, salt, and pepper.
5. Pour the egg mixture into the skillet with the vegetables. Stir gently to combine.
6. Transfer the skillet to the oven and bake for 15 minutes, or until the eggs are set.
7. Let cool for a few minutes before serving.

**Time:** 25 minutes
**Servings:** 4

**Nutritional Information (approx.):** Calories: 180 | Carbohydrates: 3g | Fiber: 1g | Sugar: 2g | Protein: 16g | Fat: 12g | (Glycemic Index: Low)

## *Moroccan Chicken with Couscous*

**Time:** 30 minutes
**Servings:** 2

**Nutritional Information (approx.):**
Calories: 450 | Carbohydrates: 45g | Fiber: 6g | Sugar: 2g | Protein: 35g | Fat: 12g | (Glycemic Index: Medium for couscous, balanced with protein and fiber)

**Ingredients:**
- 2 chicken breasts, skinless and boneless
- 1 tsp Moroccan spice blend (cumin, coriander, cinnamon)
- 1 cup whole wheat couscous
- 2 cups low-sodium chicken broth
- ½ cup diced tomatoes
- ¼ cup chopped fresh cilantro
- Salt and pepper to taste
- 1 tbsp olive oil

**Instructions:**
1. Season chicken breasts with Moroccan spice blend, salt, and pepper.
2. In a skillet, heat olive oil over medium heat. Add chicken and cook until browned on each side and cooked through, about 6-7 minutes per side. Remove and set aside.
3. In the same skillet, add chicken broth and bring to a boil. Stir in whole wheat couscous and diced tomatoes, cover, and remove from heat. Let stand for 5 minutes.
4. Fluff couscous with a fork, mix in chopped cilantro, and season with salt and pepper to taste.
5. Serve chicken sliced over couscous.

## *Seared Scallops with Cauliflower Puree*

**Ingredients:**
- 8 large sea scallops
- 1 head cauliflower, cut into florets
- 1 clove garlic, minced
- ½ cup unsweetened almond milk
- Salt and pepper to taste
- 2 tsp olive oil

**Instructions:**
1. Steam cauliflower florets until very tender, about 15 minutes.
2. In a blender, combine steamed cauliflower, garlic, almond milk, salt, and pepper. Puree until smooth.
3. Heat olive oil in a pan over high heat. Season scallops with salt and pepper. Sear scallops until golden brown, about 2 minutes per side.
4. Serve scallops over cauliflower puree.

**Time:** 25 minutes
**Servings:** 2
**Nutritional Information (approx.):**
Calories: 200 | Carbohydrates: 15g | Fiber: 7g | Sugar: 5g | Protein: 22g | Fat: 5g | (Glycemic Index: Low, with high protein and fiber content)

## *Pumpkin Chickpea Curry*

**Time:** 40 minutes
**Servings:** 4

**Nutritional Information (approx.):**
Calories: 280 | Carbohydrates: 35g | Fiber: 10g | Sugar: 8g | Protein: 9g | Fat: 12g | (Glycemic Index: Low, rich in fiber and healthy fats)

**Ingredients:**
- 1 tbsp olive oil
- 1 onion, diced
- 2 cloves garlic, minced
- 1 tbsp curry powder
- 1 can (15 oz) chickpeas, drained and rinsed
- 1 can (15 oz) pumpkin puree (not pie filling)
- 1 can (14 oz) light coconut milk
- Salt and pepper to taste
- Fresh cilantro for garnish

**Instructions:**
1. In a large pot, heat olive oil over medium heat. Add onion and garlic, sautéing until soft, about 5 minutes.
2. Stir in curry powder, cooking for another minute until fragrant.
3. Add chickpeas, pumpkin puree, and coconut milk. Season with salt and pepper.
4. Bring to a simmer and cook for 30 minutes, stirring occasionally.
5. Serve garnished with fresh cilantro.

## Stuffed Eggplant with Lentils and Walnuts

**Time:** 45 minutes
**Servings:** 2

**Nutritional Information (approx.):**
Calories: 320 | Carbohydrates: 38g | Fiber: 17g | Sugar: 13g | Protein: 14g | Fat: 16g | (Glycemic Index: Low)

**Ingredients:**
- 1 large eggplant, halved lengthwise
- ½ cup cooked lentils
- ¼ cup walnuts, chopped
- 1 small onion, finely diced
- 1 clove garlic, minced
- 1 tomato, diced
- 1 tsp olive oil
- Salt and pepper to taste
- 2 tbsp low-fat feta cheese, crumbled (optional)

**Instructions:**
1. Preheat the oven to 375°F (190°C). Scoop out the center of the eggplant halves to create a shell, leaving about ½ inch of flesh on the skin.
2. In a skillet, heat olive oil over medium heat. Sauté onion, garlic, and the scooped-out eggplant flesh until soft. Add cooked lentils, walnuts, and tomatoes. Season with salt and pepper.
3. Fill the eggplant shells with the lentil mixture. Place in a baking dish and cover with foil.
4. Bake for 35 minutes. Remove foil, sprinkle with feta, and bake for another 10 minutes, uncovered.
5. Serve warm.

## Pan-Fried Cod with Slaw

**Ingredients:**
- 2 cod fillets (6 ounces each)
- 1 tbsp olive oil
- Salt and pepper to taste
- 2 cups shredded cabbage
- 1 carrot, shredded
- 1 tbsp apple cider vinegar
- 1 tsp honey
- 1 tsp mustard
- Salt and pepper to taste

**Instructions:**
1. Season cod fillets with salt and pepper.

2. Heat olive oil in a pan over medium-high heat. Add cod fillets and cook for 4-5 minutes per side or until cooked through.

3. In a bowl, mix cabbage, carrot, apple cider vinegar, honey, and mustard. Season with salt and pepper.

4. Serve the cod over a bed of slaw.

**Time:** 20 minutes
**Servings:** 2
**Nutritional Information (approx.):**
Calories: 250 | Carbohydrates: 10g | Fiber: 3g | Sugar: 6g | Protein: 34g | Fat: 9g | (Glycemic Index: Low)

## Baked Chicken with Ratatouille

**Time:** 1 hour
**Servings:** 2
**Nutritional Information (approx.):**
Calories: 330 | Carbohydrates: 22g | Fiber: 8g | Sugar: 13g | Protein: 36g | Fat: 12g | (Glycemic Index: Low)

**Ingredients:**
- 2 chicken breasts (6 ounces each)
- 1 zucchini, sliced
- 1 eggplant, cubed
- 1 bell pepper, sliced
- 1 onion, sliced
- 2 tomatoes, diced
- 2 cloves garlic, minced
- 2 tsp olive oil
- Salt and pepper to taste
- 1 tsp dried herbs (thyme, rosemary, basil)

**Instructions:**
1. Preheat the oven to 375°F (190°C). In a large bowl, toss zucchini, eggplant, bell pepper, onion, tomatoes, and garlic with olive oil, salt, pepper, and dried herbs.
2. Spread the vegetable mixture in a large baking dish. Place the chicken breasts on top of the vegetables.
3. Bake for 45-50 minutes, or until the chicken is cooked through and the vegetables are tender.
4. Serve the chicken with the ratatouille on the side.

## *Vegetable and Tofu Pad Thai*

**Time:** 25 minutes
**Servings:** 2
**Nutritional Information (approx.):** Calories: 320 | Carbohydrates: 44g | Fiber: 4g | Sugar: 6g | Protein: 12g | Fat: 12g | (Glycemic Index: Medium)

### Ingredients:
- 4 oz flat rice noodles
- 1 cup firm tofu, pressed and cubed
- 2 cups mixed vegetables (carrot, bell pepper, bean sprouts)
- 2 tbsp low-sodium soy sauce
- 1 tbsp lime juice
- 1 tsp olive oil
- 1 garlic clove, minced
- 1 tbsp crushed peanuts (for garnish)
- Fresh cilantro (for garnish)
- Optional: chili flakes

### Instructions:
1. Cook rice noodles according to package instructions; set aside.

2. In a pan, heat olive oil over medium heat. Sauté garlic until fragrant. Add tofu and vegetables, cook until tender.

3. Add soy sauce and lime juice to the pan, stir to combine.

4. Add the cooked noodles, toss together until well mixed. Serve garnished with peanuts and cilantro.

## *Pork Chops with Apple and Fennel*

### Ingredients:
- 2 lean pork chops
- 1 apple, sliced
- 1 fennel bulb, sliced
- 1 tsp olive oil
- Salt and pepper to taste
- 1 tsp fresh thyme

### Instructions:
1. Preheat the oven to 375°F (190°C).
2. Season pork chops with salt, pepper, and thyme.
3. Heat olive oil in a skillet over medium heat. Sear pork chops for 2-3 minutes on each side.
4. In the same skillet, add apple and fennel slices. Sauté for 5 minutes.
5. Transfer pork chops back to the skillet, nestling them among the apple and fennel.
6. Bake for 15-20 minutes or until pork chops are cooked through. Serve hot.

**Time:** 30 minutes
**Servings:** 2
**Nutritional Information (approx.):** Calories: 250 | Carbohydrates: 18g | Fiber: 3g | Sugar: 12g | Protein: 22g | Fat: 10g | (Glycemic Index: Low)

## *Blackened Catfish with Collard Greens*

### Ingredients:
- 2 catfish fillets
- 1 tbsp blackening seasoning
- 1 tsp olive oil
- 4 cups collard greens, chopped
- 2 cloves garlic, minced
- Salt to taste
- 1 tbsp apple cider vinegar

### Instructions:
1. Rub catfish fillets with blackening seasoning.

2. Heat olive oil in a skillet over medium-high heat. Add catfish and cook for 3-4 minutes per side or until cooked through. Remove and set aside.

3. In the same skillet, add garlic and collard greens. Cook until greens are wilted. Season with salt and finish with apple cider vinegar.

4. Serve catfish over a bed of collard greens.

**Time:** 20 minutes
**Servings:** 2
**Nutritional Information (approx.):** Calories: 200 | Carbohydrates: 5g | Fiber: 2g | Sugar: 1g | Protein: 25g | Fat: 9g | (Glycemic Index: Low)

# *Ratatouille with Whole Grain Bread*

**Time:** 45 minutes

**Servings:** 2

**Nutritional Information (approx.):**
Calories: 260 | Carbohydrates: 40g | Fiber: 9g | Sugar: 15g | Protein: 8g | Fat: 8g | (Glycemic Index: Low)

**Ingredients:**
- 1 zucchini, sliced
- 1 eggplant, sliced
- 1 bell pepper, chopped
- 1 onion, chopped
- 2 tomatoes, chopped
- 2 cloves garlic, minced
- 2 tsp olive oil
- Salt and pepper to taste
- Fresh basil (for garnish)
- 2 slices whole grain bread

**Instructions:**
1. Preheat the oven to 375°F (190°C).
2. In a large baking dish, layer zucchini, eggplant, bell pepper, onion, and tomatoes.
3. Drizzle with olive oil, sprinkle minced garlic, salt, and pepper.
4. Cover with foil and bake for 35 minutes, or until vegetables are tender.
5. Serve hot, garnished with fresh basil alongside whole grain bread.

# SNACKS

## *Celery Sticks with Almond Butter*

**Instructions:**
1. Wash and cut the celery stalks into 3 to 4-inch sticks.
2. Spread almond butter evenly over the celery sticks.
3. Enjoy as a crunchy and satisfying snack.

**Time:** 5 minutes
**Servings:** 1

**Nutritional Information (approx.):** Calories: 190 | Carbohydrates: 8g | Fiber: 3g | Sugar: 3g | Protein: 5g | Fat: 16g | (Glycemic Index: Low)

**Ingredients:**
- 2 large celery stalks
- 2 tablespoons almond butter

## *Greek Yogurt with Mixed Berries*

**Ingredients:**
- 1 cup plain, low-fat Greek yogurt
- ½ cup mixed berries (blueberries, strawberries, raspberries)
- A drizzle of honey (optional)

**Instructions:**
1. Spoon the Greek yogurt into a bowl.
2. Top with fresh or thawed mixed berries.
3. Drizzle with a small amount of honey if desired. Serve immediately.

**Time:** 5 minutes
**Servings:** 1
**Nutritional Information (approx.):** Calories: 180 (without honey) | Carbohydrates: 20g | Fiber: 2g | Sugar: 15g | Protein: 20g | Fat: 1g | (Glycemic Index: Low)

## *Roasted Chickpeas with Paprika*

**Instructions:**
1. Preheat the oven to 375°F (190°C).
2. Pat the chickpeas dry with paper towels and remove any loose skins.
3. Toss the chickpeas with olive oil, paprika, and salt until evenly coated.
4. Spread the chickpeas on a baking sheet in a single layer.
5. Roast for 30-35 minutes, stirring halfway through, until crispy.
6. Let cool before serving.

**Ingredients:**
- 1 can (15 oz) chickpeas, drained and rinsed
- 1 tablespoon olive oil
- ½ teaspoon paprika
- Salt to taste

**Time:** 40 minutes
**Servings:** 2
**Nutritional Information (approx.):** Calories: 215 | Carbohydrates: 30g | Fiber: 8g | Sugar: 5g | Protein: 10g | Fat: 7g | (Glycemic Index: Low)

## Sliced Apples with Peanut Butter

**Instructions:**
1. Core and slice the apple into thin wedges.
2. Spread peanut butter over each apple slice.

**Time:** 5 minutes
**Servings:** 1

**Nutritional Information (approx.):** Calories: 250 | Carbohydrates: 28g | Fiber: 5g | Sugar: 19g | Protein: 8g | Fat: 14g | (Glycemic Index: Medium for apples, but the addition of peanut butter lowers the overall GI due to fat and protein slowing down the sugar absorption.)

**Ingredients:**
- 1 medium apple, sliced
- 2 tablespoons unsweetened peanut butter

## Cucumber and Hummus Bites

**Ingredients:**
- 1 large cucumber, sliced into rounds
- ½ cup hummus

**Instructions:**
1. Slice the cucumber into ½-inch thick rounds.
2. Top each cucumber round with a spoonful of hummus.

**Time:** 10 minutes
**Servings:** 2

**Nutritional Information (approx.):** Calories: 150 per serving | Carbohydrates: 12g | Fiber: 5g | Sugar: 2g | Protein: 7g | Fat: 9g | (Glycemic Index: Low, cucumbers are low in carbs and the fiber in hummus helps stabilize blood sugar levels.)

## Cherry Tomatoes Stuffed with Cottage Cheese

**Instructions:**
1. Slice the tops off the cherry tomatoes and scoop out the seeds with a small spoon to create a hollow.
2. Season the cottage cheese with salt and pepper.
3. Stuff each cherry tomato with the seasoned cottage cheese using a small spoon.
4. Garnish with fresh herbs if desired. Serve chilled.

**Time:** 15 minutes
**Servings:** 2

**Ingredients:**
- 12 cherry tomatoes
- ½ cup low-fat cottage cheese
- Salt and pepper to taste
- Fresh herbs for garnish (optional)

**Nutritional Information (approx.):** Calories: 90 per serving | Carbohydrates: 6g | Fiber: 1g | Sugar: 4g | Protein: 12g | Fat: 1g | (Glycemic Index: Low, both cherry tomatoes and cottage cheese are low-GI, making this snack ideal for blood sugar management.)

## *Mixed Nuts and Seeds*

**Ingredients:**

- ½ cup almonds
- ½ cup walnuts
- ¼ cup pumpkin seeds
- ¼ cup sunflower seeds
- 1 tsp olive oil
- A pinch of salt (optional)

**Instructions:**
1. Preheat your oven to 350°F (175°C).
2. In a bowl, mix almonds, walnuts, pumpkin seeds, and sunflower seeds with olive oil and a pinch of salt if desired.
3. Spread the mixture evenly on a baking sheet and bake for about 8-10 minutes, or until lightly toasted.
4. Let cool before serving.

**Time:** 10 minutes
**Servings:** 4

**Nutritional Information (approx.):** Calories: 240 | Carbohydrates: 9g | Fiber: 4g | Sugar: 2g | Protein: 7g | Fat: 20g | (Glycemic Index: Low)

## *Baked Kale Chips*

**Ingredients:**

- 1 bunch of kale, washed and dried
- 1 tbsp olive oil
- A pinch of salt

**Instructions:**
1. Preheat the oven to 300°F (150°C).
2. Remove the stems from the kale and tear the leaves into bite-sized pieces.
3. Toss kale pieces with olive oil and salt in a bowl.
4. Arrange the kale on a baking sheet in a single layer.
5. Bake for 10-15 minutes, or until edges are slightly brown but not burnt.
6. Let cool for a few minutes before serving.

**Time:** 20 minutes
**Servings:** 2
**Nutritional Information (approx.):** Calories: 80 | Carbohydrates: 10g | Fiber: 2g | Sugar: 0g | Protein: 3g | Fat: 5g | (Glycemic Index: Low)

## *Edamame with Sea Salt*

**Ingredients:**
- 1 cup frozen edamame (in pods)
- 1 tsp sea salt

**Instructions:**
1. Bring a pot of water to boil and add the frozen edamame.

2. Cook for 5 minutes, or until edamame is tender.

3. Drain the edamame and sprinkle with sea salt.

4. Serve warm.

**Time:** 10 minutes
**Servings:** 2
**Nutritional Information (approx.):** Calories: 120 | Carbohydrates: 9g | Fiber: 4g | Sugar: 2g | Protein: 11g | Fat: 5g | (Glycemic Index: Low)

## *Avocado and Egg Salad on Whole Grain Crackers*

**Ingredients:**
- 1 ripe avocado, mashed
- 2 hard-boiled eggs, chopped
- 1 tablespoon lemon juice
- Salt and pepper to taste
- 4 whole grain crackers

**Instructions:**
1. In a bowl, mix the mashed avocado, chopped eggs, lemon juice, salt, and pepper until well combined.
2. Spoon the mixture onto whole grain crackers.
3. Serve immediately for best texture.

**Time:** 10 minutes
**Servings:** 2

**Nutritional Information (approx.):** Calories: 240 per serving | Carbohydrates: 20g | Fiber: 7g | Sugar: 2g | Protein: 10g | Fat: 15g | (Glycemic Index: Low)

## *Carrot Sticks with Guacamole*

**Ingredients:**
- 2 medium carrots, cut into sticks
- ½ cup guacamole

**Instructions:**
1. Peel the carrots and cut them into sticks.
2. Serve with a side of guacamole for dipping.

**Time:** 5 minutes
**Servings:** 2
**Nutritional Information (approx.):** Calories: 150 per serving | Carbohydrates: 17g | Fiber: 6g | Sugar: 5g | Protein: 2g | Fat: 9g | (Glycemic Index: Low)

## *Zucchini and Parmesan Crisps*

**Ingredients:**
- 2 medium zucchinis, thinly sliced
- ¼ cup grated Parmesan cheese
- Salt to taste
- Cooking spray or 1 tsp olive oil

**Instructions:**
1. Preheat oven to 425°F (220°C). Line a baking sheet with parchment paper and lightly grease with cooking spray or olive oil.
2. Arrange zucchini slices in a single layer on the baking sheet. Sprinkle with salt.
3. Bake for 10 minutes. Remove from oven, flip each slice, and sprinkle with grated Parmesan cheese.
4. Bake for another 5-10 minutes or until crispy and golden.
5. Serve immediately.

**Time:** 20 minutes
**Servings:** 2

**Nutritional Information (approx.):** Calories: 100 per serving | Carbohydrates: 4g | Fiber: 1g | Sugar: 2g | Protein: 7g | Fat: 6g | (Glycemic Index: Low)

## *Whole Grain Toast with Ricotta and Berries*

**Instructions:**
1. Toast the whole grain bread to your liking.
2. Spread the low-fat ricotta cheese evenly over the toast.
3. Top with mixed berries.
4. Drizzle a tiny amount of honey over the top if desired.

**Time:** 5 minutes
**Servings:** 2

**Nutritional Information (approx.):** Calories: 180 | Carbohydrates: 25g | Fiber: 5g | Sugar: 8g (includes natural sugars from berries and a minimal amount of honey) | Protein: 10g | Fat: 4g | (Glycemic Index: Low)

**Ingredients:**
- 1 slice whole grain bread
- 2 tablespoons low-fat ricotta cheese
- ¼ cup mixed berries (blueberries, raspberries)
- A drizzle of honey (optional, use sparingly)

## *Frozen Grapes*

**Ingredients:**
- 1 cup grapes (green or red)

**Instructions:**
1. Wash the grapes thoroughly and remove them from the stem.
2. Pat dry and spread out on a baking sheet lined with parchment paper.
3. Freeze for at least 2 hours or until solid.
4. Serve as a refreshing snack.

**Time:** 2 hours (freezing time)
**Servings:** 2
**Nutritional Information (approx.):** Calories: 62 | Carbohydrates: 16g | Fiber: 1g | Sugar: 15g (natural sugars) | Protein: 0.6g | Fat: 0.3g | (Glycemic Index: Low)

## *Mini Bell Peppers with Tuna Salad*

**Instructions:**
1. In a bowl, mix together the drained tuna, low-fat mayonnaise, Greek yogurt, and season with salt and pepper. Add parsley if using.
2. Fill each mini bell pepper half with the tuna mixture.
3. Serve chilled or at room temperature.

**Time:** 10 minutes
**Servings:** 2

**Nutritional Information (approx.):** Calories: 150 | Carbohydrates: 10g | Fiber: 3g | Sugar: 6g (natural sugars from bell peppers) | Protein: 20g | Fat: 3g | (Glycemic Index: Low)

**Ingredients:**
- 4 mini bell peppers, halved and seeds removed
- 1 can (5 ounces) tuna in water, drained
- 1 tablespoon low-fat mayonnaise
- 1 tablespoon plain Greek yogurt
- Salt and pepper to taste
- 1 tablespoon chopped fresh parsley (optional)

## *Watermelon and Feta Cheese Skewers*

**Ingredients:**
- 1 cup watermelon, cut into cubes
- ½ cup low-fat feta cheese, cut into cubes
- Fresh basil leaves
- Balsamic glaze for drizzling (optional)

**Instructions:**
1. Skewer alternating pieces of watermelon, feta cheese, and basil leaves onto small skewers or toothpicks.
2. Drizzle with balsamic glaze if desired before serving.

**Time:** 10 minutes
**Servings:** 2

**Nutritional Information (approx.):** Calories: 100 per serving | Carbohydrates: 12g | Fiber: 1g | Sugar: 10g | Protein: 6g | Fat: 3g | (Glycemic Index: Low; watermelon's GI is balanced by the protein and fat in feta cheese)

## *Almond and Date Energy Balls*

**Ingredients:**
- ½ cup dates, pitted
- ¼ cup raw almonds
- 1 tbsp chia seeds
- 1 tbsp unsweetened cocoa powder
- A pinch of salt

**Instructions:**
1. In a food processor, combine dates, almonds, chia seeds, cocoa powder, and salt. Process until the mixture sticks together.

2. Roll the mixture into balls, about 1 tablespoon per ball.

3. Chill in the refrigerator for at least 30 minutes before serving.

**Time:** 15 minutes (plus chilling)
**Servings:** 2 (makes about 6 balls)
**Nutritional Information (approx.):** Calories: 150 per serving | Carbohydrates: 18g | Fiber: 4g | Sugar: 12g (natural sugars from dates) | Protein: 4g | Fat: 7g | (Glycemic Index: Medium; balanced by fiber and healthy fats)

## *Cottage Cheese with Sliced Peaches*

**Ingredients:**
- ½ cup low-fat cottage cheese
- 1 medium peach, sliced
- A sprinkle of cinnamon (optional)

**Instructions:**
1. Place the cottage cheese in a bowl.
2. Top with fresh peach slices.
3. Sprinkle with cinnamon if desired. Serve.

**Time:** 5 minutes
**Servings:** 1

**Nutritional Information (approx.):** Calories: 150 | Carbohydrates: 20g | Fiber: 2g | Sugar: 18g | Protein: 14g | Fat: 2g | (Glycemic Index: Medium due to the natural sugars in peaches, but balanced by the protein in the cottage cheese)

## *Hard-Boiled Eggs with a Pinch of Paprika*

**Ingredients:**
- 4 large eggs
- Pinch of paprika
- Salt to taste

**Instructions:**
1. Place eggs in a saucepan and cover with cold water by an inch. Bring to a boil over medium-high heat.
2. Once boiling, cover and remove from heat. Let sit for 9 minutes.
3. Transfer eggs to a bowl of ice water and chill for a few minutes. Peel the eggs.
4. Slice in half, season with a pinch of paprika and salt to taste. Serve.

**Time:** 12 minutes
**Servings:** 2
**Nutritional Information (approx.):** Calories: 140 | Carbohydrates: 1g | Fiber: 0g | Sugar: 1g | Protein: 12g | Fat: 10g | (Glycemic Index: Very Low)

## *Pumpkin Seeds and Sunflower Seeds Mix*

**Ingredients:**
- ½ cup unsalted pumpkin seeds
- ½ cup unsalted sunflower seeds
- Optional: pinch of salt, paprika, or cinnamon for seasoning

**Instructions:**
1. Mix pumpkin and sunflower seeds in a bowl. Season with salt, paprika, or cinnamon if desired.
2. For roasted seeds, spread on a baking sheet and roast at 350°F for 10-15 minutes or until golden. Let cool before serving.

**Time:** 5 minutes (plus roasting time if preferred)
**Servings:** 4
**Nutritional Information (approx.):** Calories: 205 | Carbohydrates: 7g | Fiber: 3g | Sugar: 1g | Protein: 9g | Fat: 17g | (Glycemic Index: Low)

## *Caprese Salad Skewers*

**Ingredients:**
- 16 cherry tomatoes
- 16 small mozzarella balls
- 16 fresh basil leaves
- 2 tablespoons balsamic vinegar
- 1 tablespoon olive oil
- Salt and pepper to taste

**Instructions:**
1. Thread a cherry tomato, a basil leaf, and a mozzarella ball onto small skewers or toothpicks. Repeat until all ingredients are used.
2. Drizzle with balsamic vinegar and olive oil. Season with salt and pepper. Serve immediately.

**Time:** 10 minutes
**Servings:** 4

**Nutritional Information (approx.):** Calories: 150 | Carbohydrates: 5g | Fiber: 1g | Sugar: 3g | Protein: 9g | Fat: 11g | (Glycemic Index: Low)

## *Whole Wheat Pita with Baba Ganoush*

**Ingredients:**

- 1 large eggplant (for Baba Ganoush, pre-roasted)
- 2 whole wheat pitas
- 2 tablespoons tahini
- 1 garlic clove, minced
- Juice of 1 lemon
- Salt and pepper to taste
- 1 tablespoon olive oil
- A pinch of paprika (optional for garnish)

**Instructions:**

1. Prepare Baba Ganoush by blending the roasted eggplant pulp with tahini, garlic, lemon juice, salt, pepper, and olive oil until smooth.
2. Warm whole wheat pitas in the oven or on a skillet.
3. Spread a generous amount of Baba Ganoush onto each pita.
4. Garnish with paprika if desired. Serve immediately.

**Time:** 30 minutes (for Baba Ganoush, excluding eggplant roasting)
**Servings:** 2

**Nutritional Information (approx.):** Calories: 220 per serving | Carbohydrates: 35g | Fiber: 7g | Sugar: 8g | Protein: 9g | Fat: 8g | (Glycemic Index: Medium due to whole wheat pita but balanced with high fiber and healthy fats)

## *Crispy Brussels Sprouts with Balsamic Glaze*

**Ingredients:**

- 2 cups Brussels sprouts, halved
- 2 tablespoons olive oil
- Salt and pepper to taste
- 2 tablespoons balsamic vinegar

**Instructions:**

1. Preheat oven to 400°F (200°C).
2. Toss Brussels sprouts with olive oil, salt, and pepper. Spread on a baking sheet.
3. Roast for 20 minutes, or until crispy and golden.
4. Drizzle with balsamic vinegar before serving.

**Time:** 25 minutes
**Servings:** 2
**Nutritional Information (approx.):** Calories: 150 per serving | Carbohydrates: 15g | Fiber: 4g | Sugar: 5g | Protein: 4g | Fat: 9g | (Glycemic Index: Low)

## *Sliced Pear with Cheese*

**Ingredients:**

- 1 medium pear, sliced
- 1 ounce of low-fat cheese, sliced

**Instructions:**

1 Slice the pear and cheese.
2. Arrange pear slices on a plate and top each with a slice of cheese.
3. Serve as a refreshing and balanced snack.

**Time:** 5 minutes
**Servings:** 1
**Nutritional Information (approx.):** Calories: 180 | Carbohydrates: 22g | Fiber: 5g | Sugar: 15g | Protein: 7g | Fat: 6g | (Glycemic Index: Low to Medium, balanced with fiber and protein)

## *Sweet Potato Toast with Avocado*

**Ingredients:**
- 1 large sweet potato, sliced lengthwise into ¼ inch slices
- ½ ripe avocado
- Salt, pepper, and chili flakes to taste
- A squeeze of lemon juice (optional)

**Instructions:**
1. Toast the sweet potato slices in a toaster or oven at 400°F until tender and slightly crispy, about 10-15 minutes.
2. Mash the avocado and season with salt, pepper, chili flakes, and lemon juice.
3. Spread the mashed avocado over the sweet potato slices. Serve immediately.

**Time:** 15 minutes
**Servings:** 1

**Nutritional Information (approx.):** Calories: 200 | Carbohydrates: 30g | Fiber: 7g | Sugar: 5g | Protein: 3g | Fat: 10g | (Glycemic Index: Medium - Sweet potatoes have a lower GI than regular potatoes, and the fiber content helps balance blood sugar levels.)

## *Ricotta and Tomato on Whole Grain Toast*

**Ingredients:**
- 1 slice whole grain bread, toasted
- ¼ cup low-fat ricotta cheese
- 1 small tomato, sliced
- Salt and pepper to taste
- Fresh basil leaves (optional)

**Instructions:**
1. Spread the ricotta cheese on the toasted whole grain bread.
2. Top with tomato slices, season with salt and pepper, and garnish with fresh basil if using.
3. Serve immediately.

**Time:** 5 minutes
**Servings:** 1
**Nutritional Information (approx.):** Calories: 180 | Carbohydrates: 20g | Fiber: 4g | Sugar: 4g | Protein: 10g | Fat: 6g | (Glycemic Index: Low - Whole grain bread has a lower GI, and the protein from ricotta helps moderate blood sugar levels.)

## *Chia Seed Pudding with Coconut Milk*

**Ingredients:**
- ¼ cup chia seeds
- 1 cup unsweetened coconut milk
- 1 tablespoon maple syrup (optional, can adjust for less or substitute with a low-GI sweetener)
- ½ teaspoon vanilla extract
- Toppings of choice: berries, nuts, seeds

**Instructions:**
1. In a bowl, mix together chia seeds, coconut milk, maple syrup (if using), and vanilla extract.
2. Cover and refrigerate overnight, or at least 8 hours, until it achieves a pudding-like consistency.
3. Stir well before serving and add toppings of your choice.

**Time:** Overnight (8 hours)
**Servings:** 2

**Nutritional Information (approx.):** Calories: 200 (per serving) | Carbohydrates: 18g | Fiber: 10g | Sugar: 3g (without maple syrup) | Protein: 4g | Fat: 12g | (Glycemic Index: Low - The high fiber content in chia seeds helps to prevent blood sugar spikes.)

## Mini Quinoa and Vegetable Muffins

**Ingredients:**
- 1 cup cooked quinoa
- 2 eggs, beaten
- ½ cup finely chopped mixed vegetables (carrot, zucchini, bell pepper)
- ¼ cup grated low-fat cheese
- 2 tbsp chopped fresh herbs (parsley or chives)
- Salt and pepper to taste

**Instructions:**
1. Preheat oven to 375°F (190°C). Grease a mini muffin tin or line with muffin cups.
2. In a large bowl, combine the cooked quinoa, beaten eggs, chopped vegetables, cheese, and herbs. Season with salt and pepper.
3. Spoon the mixture into the prepared muffin tin, filling each cup to the top.
4. Bake for 15-20 minutes, or until the tops are golden and a toothpick inserted into the center of a muffin comes out clean.
5. Let cool for 5 minutes before serving.

**Time:** 30 minutes
**Servings:** 12 muffins

**Nutritional Information (approx.):** Calories: 70 | Carbohydrates: 8g | Fiber: 1g | Sugar: 1g | Protein: 4g | Fat: 2g | (Glycemic Index: Low)

## Spicy Roasted Almonds

**Ingredients:**
- 1 cup raw almonds
- 1 tsp olive oil
- ½ tsp smoked paprika
- ¼ tsp garlic powder
- ¼ tsp chili powder
- ¼ tsp salt

**Instructions:**
1. Preheat oven to 350°F (175°C). Line a baking sheet with parchment paper.
2. In a bowl, mix almonds with olive oil, smoked paprika, garlic powder, chili powder, and salt until evenly coated.
3. Spread the almonds on the prepared baking sheet in a single layer.
4. Roast in the oven for 10-15 minutes, stirring once, until golden and fragrant.
5. Let cool before serving.

**Time:** 20 minutes
**Servings:** 4
**Nutritional Information (approx.):** Calories: 170 | Carbohydrates: 6g | Fiber: 3g | Sugar: 1g | Protein: 6g | Fat: 15g | (Glycemic Index: Low)

## Raspberry and Yogurt Parfait

**Instructions:**
1. In a glass or jar, layer half of the Greek yogurt at the bottom.
2. Add a layer of fresh raspberries, then sprinkle with 1 tablespoon of granola.
3. Repeat the layers with the remaining yogurt, raspberries, and granola.
4. Drizzle with a little honey on top if desired.

**Time:** 10 minutes
**Servings:** 1

**Ingredients:**
- ¾ cup low-fat Greek yogurt
- ½ cup fresh raspberries
- 2 tbsp granola (no added sugar)
- A drizzle of honey (optional)

**Nutritional Information (approx.):** Calories: 200 | Carbohydrates: 25g | Fiber: 4g | Sugar: 16g (natural sugars from the raspberries and yogurt; adjust if adding honey) | Protein: 15g | Fat: 4g | (Glycemic Index: Medium due to the natural sugars in the raspberries and yogurt, balanced by the high protein content)

## Stuffed Mini Peppers with Quinoa and Black Beans

**Ingredients:**
- 12 mini bell peppers, halved and seeded
- 1 cup cooked quinoa
- ½ cup black beans, rinsed and drained
- ¼ cup corn kernels
- ¼ cup finely chopped onion
- ½ teaspoon ground cumin
- Salt and pepper to taste
- ¼ cup shredded low-fat cheese

**Instructions:**
1. Preheat oven to 375°F (190°C).
2. In a bowl, mix quinoa, black beans, corn, onion, cumin, salt, and pepper.
3. Stuff each pepper half with the quinoa mixture and place on a baking sheet.
4. Sprinkle shredded cheese on top of each stuffed pepper.
5. Bake for 20 minutes or until peppers are tender.
6. Serve warm.

**Time:** 30 minutes
**Servings:** 4
**Nutritional Information (approx.):** Calories: 200 | Carbohydrates: 30g | Fiber: 7g | Sugar: 5g | Protein: 9g | Fat: 4g | (Glycemic Index: Low)

## Baked Avocado Fries with Spicy Mayo Dip

**Ingredients:**
- 1 ripe avocado, sliced into wedges
- ½ cup almond flour
- 1 egg, beaten
- Salt and pepper to taste
- ½ cup Greek yogurt
- 1 tablespoon Sriracha sauce

**Instructions:**
1. Preheat oven to 400°F (200°C). Line a baking sheet with parchment paper.
2. Season avocado slices with salt and pepper.
3. Dip avocado slices in beaten egg, then coat with almond flour. Place on the prepared baking sheet.
4. Bake for 15 minutes or until golden and crispy.
5. Mix Greek yogurt and Sriracha sauce for the dip.
6. Serve avocado fries with spicy mayo dip.

**Time:** 25 minutes
**Servings:** 2
**Nutritional Information (approx.):** Calories: 280 | Carbohydrates: 18g | Fiber: 9g | Sugar: 3g | Protein: 10g | Fat: 20g | (Glycemic Index: Low)

## Spinach and Feta Stuffed Mushrooms

**Ingredients:**
- 16 large mushrooms, stems removed
- 2 cups spinach, chopped
- ½ cup crumbled feta cheese
- ¼ cup diced onions
- 1 clove garlic, minced
- 1 tablespoon olive oil
- Salt and pepper to taste

**Instructions:**
1. Preheat oven to 375°F (190°C).
2. In a skillet, heat olive oil over medium heat. Sauté onions and garlic until soft.
3. Add spinach and cook until wilted. Remove from heat and let cool slightly.
4. Stir feta cheese into the spinach mixture. Season with salt and pepper.
5. Stuff each mushroom cap with the spinach and feta mixture.
6. Place stuffed mushrooms on a baking sheet and bake for 15 minutes.
7. Serve warm.

**Time:** 25 minutes
**Servings:** 4
**Nutritional Information (approx.):** Calories: 150 | Carbohydrates: 10g | Fiber: 3g | Sugar: 4g | Protein: 8g | Fat: 10g | (Glycemic Index: Low)

## Crispy Parmesan Zucchini Rounds

**Ingredients:**
- 2 medium zucchinis, sliced into rounds
- ¼ cup grated Parmesan cheese
- 1 tsp garlic powder
- Salt and pepper to taste
- Olive oil spray

**Instructions:**
1. Preheat oven to 425°F (220°C). Line a baking sheet with parchment paper.
2. In a bowl, mix Parmesan cheese, garlic powder, salt, and pepper.
3. Place zucchini rounds on the prepared baking sheet. Lightly spray with olive oil.
4. Sprinkle the Parmesan mixture over the zucchini rounds.
5. Bake for 15 minutes or until crispy and golden.
6. Serve immediately.

**Time:** 20 minutes
**Servings:** 2
**Nutritional Information (approx.):** Calories: 90 | Carbohydrates: 7g | Fiber: 2g | Sugar: 4g | Protein: 6g | Fat: 5g | (Glycemic Index: Low)

## Spiced Pumpkin Seeds

**Ingredients:**
- 1 cup raw pumpkin seeds
- 1 tsp olive oil
- ½ tsp paprika
- ¼ tsp ground cumin
- Pinch of cayenne pepper (optional)
- Salt to taste

**Instructions:**
1. Preheat oven to 300°F (150°C). Line a baking sheet with parchment paper.
2. In a bowl, toss pumpkin seeds with olive oil, paprika, cumin, cayenne pepper, and salt.
3. Spread the seeds in a single layer on the baking sheet.
4. Bake for 20-25 minutes, stirring occasionally, until golden and crunchy.
5. Let cool before serving.

**Time:** 30 minutes
**Servings:** 4
**Nutritional Information (approx.):** Calories: 180 | Carbohydrates: 3g | Fiber: 2g | Sugar: 0g | Protein: 9g | Fat: 15g | (Glycemic Index: Low)

## Greek Yogurt with Honey and Cinnamon

**Instructions:**
1. Place Greek yogurt in a serving bowl.

2. Drizzle honey over the yogurt.

3. Sprinkle with ground cinnamon.

4. Stir lightly before serving.

**Ingredients:**
- 1 cup low-fat Greek yogurt
- 1 tbsp honey
- ½ tsp ground cinnamon

**Time:** 5 minutes
**Servings:** 1
**Nutritional Information (approx.):** Calories: 150 | Carbohydrates: 18g | Fiber: 0g | Sugar: 17g (natural sugars from honey; monitor if closely managing blood sugar levels) | Protein: 20g | Fat: 0g | (Glycemic Index: Medium due to honey, but the high protein content helps moderate blood sugar response)

## Rye Crispbread with Smoked Salmon and Cream Cheese

**Instructions:**
1. Spread the low-fat cream cheese evenly over the rye crispbread slices.
2. Place the smoked salmon on top of the cream cheese.
3. Garnish with fresh dill and a sprinkle of black pepper.
4. Serve immediately.

**Time:** 5 minutes
**Servings:** 1

**Nutritional Information (approx.):** Calories: 200 | Carbohydrates: 20g | Fiber: 4g | Sugar: 2g | Protein: 15g | Fat: 6g | (Glycemic Index: Low)

**Ingredients:**
- 2 slices rye crispbread
- 2 ounces smoked salmon
- 1 tablespoon low-fat cream cheese
- Fresh dill for garnish
- Black pepper to taste

## Beet Chips with Sea Salt

**Ingredients:**
- 2 large beets, thinly sliced
- 1 tablespoon olive oil
- Sea salt to taste

**Instructions:**
1. Preheat your oven to 375°F (190°C).
2. Toss the beet slices with olive oil and spread them in a single layer on a baking sheet lined with parchment paper.
3. Bake for 20-25 minutes, turning halfway through, until crisp.
4. Sprinkle with sea salt while still warm.
5. Let cool before serving.

**Time:** 45 minutes
**Servings:** 2
**Nutritional Information (approx.):** Calories: 110 per serving | Carbohydrates: 16g | Fiber: 4g | Sugar: 11g | Protein: 2g | Fat: 5g | (Glycemic Index: Low)

## Pear Slices with Blue Cheese

**Instructions:**
1. Arrange the pear slices on a plate.
2. Sprinkle with crumbled blue cheese.
3. Serve as a fresh, tangy snack or appetizer.

**Time:** 5 minutes
**Servings:** 1
**Nutritional Information (approx.):** Calories: 150 | Carbohydrates: 22g | Fiber: 5g | Sugar: 15g | Protein: 7g | Fat: 6g | (Glycemic Index: Medium)

**Ingredients:**
- 1 medium pear, sliced
- 1 ounce blue cheese, crumbled

## *Roasted Cauliflower Bites with Curry Powder*

**Ingredients:**

- 1 head cauliflower, cut into bite-sized florets
- 1 tablespoon olive oil
- 1 teaspoon curry powder
- Salt and pepper to taste

**Instructions:**

1. Preheat your oven to 425°F (220°C).
2. Toss the cauliflower florets with olive oil, curry powder, salt, and pepper until evenly coated.
3. Spread on a baking sheet in a single layer.
4. Roast for 20-25 minutes, or until tender and golden brown, stirring halfway through.
5. Serve warm.

**Time:** 3 minutes
**Servings:** 2

**Nutritional Information (approx.):** Calories: 120 per serving | Carbohydrates: 13g | Fiber: 5g | Sugar: 5g | Protein: 4g | Fat: 7g | (Glycemic Index: Low)

# DESSERTS

## *Baked Apples with Cinnamon and Walnuts*

**Instructions:**
1. Preheat oven to 350°F (175°C). Place the cored apples in a baking dish.
2. Mix the walnuts, cinnamon, and sugar substitute together. Stuff this mixture into the center of each apple.
3. Add a splash of water to the bottom of the dish to prevent the apples from sticking.
4. Bake for 20-25 minutes, or until the apples are tender.
5. Serve warm.

**Time:** 30 minutes
**Servings:** 2

**Nutritional Information (approx.):** Calories: 120 | Carbohydrates: 18g | Fiber: 4g | Sugar: 12g (natural sugars from apples) | Protein: 2g | Fat: 6g | (Glycemic Index: Low to Medium)

**Ingredients:**
- 2 medium-sized apples, cored
- 2 tablespoons chopped walnuts
- ½ teaspoon ground cinnamon
- 1 tablespoon sugar substitute (suitable for baking)
- A splash of water

## *Dark Chocolate and Almond Clusters*

**Ingredients:**
- 2 ounces dark chocolate (70% cocoa or higher), melted
- ½ cup whole almonds
- A pinch of sea salt

**Instructions:**
1. Line a baking sheet with parchment paper.
2. Mix the almonds into the melted dark chocolate, ensuring each almond is coated.
3. Spoon small clusters of the almond-chocolate mixture onto the prepared baking sheet. Sprinkle with a pinch of sea salt.
4. Refrigerate until set, about 10-15 minutes.
5. Serve chilled.

**Time:** 15 minutes (plus cooling)
**Servings:** 4
**Nutritional Information (approx.):** Calories: 150 | Carbohydrates: 9g | Fiber: 3g | Sugar: 4g | Protein: 4g | Fat: 12g | (Glycemic Index: Low)

## *Berry and Chia Seed Compote*

**Instructions:**
1. In a small saucepan, combine the berries, chia seeds, sugar substitute, and water.
2. Bring to a simmer over medium heat, stirring frequently.
3. Cook for 5-7 minutes, or until the berries are soft and the mixture has thickened.
4. Remove from heat and let cool. The compote will thicken further as it cools.
5. Refrigerate until chilled. Serve cold.

**Time:** 15 minutes (plus chilling)
**Servings:** 2
**Nutritional Information (approx.):** Calories: 100 | Carbohydrates: 15g | Fiber: 7g | Sugar: 6g (natural sugars from berries) | Protein: 3g | Fat: 4.5g | (Glycemic Index: Low)

**Ingredients:**
- 1 cup mixed berries (fresh or frozen)
- 2 tablespoons chia seeds
- 1 tablespoon sugar substitute
- ½ cup water

## Peach Cobbler with Oatmeal Crust

**Time:** 45 minutes
**Servings:** 6
**Nutritional Information (approx.):**
Calories: 180 | Carbohydrates: 27g | Fiber: 4g | Sugar: 16g | Protein: 4g | Fat: 7g | (Glycemic Index: Medium-Low)

**Ingredients:**
- 4 cups sliced peaches (fresh or unsweetened frozen)
- 1 cup rolled oats
- ½ cup almond flour
- ¼ cup unsweetened applesauce
- 2 tablespoons honey (or a suitable diabetic-friendly sweetener)
- ½ teaspoon cinnamon
- ¼ teaspoon nutmeg
- Cooking spray

**Instructions:**
1. Preheat your oven to 375°F (190°C). Lightly spray a baking dish with cooking spray.
2. Arrange the peach slices evenly in the bottom of the dish.
3. In a bowl, mix rolled oats, almond flour, applesauce, honey, cinnamon, and nutmeg until well combined. Spread this mixture over the peaches.
4. Bake for 30-35 minutes, until the topping is golden and the peaches are tender.
5. Serve warm.

## Carrot Cake with Cream Cheese Frosting

**Ingredients:**
**For the cake:**
- 2 cups grated carrots
- 1 cup whole wheat flour
- ½ cup almond flour
- ¼ cup unsweetened applesauce
- 2 eggs
- ¼ cup olive oil
- ½ cup erythritol (or another diabetic-friendly sweetener)
- 1 teaspoon baking soda
- 1 teaspoon cinnamon
- ½ teaspoon nutmeg

**For the frosting:**
- 1 cup low-fat cream cheese
- 2 tablespoons erythritol (powdered)
- 1 teaspoon vanilla extract

**Instructions:**
1. Preheat your oven to 350°F (175°C). Grease and flour a 9-inch cake pan.
2. Combine all cake ingredients in a large bowl until well mixed. Pour into the prepared pan.
3. Bake for 35-40 minutes, until a toothpick inserted into the center comes out clean.
4. For the frosting, beat together the cream cheese, powdered erythritol, and vanilla until smooth.
5. Once the cake is cooled, spread the frosting evenly over the top.
6. Serve and enjoy.

**Time:** 1 hour
**Servings:** 12

**Nutritional Information (approx.):**
Calories: 200 | Carbohydrates: 18g | Fiber: 3g | Sugar: 5g | Protein: 6g | Fat: 12g | (Glycemic Index: Low))

## Frozen Yogurt Bark with Mixed Berries

**Instructions:**
1. Mix the Greek yogurt with the honey until well combined.
2. Spread the yogurt mixture on a baking sheet lined with parchment paper, about ½ inch thick.
3. Sprinkle the mixed berries and sliced almonds evenly over the yogurt.
4. Freeze for at least 2 hours, until firm.
5. Break into pieces and serve.

**Time:** 2 hours 15 minutes (includes freezing time)
**Servings:** 8
**Nutritional Information (approx.):** Calories: 100 | Carbohydrates: 12g | Fiber: 2g | Sugar: 9g | Protein: 8g | Fat: 3g | (Glycemic Index: Low)

**Ingredients:**
- 2 cups plain Greek yogurt
- 2 tablespoons honey (or a suitable diabetic-friendly sweetener)
- ½ cup mixed berries (blueberries, raspberries, chopped strawberries)
- ¼ cup sliced almonds

# Almond Flour Chocolate Chip Cookies

**Ingredients:**
- 2 cups almond flour
- 1/3 cup sugar substitute (e.g., stevia or monk fruit sweetener)
- 1 tsp baking powder
- ¼ tsp salt
- 1 large egg
- 3 tbsp coconut oil, melted
- 1 tsp vanilla extract
- ¼ cup dark chocolate chips (at least 70% cocoa)

**Instructions:**
1. Preheat oven to 350°F (175°C). Line a baking sheet with parchment paper.
2. In a bowl, mix almond flour, sugar substitute, baking powder, and salt.
3. Beat in the egg, melted coconut oil, and vanilla extract until well combined.
4. Fold in the chocolate chips.
5. Scoop tablespoonfuls of dough onto the prepared baking sheet. Flatten slightly.
6. Bake for 10-12 minutes or until edges are golden. Let cool before serving.

**Time:** 20 minutes
**Servings:** 12 cookies

**Nutritional Information (approx.):** Calories: 160 | Carbohydrates: 8g | Fiber: 3g | Sugar: 2g (from chocolate chips) | Protein: 5g | Fat: 14g | (Glycemic Index: Low)

# Baked Pears with Honey and Greek Yogurt

**Ingredients:**
- 2 ripe pears, halved and cored
- 2 tsp honey
- ½ tsp ground cinnamon
- 1 cup low-fat Greek yogurt

**Instructions:**
1. Preheat oven to 375°F (190°C). Arrange pear halves on a baking dish.
2. Drizzle honey over pears and sprinkle with cinnamon.
3. Bake for 20-25 minutes, until pears are soft.
4. Serve warm with a dollop of Greek yogurt on each half.

**Time:** 30 minutes
**Servings:** 4
**Nutritional Information (approx.):** Calories: 120 | Carbohydrates: 22g | Fiber: 3g | Sugar: 17g | Protein: 7g | Fat: 1g | (Glycemic Index: Medium, moderated by the protein in the Greek yogurt)

# Coconut Milk Popsicles with Kiwi

**Ingredients:**
- 1 can (13.5 oz) full-fat coconut milk
- 2 tbsp sugar substitute (e.g., stevia or monk fruit sweetener)
- 1 tsp vanilla extract
- 2 kiwis, peeled and thinly sliced

**Instructions:**
1. In a blender, combine coconut milk, sugar substitute, and vanilla extract. Blend until smooth.
2. Place a few kiwi slices into each popsicle mold.
3. Pour the coconut milk mixture into the molds, over the kiwi slices.
4. Insert popsicle sticks and freeze for at least 4 hours, until solid.
5. To serve, run warm water over the outside of the molds for a few seconds to release the popsicles.

**Time:** 4 hours (including freezing time)
**Servings:** 6 popsicles
**Nutritional Information (approx.):** Calories: 180 | Carbohydrates: 9g | Fiber: 1g | Sugar: 3g | Protein: 2g | Fat: 16g | (Glycemic Index: Low)

## Flourless Peanut Butter Cookies

**Ingredients:**
- 1 cup natural peanut butter (unsweetened)
- 1/3 cup erythritol (or another diabetic-friendly sweetener)
- 1 large egg
- 1 tsp vanilla extract
- A pinch of salt

**Instructions:**
1. Preheat the oven to 350°F (175°C) and line a baking sheet with parchment paper.
2. In a bowl, mix together peanut butter, erythritol, egg, vanilla extract, and a pinch of salt until well combined.
3. Scoop tablespoonfuls of the dough onto the prepared baking sheet. Press down with a fork to make a crisscross pattern.
4. Bake for 10-12 minutes, or until the edges start to brown.
5. Let cool on the baking sheet for 5 minutes, then transfer to a wire rack to cool completely.

**Time:** 20 minutes
**Servings:** 12 cookies
**Nutritional Information (approx.):** Calories: 160 | Carbohydrates: 5g (Net Carbs: 3g) | Fiber: 2g | Sugar: 1g | Protein: 7g | Fat: 12g | (Glycemic Index: Low)

## Avocado Chocolate Mousse

**Ingredients:**
- 1 ripe avocado
- 2 tablespoons cocoa powder (unsweetened)
- 2 tablespoons almond milk (unsweetened)
- 2 tablespoons erythritol (powdered)
- 1/2 tsp vanilla extract

**Instructions:**
1. Scoop the avocado flesh into a blender. Add cocoa powder, almond milk, erythritol, and vanilla extract.
2. Blend until smooth and creamy.
3. Divide the mousse between two serving dishes and chill for at least 1 hour before serving.

**Time:** 10 minutes + chilling
**Servings:** 2
**Nutritional Information (approx.):** Calories: 200 | Carbohydrates: 12g (Net Carbs: 5g) | Fiber: 7g | Sugar: 1g | Protein: 3g | Fat: 15g | (Glycemic Index: Low)

## Raspberry Sorbet

**Ingredients:**
- 2 cups fresh raspberries
- 1/3 cup water
- 1/3 cup erythritol
- 1 tablespoon lemon juice

**Instructions:**
1. In a saucepan over medium heat, combine water and erythritol, stirring until the erythritol dissolves. Remove from heat and cool to room temperature.
2. Blend the raspberries, lemon juice, and erythritol syrup until smooth.
3. Strain the mixture through a fine mesh sieve to remove the seeds.
4. Pour into a shallow container and freeze for 1 hour. Stir the mixture and freeze again, repeating this process every 30 minutes for about 3 hours, until firm but scoopable.
5. Serve immediately or store in the freezer in an airtight container.

**Time:** 3 hours (including freezing time)
**Servings:** 4

**Nutritional Information (approx.):** Calories: 50 | Carbohydrates: 12g (Net Carbs: 7g) | Fiber: 5g | Sugar: 5g (natural sugars from raspberries) | Protein: 1g | Fat: 0.5g | (Glycemic Index: Low)

## Lemon and Poppy Seed Muffins

**Time:** 30 minutes
**Servings:** 6

**Nutritional Information (approx.):** Calories: 150 | Carbohydrates: 10g | Fiber: 4g | Sugar: 2g | Protein: 6g | Fat: 10g | (Glycemic Index: Low)

**Ingredients:**
- 1 cup almond flour
- ¼ cup coconut flour
- 2 tablespoons poppy seeds
- 1 teaspoon baking powder
- ¼ teaspoon salt
- 3 tablespoons fresh lemon juice
- 2 tablespoons lemon zest
- 2 eggs
- ¼ cup unsweetened almond milk
- ¼ cup erythritol (or another low-GI sweetener)
- 2 tablespoons unsweetened applesauce

**Instructions:**
1. Preheat the oven to 350°F (175°C). Line a muffin tin with 6 paper liners.
2. In a large bowl, combine almond flour, coconut flour, poppy seeds, baking powder, and salt.
3. In another bowl, whisk together lemon juice, lemon zest, eggs, almond milk, erythritol, and applesauce until well combined.
4. Mix the wet ingredients into the dry ingredients until just combined.
5. Divide the batter evenly among the prepared muffin cups.
6. Bake for 20-25 minutes, or until a toothpick inserted into the center of a muffin comes out clean.
7. Let cool before serving.

## Oatmeal and Banana Cookies

**Ingredients:**
- 2 ripe bananas, mashed
- 1 cup rolled oats
- ½ teaspoon cinnamon
- ¼ cup walnuts, chopped
- ¼ cup dark chocolate chips (at least 70% cocoa)

**Instructions:**
1. Preheat the oven to 350°F (175°C). Line a baking sheet with parchment paper.
2. In a bowl, combine mashed bananas, rolled oats, and cinnamon.
3. Fold in the walnuts and dark chocolate chips.
4. Drop tablespoon-sized portions of the mixture onto the prepared baking sheet.
5. Bake for 15-18 minutes, or until the edges are golden.
6. Let cool before serving.

**Time:** 25 minutes
**Servings:** 12
**Nutritional Information (approx.):** Calories: 80 | Carbohydrates: 12g | Fiber: 2g | Sugar: 4g | Protein: 2g | Fat: 3g | (Glycemic Index: Medium)

## Grilled Peaches with Cinnamon

**Ingredients:**
- 2 large peaches, halved and pitted
- 1 teaspoon cinnamon
- 2 teaspoons honey (optional, for those who can incorporate a small amount of sugar)
- ¼ cup low-fat Greek yogurt (for serving)

**Instructions:**
1. Preheat the grill to medium heat.
2. Sprinkle the cut side of each peach half with cinnamon.
3. Place peaches on the grill, cut side down, and grill for 4-5 minutes until slightly soft and char marks form.
4. Flip and grill for another 3-4 minutes.
5. Drizzle a small amount of honey over each peach half if using.
6. Serve with a dollop of Greek yogurt on each half.

**Time:** 15 minutes
**Servings:** 4

**Nutritional Information (approx.):** Calories: 60 (without honey) | Carbohydrates: 14g | Fiber: 2g | Sugar: 12g (natural sugars from peaches) | Protein: 1g | Fat: 0.5g | (Glycemic Index: Medium due to natural fruit sugars, balanced by protein in Greek yogurt)

## Berry Crisp with Almond Topping

**Time:** 35 minutes
**Servings:** 4
**Nutritional Information (approx.):** Calories: 150 | Carbohydrates: 18g | Fiber: 4g | Sugar: 8g (natural sugars from berries) | Protein: 4g | Fat: 8g | (Glycemic Index: Medium, balanced with fiber and protein)

**Ingredients:**
- 2 cups mixed berries (fresh or frozen)
- 1 tablespoon cornstarch
- ¼ cup almond flour
- ¼ cup rolled oats
- 2 tablespoons sliced almonds
- 1 tablespoon melted coconut oil
- 2 tablespoons monk fruit sweetener
- ½ teaspoon cinnamon

**Instructions:**
1. Preheat oven to 375°F (190°C). Mix berries with cornstarch and pour into a baking dish.

2. In a bowl, combine almond flour, rolled oats, sliced almonds, coconut oil, monk fruit sweetener, and cinnamon until crumbly. Sprinkle over the berries.

3. Bake for 25-30 minutes until the topping is golden and the berries are bubbling. Let cool slightly before serving.

## Mango and Sticky Rice

**Ingredients:**
- ½ cup long-grain brown rice, soaked for 2 hours
- 1 cup water
- ½ cup light coconut milk
- 1 tablespoon monk fruit sweetener
- 1 ripe mango, sliced
- Sesame seeds for garnish (optional)

**Instructions:**
1. Rinse the soaked rice and cook in water until tender and sticky, about 20 minutes.

2. In a separate saucepan, warm coconut milk with monk fruit sweetener until dissolved. Mix half with the cooked rice.

3. Serve rice with mango slices on top. Drizzle with the remaining coconut milk. Garnish with sesame seeds if desired.

**Time:** 30 minutes + soaking
**Servings:** 2
**Nutritional Information (approx.):** Calories: 200 | Carbohydrates: 40g | Fiber: 3g | Sugar: 15g (natural sugars from mango) | Protein: 3g | Fat: 4g | (Glycemic Index: Medium, moderated by the fiber in brown rice and fat in coconut milk)

## Chocolate-Dipped Strawberries

**Instructions:**
1. Wash and dry strawberries. Melt dark chocolate and coconut oil together in a double boiler or microwave, stirring until smooth.
2. Dip each strawberry into the melted chocolate, coating half the strawberry. Place on a parchment-lined tray.
3. Sprinkle with a tiny pinch of flaky sea salt (optional). Chill in the refrigerator until the chocolate sets, about 15 minutes.

**Time:** 15 minutes + chilling
**Servings:** 4

**Ingredients:**
- 12 large strawberries
- 50g dark chocolate (70% cocoa or higher)
- 1 teaspoon coconut oil
- Flaky sea salt for garnish (optional)

**Nutritional Information (approx.):** Calories: 100 | Carbohydrates: 12g | Fiber: 2g | Sugar: 8g (mostly natural sugars from strawberries) | Protein: 1g | Fat: 6g | (Glycemic Index: Low, thanks to the high cocoa content in dark chocolate and the natural sugars in strawberries)

## Pumpkin Pie with Whole Wheat Crust

**Time:** 1 hour 20 minutes (includes baking and cooling)
**Servings:** 8

**Nutritional Information (approx.):** Calories: 180 | Carbohydrates: 20g | Fiber: 4g | Sugar: 3g (natural sugars from pumpkin) | Protein: 5g | Fat: 9g | (Glycemic Index: Medium)

**Ingredients:**
**For the crust:**
- 1 cup whole wheat flour
- ¼ cup cold water
- ¼ cup olive oil
- ½ teaspoon salt

**For the filling:**
- 2 cups pumpkin puree
- ¾ cup almond milk
- ½ cup granulated stevia (or sweetener of choice, equivalent to sugar)
- 2 eggs
- 1 teaspoon cinnamon
- ½ teaspoon ground ginger
- ¼ teaspoon ground cloves
- ¼ teaspoon salt

**Instructions:**
1. Preheat the oven to 350°F (175°C).

2. **For the crust:** Mix flour and salt, then add olive oil and water until dough forms. Press into a 9-inch pie dish.

3. **For the filling:** Combine all filling ingredients in a bowl and mix until smooth. Pour into the crust.

4. Bake for 50 minutes or until the filling is set. Let cool before serving.

## No-Bake Cheesecake with Berry Compote

**Ingredients:**
**For the base:**
- 1 cup almond flour
- 2 tablespoons melted coconut oil
- 2 tablespoons granulated stevia

**For the filling:**
- 2 cups low-fat cream cheese, softened
- ½ cup Greek yogurt
- ½ cup granulated stevia
- 1 teaspoon vanilla extract

**For the compote:**
- 2 cups mixed berries (frozen or fresh)
- 2 tablespoons water
- 1 tablespoon lemon juice
- 2 tablespoons granulated stevia

**Instructions:**
1. Mix almond flour, coconut oil, and stevia for the base. Press into the bottom of a springform pan. Chill for 30 minutes.

2. Beat cream cheese, Greek yogurt, stevia, and vanilla for the filling until smooth. Spread over the base. Chill for 2 hours.

3. For the compote, simmer berries, water, lemon juice, and stevia until thickened. Cool before topping the cheesecake.

**Time:** 2 hours 30 minutes (includes chilling)
**Servings:** 8

**Nutritional Information (approx.):** Calories: 220 | Carbohydrates: 15g | Fiber: 3g | Sugar: 8g | Protein: 8g | Fat: 15g | (Glycemic Index: Low)

## *Apple Crisp with Almond Flour Topping*

**Time:** 45 minutes
**Servings:** 8
**Nutritional Information (approx.):**
Calories: 200 | Carbohydrates: 22g | Fiber:
5g | Sugar: 12g (natural sugars from apples)
| Protein: 4g | Fat: 11g | (Glycemic Index:
Medium)

**Ingredients:**
**For the filling:**
- 4 medium apples, peeled and sliced
- 2 tablespoons lemon juice
- 2 tablespoons granulated stevia
- 1 teaspoon cinnamon

**For the topping:**
- 1 cup almond flour
- ½ cup rolled oats
- ¼ cup melted unsalted butter
- 3 tablespoons granulated stevia
- ½ teaspoon cinnamon

**Instructions:**
1. Preheat the oven to 375°F (190°C).

2. Toss apple slices with lemon juice, stevia, and cinnamon. Place in a baking dish.

3. Mix topping ingredients until crumbly. Sprinkle over the apples.
4. Bake for 30 minutes, or until the topping is golden and apples are tender.

## *Cherry and Almond Galette*

**Ingredients:**
- 1 cup fresh cherries, pitted and halved
- 1 pre-made whole wheat pie crust
- 2 tbsp almond flour
- 1 tbsp stevia (granulated)
- 1 tsp almond extract
- 1 egg (for egg wash)
- Slivered almonds for garnish

**Instructions:**
1. Preheat your oven to 375°F (190°C).
2. Mix cherries with stevia and almond extract. Let sit for 10 minutes.
3. Roll out the pie crust on a baking sheet lined with parchment paper. Sprinkle almond flour in the center, leaving a 2-inch border.
4. Arrange cherry mixture over almond flour. Fold the edges of the crust over the filling.
5. Brush the crust with egg wash and sprinkle slivered almonds on top.
6. Bake for 25 minutes or until the crust is golden brown. Let cool before serving.

**Time:** 35 minutes
**Servings:** 4
**Nutritional Information (approx.):** Calories: 200 | Carbohydrates: 22g | Fiber: 3g | Sugar: 8g (Natural sugars from cherries) | Protein: 5g | Fat: 11g | (Glycemic Index: Medium)

## Baked Custard with Nutmeg

**Ingredients:**
- 4 eggs
- 2 cups almond milk
- 2 tbsp stevia (granulated)
- ½ tsp ground nutmeg
- 1 tsp vanilla extract

**Instructions:**

1. Preheat your oven to 350°F (175°C).

2. Whisk together eggs, almond milk, stevia, nutmeg, and vanilla extract until well combined.

3. Pour into 4 ramekins. Place ramekins in a baking dish and fill the dish with hot water halfway up the sides of the ramekins.

4. Bake for 35 minutes or until set. Cool slightly before serving. Sprinkle with extra nutmeg if desired.

**Time:** 45 minutes
**Servings:** 4
**Nutritional Information (approx.):** Calories: 120 | Carbohydrates: 3g | Fiber: 0g | Sugar: 1g | Protein: 7g | Fat: 8g | (Glycemic Index: Low)

## Chocolate Avocado Pudding

**Ingredients:**
- 2 ripe avocados, peeled and pitted
- ¼ cup unsweetened cocoa powder
- ¼ cup almond milk
- 3 tbsp stevia (granulated)
- 1 tsp vanilla extract

**Instructions:**

1. Blend avocados, cocoa powder, almond milk, stevia, and vanilla extract in a food processor until smooth.
2. Divide the mixture into 4 small bowls. Cover and refrigerate for at least 1 hour.
3. Serve chilled, garnished with a few raspberries or a mint leaf.

**Time:** 10 minutes + chilling
**Servings:** 4

**Nutritional Information (approx.):** Calories: 160 | Carbohydrates: 12g | Fiber: 7g | Sugar: 1g | Protein: 3g | Fat: 12g | (Glycemic Index: Low)

## Fruit Salad with Mint and Lime

**Ingredients:**
- 1 cup strawberries, hulled and quartered
- 1 cup blueberries
- 1 kiwi, peeled and sliced
- 1 tablespoon fresh lime juice
- 1 teaspoon lime zest
- 1 tablespoon fresh mint leaves, chopped
- 1 teaspoon honey (optional, for those managing their sugar intake)

**Instructions:**

1. In a large bowl, combine the strawberries, blueberries, and kiwi.
2. In a small bowl, whisk together the lime juice, lime zest, and honey (if using) until well combined.
3. Pour the lime mixture over the fruit and gently toss to coat.
4. Sprinkle with chopped mint leaves and serve.

**Time:** 10 minutes
**Servings:** 2

**Nutritional Information (approx.):** Calories: 110 | Carbohydrates: 27g | Fiber: 5g | Sugar: 17g (natural sugars from fruit) | Protein: 2g | Fat: 0.5g | (Glycemic Index: Low to Medium, depending on fruit ripeness)

## Ingredients:

- 2 cups finely grated zucchini
- 1 cup whole wheat flour
- ½ cup unsweetened cocoa powder
- ¾ teaspoon baking soda
- ½ teaspoon salt
- ¼ cup coconut oil, melted
- ¼ cup unsweetened apple sauce
- ½ cup erythritol (or another sugar substitute safe for diabetes)
- 2 teaspoons vanilla extract
- ½ cup sugar-free dark chocolate chips

## Instructions:

1. Preheat the oven to 350°F (175°C). Line an 8x8 inch baking pan with parchment paper.
2. In a large bowl, combine the whole wheat flour, cocoa powder, baking soda, and salt.
3. Stir in the grated zucchini, melted coconut oil, apple sauce, erythritol, and vanilla extract until well combined.
4. Fold in the chocolate chips and pour the batter into the prepared baking pan.
5. Bake for 25-30 minutes or until a toothpick inserted into the center comes out mostly clean.
6. Let cool before slicing into squares.

**Time:** 35 minutes
**Servings:** 12
**Nutritional Information (approx.):** Calories: 120 | Carbohydrates: 15g | Fiber: 3g | Sugar: 2g (erythritol not counted as sugar) | Protein: 3g | Fat: 7g | (Glycemic Index: Low)

## *Peanut Butter and Banana Ice Cream*

## Instructions:

1. Place the frozen banana slices and peanut butter in a blender or food processor.
2. Blend until smooth, adding a splash of almond milk if necessary to help with blending.
3. Serve immediately for a soft-serve texture or freeze for an additional hour for a firmer ice cream.

**Time:** 5 minutes (plus freezing time)
**Servings:** 2
**Nutritional Information (approx.):** Calories: 210 Carbohydrates: 27g Fiber: 4g Sugar: 14g (natural sugars from banana) Protein: 6g Fat: 10g (Glycemic Index: Medium, balanced with fiber and healthy fats)

## Ingredients:

- 2 ripe bananas, sliced and frozen
- 2 tablespoons natural peanut butter
- A splash of almond milk (if needed for blending)

## Blackberry and Lemon Bars

**Ingredients:**
- 1 cup almond flour
- ¼ cup coconut oil, melted
- 1 tablespoon stevia
- 2 eggs
- 1 cup fresh blackberries
- Zest and juice of 1 lemon
- 1 teaspoon vanilla extract

**Instructions:**
1. Preheat oven to 350°F (175°C). Line an 8x8 inch baking pan with parchment paper.
2. Mix almond flour, melted coconut oil, and ½ tablespoon of stevia to create the crust. Press into the bottom of the prepared pan.
3. Bake for 15 minutes until slightly golden. Remove from oven and let cool.
4. In a bowl, beat eggs with the remaining stevia, lemon zest, lemon juice, and vanilla extract. Stir in blackberries.
5. Pour the blackberry mixture over the cooled crust and return to the oven. Bake for an additional 20-25 minutes until set.
6. Let cool before slicing into bars.

**Time:** 45 minutes
**Servings:** 8
**Nutritional Information (approx.):** Calories: 200 | Carbohydrates: 10g | Fiber: 4g | Sugar: 3g (natural sugars) | Protein: 6g | Fat: 15g | (Glycemic Index: Low)

## Coconut and Date Truffles

**Ingredients:**
- 1 cup pitted dates, soaked in warm water for 10 minutes and drained
- ½ cup unsweetened shredded coconut, plus extra for coating
- 1 tablespoon coconut oil
- 1 teaspoon vanilla extract
- Pinch of salt

**Instructions:**
1. In a food processor, blend soaked dates, shredded coconut, coconut oil, vanilla extract, and salt until the mixture sticks together.
2. Using your hands, roll the mixture into small balls.
3. Roll the truffles in additional shredded coconut to coat.
4. Chill in the refrigerator for at least 30 minutes before serving.

**Time:** 20 minutes (plus chilling)
**Servings:** 10
**Nutritional Information (approx.):** Calories: 90 | Carbohydrates: 15g | Fiber: 3g | Sugar: 12g (natural sugars) | Protein: 1g | Fat: 4g | (Glycemic Index: Medium)

## Stewed Plums with Vanilla

**Ingredients:**
- 8 ripe plums, pitted and quartered
- ¼ cup water
- 1 vanilla bean, split and seeds scraped
- 1 tablespoon stevia (adjust to taste)

**Instructions:**
1. In a saucepan over medium heat, combine plums, water, vanilla bean (pod and seeds), and stevia.
2. Bring to a simmer and cook for 20 minutes, or until the plums are soft and the liquid has slightly thickened.
3. Remove the vanilla bean pod before serving. Serve warm or chilled.

**Time:** 25 minutes
**Servings:** 4
**Nutritional Information (approx.):** Calories: 60 | Carbohydrates: 14g | Fiber: 2g | Sugar: 12g (natural sugars) | Protein: 1g | Fat: 0g | (Glycemic Index: Low to Medium)

## No-Bake Coconut Bars

**Ingredients:**
- 2 cups unsweetened shredded coconut
- ¼ cup coconut oil, melted
- 2 tablespoons almond flour
- 1 tablespoon monk fruit sweetener
- ½ teaspoon vanilla extract

**Instructions:**
1. In a mixing bowl, combine shredded coconut, coconut oil, almond flour, monk fruit sweetener, and vanilla extract. Mix well.
2. Press the mixture firmly into a lined 8x8 inch baking pan.
3. Refrigerate for at least 1 hour or until firm. Slice into 12 bars and serve.

**Time:** 1 hour 20 minutes (includes chilling)
**Servings:** 12 bars

**Nutritional Information (approx.):** Calories: 150 | Carbohydrates: 4g | Fiber: 2g | Sugar: 1g | Protein: 1g | Fat: 14g | (Glycemic Index: Low)

## Raspberry Almond Thumbprint Cookies

**Ingredients:**
- 1 cup almond flour
- ¼ cup coconut flour
- ¼ cup unsalted butter, softened
- 3 tablespoons erythritol
- 1 teaspoon vanilla extract
- ½ cup sugar-free raspberry jam

**Instructions:**
1. Preheat oven to 350°F (175°C). Line a baking sheet with parchment paper.
2. In a bowl, mix almond flour, coconut flour, butter, erythritol, and vanilla extract until dough forms.
3. Roll dough into 15 balls and place on the baking sheet. Press your thumb into the center of each ball to create a well. Fill each well with raspberry jam.
4. Bake for 12-15 minutes or until edges are golden. Cool before serving.

**Time:** 30 minutes
**Servings:** 15 cookies
**Nutritional Information (approx.):** Calories: 100 | Carbohydrates: 6g | Fiber: 2g | Sugar: 1g | Protein: 2g | Fat: 8g | (Glycemic Index: Low)

## Greek Yogurt Cheesecake with Strawberry Compote

**Time:** 2 hours 30 minutes (includes chilling)
**Servings:** 8
**Nutritional Information (approx.):** Calories: 120 | Carbohydrates: 12g | Fiber: 1g | Sugar: 10g | Protein: 9g | Fat: 3g | (Glycemic Index: Medium, balanced by protein)

**Ingredients:**
**For the cheesecake:**
- 2 cups Greek yogurt
- ¼ cup honey
- 2 eggs
- 1 teaspoon vanilla extract

**For the compote:**
- 1 cup strawberries, sliced
- 1 tablespoon lemon juice
- 1 tablespoon erythritol

**Instructions:**
1. Preheat oven to 325°F (163°C). Grease an 8-inch springform pan.
2. In a bowl, whisk together Greek yogurt, honey, eggs, and vanilla extract. Pour into the prepared pan.
3. Bake for 30 minutes. Turn off the oven and leave the cheesecake inside for another hour without opening the door. Chill in the refrigerator.
4. For the compote, combine strawberries, lemon juice, and erythritol in a saucepan over medium heat. Simmer until strawberries are soft. Cool and pour over chilled cheesecake.

## Chocolate Zucchini Cake

**Ingredients:**

- 1½ cups grated zucchini
- 1 cup almond flour
- ½ cup unsweetened cocoa powder
- ¼ cup coconut oil, melted
- ¼ cup monk fruit sweetener
- 2 eggs
- 1 tsp baking powder
- ½ tsp vanilla extract
- Pinch of salt

**Instructions:**

1. Preheat the oven to 350°F (175°C). Grease a 9-inch cake pan.
2. In a bowl, mix together the almond flour, cocoa powder, baking powder, and salt.
3. In another bowl, whisk the eggs with the monk fruit sweetener and vanilla extract. Stir in the melted coconut oil.
4. Combine the wet and dry ingredients until just mixed. Fold in the grated zucchini.
5. Pour the batter into the prepared pan and bake for 25-30 minutes, or until a toothpick comes out clean.
Let cool before serving.

**Time:** 40 minutes
**Servings:** 8

**Nutritional Information (approx.):** Calories: 180 | Carbohydrates: 12g | Fiber: 4g | Sugar: 3g (natural sugars) | Protein: 6g | Fat: 14g | (Glycemic Index: Low)

## Apple Nachos with Peanut Butter and Chocolate

**Ingredients:**

- 2 medium apples, thinly sliced
- 2 tbsp natural peanut butter, melted
- 1 tbsp dark chocolate chips, melted
- 1 tbsp chopped nuts (walnuts or almonds)

**Instructions:**

1. Arrange apple slices on a plate.
2. Drizzle melted peanut butter and chocolate over the apple slices.
3. Sprinkle chopped nuts on top.
4. Serve immediately.

**Time:** 10 minutes
**Servings:** 2

**Nutritional Information (approx.):** Calories: 210 | Carbohydrates: 25g | Fiber: 5g | Sugar: 18g (natural sugars) | Protein: 4g | Fat: 12g | (Glycemic Index: Medium, moderated by the fiber in apples and protein in peanut butter)

## *Banana Split with Greek Yogurt and Nuts*

**Ingredients:**
- 1 medium banana, split lengthwise
- ½ cup plain Greek yogurt
- 1 tbsp chopped nuts (almonds, walnuts)
- A sprinkle of cinnamon
- A few dark chocolate shavings

**Instructions:**
1. Place the split banana on a plate.
2. Top with Greek yogurt.
3. Sprinkle with chopped nuts, cinnamon, and chocolate shavings.
4. Serve immediately.

**Time:** 5 minutes
**Servings:** 1

**Nutritional Information (approx.):** Calories: 220 | Carbohydrates: 30g | Fiber: 4g | Sugar: 16g (natural sugars) | Protein: 12g | Fat: 8g | (Glycemic Index: Low to Medium, balanced by the protein in Greek yogurt and the fiber in the banana)

## *Matcha Green Tea Ice Cream*

**Ingredients:**
- 2 cups unsweetened almond milk
- 1 ripe avocado
- 2 tbsp matcha green tea powder
- ¼ cup erythritol (or another low-GI sweetener)
- 1 tsp vanilla extract

**Instructions:**
1. Blend almond milk, avocado, matcha powder, erythritol, and vanilla in a blender until smooth.
2. Pour the mixture into an ice cream maker and churn according to the manufacturer's instructions until it reaches a soft-serve consistency.
3. Transfer to a freezer-safe container and freeze until firm, about 4 hours.
4. Serve with a sprinkle of matcha powder on top.

**Time:** 20 minutes (plus freezing time)
**Servings:** 2
**Nutritional Information (approx.):** Calories: 180 | Carbohydrates: 9g | Fiber: 4g | Sugar: 1g | Protein: 3g | Fat: 15g | (Glycemic Index: Low)

## *Orange and Almond Cake*

**Ingredients:**
- 2 oranges, boiled and pureed
- 3 cups almond flour
- 1 cup erythritol
- 5 eggs
- 1 tsp baking powder
- 1 tsp vanilla extract

**Instructions:**
1. Preheat the oven to 350°F (175°C). Grease and line an 8-inch round cake pan.
2. In a large bowl, mix the almond flour, erythritol, and baking powder.
3. Stir in the eggs, orange puree, and vanilla extract until well combined.
4. Pour the batter into the prepared pan and bake for 30-35 minutes, or until a toothpick inserted into the center comes out clean.
5. Allow to cool before serving.

**Time:** 40 minutes
**Servings:** 8
**Nutritional Information (approx.):** Calories: 280 | Carbohydrates: 15g | Fiber: 6g | Sugar: 6g (natural sugars from oranges) | Protein: 10g | Fat: 22g | (Glycemic Index: Medium-Low)

## Blueberry Lemon Chia Pudding

**Ingredients:**
- 1 cup unsweetened almond milk
- ¼ cup chia seeds
- ½ cup fresh blueberries
- 2 tbsp lemon juice
- Zest of 1 lemon
- 2 tbsp erythritol

**Instructions:**
1. In a bowl, whisk together almond milk, chia seeds, lemon juice, lemon zest, and erythritol. Let sit for 5 minutes, then stir again to prevent clumping.
2. Fold in the blueberries, then divide the mixture between two cups.
3. Refrigerate for at least 4 hours or overnight until set.
4. Serve chilled, garnished with extra blueberries and lemon zest.

**Time:** 15 minutes (plus chilling time)
**Servings:** 2

**Nutritional Information (approx.):** Calories: 150 | Carbohydrates: 14g | Fiber: 8g | Sugar: 4g | Protein: 4g | Fat: 9g | (Glycemic Index: Low)


## Carrot and Pineapple Cake

**Ingredients:**
- 1 ½ cups almond flour
- ½ cup coconut flour
- 1 tsp baking soda
- 2 tsp cinnamon
- ½ tsp nutmeg
- ¼ tsp salt
- 3 eggs
- ¼ cup unsweetened applesauce
- ¼ cup olive oil
- ½ cup erythritol (or other low-GI sweetener)
- 1 tsp vanilla extract
- 1 cup grated carrots
- ½ cup crushed pineapple, drained
- ¼ cup chopped walnuts (optional)

**Instructions:**
1. Preheat your oven to 350°F (175°C). Grease and flour a 9-inch round cake pan.
2. In a large bowl, whisk together almond flour, coconut flour, baking soda, cinnamon, nutmeg, and salt.
3. In a separate bowl, beat eggs, applesauce, olive oil, erythritol, and vanilla extract until smooth. Stir into the dry ingredients until just moistened. Fold in the carrots, pineapple, and walnuts.
4. Pour into the prepared cake pan. Bake for 45-50 minutes or until a toothpick inserted into the center comes out clean.
5. Let cool in the pan for 10 minutes, then transfer to a wire rack to cool completely.

**Time:** 1 hour
**Servings:** 8

**Nutritional Information (approx.):** Calories: 240 | Carbohydrates: 18g | Fiber: 6g | Sugar: 8g (natural sugars from carrots and pineapple) | Protein: 7g | Fat: 16g | Glycemic Index: Medium-Low (due to the use of low-GI sweeteners and high fiber content from almond and coconut flours)

# Part VI
# 60 Days Meal Plan

## INTRODUCTION TO THE 60-DAY MEAL PLAN

As we navigate through these two months together, you'll find meals crafted to balance the intricate dance of glycemic control with the joy of eating. Each dish is selected for its ability to support blood sugar management while delighting the senses. From hearty breakfasts to satisfying dinners, and yes, even the occasional indulgent dessert, this plan embraces the philosophy that managing diabetes doesn't mean forsaking delicious food.

### *Notes for Continued Success:*

- **Variety is Key:** A colorful diet is a healthy one. Incorporate a wide range of fruits, vegetables, whole grains, lean proteins, and healthy fats to keep meals interesting and nutritionally sound.

- **Dessert Moderation:** Desserts, thoughtfully chosen for their lower glycemic impact, are included sparingly. Enjoy these treats mindfully, appreciating each bite.

- **Listen to Your Body:** Individual responses to foods can vary. Adjust this meal plan based on how different foods and meals affect your blood sugar levels and overall well-being.

- **Stay Active:** Pairing this meal plan with regular physical activity amplifies its benefits, aiding in blood sugar management and boosting overall health.

- **Hydration and Activity:** Drink plenty of water and engage in regular physical activity that you enjoy. This combination is potent for managing type 2 diabetes.

- **Adjust Portions and Meal Prep:** Tailor portion sizes to your needs and consider meal prepping to ease daily decisions and maintain focus on your health goals.

- **Monitor Blood Sugar Levels:** Keeping a close eye on how different meals influence your blood sugar can offer invaluable insights into personalizing your diet for optimal control.

- **Flexibility and Mindful Eating:** Feel free to swap snack options and listen to your body's hunger and satiety signals. Eating should be a source of pleasure as well as nourishment.

# MEAL PLAN

## Week 1

**Day 1:**

- **Breakfast:** Oatmeal with Almonds and Berries
- **Snack:** Greek Yogurt with Mixed Berries
- **Lunch:** Mixed Bean Salad with a Lemon-Tahini Dressing
- **Snack:** Celery Sticks with Almond Butter
- **Dinner:** Grilled Lemon-Garlic Salmon with Asparagus
- **Dessert:** Baked Apples with Cinnamon and Walnuts

**Day 2:**

- **Breakfast:** Spinach and Feta Egg Muffins
- **Snack:** Roasted Chickpeas with Paprika
- **Lunch:** Quinoa Tabbouleh with Chickpeas
- **Snack:** Sliced Apples with Peanut Butter
- **Dinner:** Stir-Fried Chicken and Broccoli with Brown Rice

**Day 3:**

- **Breakfast:** Chia Seed Pudding with Coconut Milk
- **Snack:** Cucumber and Hummus Bites
- **Lunch:** Grilled Chicken Caesar Salad with Kale
- **Snack:** Cherry Tomatoes Stuffed with Cottage Cheese
- **Dinner:** Eggplant Parmesan with Whole Wheat Pasta
- **Dessert:** Berry and Chia Seed Compote

**Day 4:**

- **Breakfast:** Whole Grain Avocado Toast
- **Snack:** Mixed Nuts and Seeds
- **Lunch:** Vegetable Stir-Fry with Tofu and Brown Rice
- **Snack:** Baked Kale Chips
- **Dinner:** Baked Cod with Roasted Vegetables

**Day 5:**

- **Breakfast:** Greek Yogurt with Walnut and Apple
- **Snack:** Edamame with Sea Salt
- **Lunch:** Lentil Soup with Spinach and Carrots
- **Snack:** Avocado and Egg Salad on Whole Grain Crackers

- **Dinner:** Vegetable and Bean Casserole
- **Dessert:** Almond Flour Chocolate Chip Cookies

**Day 6:**

- **Breakfast:** Quinoa Breakfast Bowl with Mixed Berries
- **Snack:** Carrot Sticks with Guacamole
- **Lunch:** Turkey and Avocado Wrap
- **Snack:** Zucchini and Parmesan Crisps
- **Dinner:** Spaghetti Squash and Meatballs

**Day 7:**

- **Breakfast:** Egg White Omelet with Mixed Vegetables
- **Snack:** Whole Grain Toast with Ricotta and Berries
- **Lunch:** Vegetable and Hummus Whole Wheat Pita
- **Snack:** Frozen Grapes
- **Dinner:** Zucchini Lasagna with Ground Turkey
- **Dessert:** Almond Flour Chocolate Chip Cookies

**Day 8:**

- **Breakfast:** Low-GI Berry Smoothie
- **Snack:** Greek Yogurt with Honey and Cinnamon
- **Lunch**: Salmon Nicoise Salad
- **Snack:** Pear Slices with Blue Cheese
- **Dinner:** Grilled Tofu with Quinoa and Green Beans

**Day 9:**

- **Breakfast:** Cottage Cheese with Sliced Peaches
- **Snack:** Cherry Tomatoes Stuffed with Cottage Cheese
- **Lunch:** Spicy Black Bean and Quinoa Bowl
- **Snack:** Almond and Date Energy Balls
- **Dinner:** Roasted Chicken with Sweet Potatoes and Brussels Sprouts
- **Dessert:** Dark Chocolate and Almond Clusters

**Day 10:**

- **Breakfast:** Almond Butter and Banana Whole Grain Pancakes
- **Snack:** Roasted Chickpeas with Paprika
- **Lunch:** Mediterranean Chickpea and Feta Salad
- **Snack:** Mini Bell Peppers with Tuna Salad
- **Dinner:** Vegetable Curry with Brown Basmati Rice

**Day 11:**

- **Breakfast:** Buckwheat Porridge with Almonds
- **Snack:** Mixed Nuts and Seeds
- **Lunch:** Balsamic Grilled Vegetable Plate
- **Snack:** Frozen Grapes
- **Dinner:** Turkey Chili with Beans and Vegetables
- **Dessert:** Peach Cobbler with Oatmeal Crust

**Day 12:**

- **Breakfast:** Savory Mashed Cauliflower with Poached Eggs
- **Snack:** Baked Kale Chips
- **Lunch:** Chicken, Apple, and Walnut Salad
- **Snack:** Sliced Apples with Peanut Butter

- **Dinner:** Stuffed Acorn Squash with Quinoa and Kale

**Day 13:**

- **Breakfast:** Kale and Mushroom Frittata
- **Snack:** Edamame with Sea Salt
- **Lunch:** Asian Lettuce Wraps with Ground Turkey
- **Snack:** Greek Yogurt with Mixed Berries
- **Dinner:** Pan-Seared Tilapia with Lemon and Capers
- **Dessert:** Frozen Yogurt Bark with Mixed Berries

**Day 14:**

- **Breakfast:** Steel-Cut Oats with Cinnamon and Flaxseed
- **Snack:** Cucumber and Hummus Bites
- **Lunch:** Broccoli and Almond Soup
- **Snack:** Celery Sticks with Almond Butter
- **Dinner:** Vegetarian Stuffed Peppers

**Day 15:**

- **Breakfast:** Mushroom and Spinach Breakfast Skillet
- **Snack:** Baked Avocado Fries with Spicy Mayo Dip
- **Lunch:** Grilled Shrimp and Mango Salad
- **Snack:** Cherry Tomatoes Stuffed with Cottage Cheese
- **Dinner:** Grilled Lemon-Garlic Salmon with Asparagus

**Day 16:**

- **Breakfast:** Whole Grain Avocado Toast
- **Snack:** Greek Yogurt with Mixed Berries
- **Lunch:** Vegetable Stir-Fry with Tofu and Brown Rice
- **Snack:** Sliced Apples with Peanut Butter
- **Dinner:** Eggplant Parmesan with Whole Wheat Pasta
- **Dessert:** Baked Pears with Honey and Greek Yogurt

**Day 17:**

- **Breakfast:** Low-GI Mango and Chia Seed Smoothie
- **Snack:** Edamame with Sea Salt
- **Lunch:** Spicy Black Bean and Quinoa Bowl
- **Snack:** Almond and Date Energy Balls
- **Dinner:** Baked Cod with Roasted Vegetables

**Day 18:**

- **Breakfast:** Scrambled Tofu with Spinach and Tomatoes
- **Snack:** Whole Wheat Pita with Baba Ganoush
- **Lunch:** Mediterranean Chickpea and Feta Salad
- **Snack:** Raw Veggies with Hummus
- **Dinner:** Stir-Fried Chicken and Broccoli with Brown Rice

**Day 19:**

- **Breakfast:** Quinoa Breakfast Bowl with Mixed Berries
- **Snack:** Mixed Nuts and Seeds
- **Lunch:** Lentil Soup with Spinach and Carrots
- **Snack:** Greek Yogurt with Honey and Cinnamon
- **Dinner:** Zucchini Lasagna with Ground Turkey

**Day 20:**

- **Breakfast:** Whole Wheat Vegetable Upma
- **Snack:** Carrot Sticks with Guacamole
- **Lunch:** Grilled Chicken Caesar Salad with Kale
- **Snack:** Sliced Pear with Cheese
- **Dinner:** Vegetable and Bean Casserole
- **Dessert:** Almond Flour Chocolate Chip Cookies

**Day 21:**

- **Breakfast:** Buckwheat Porridge with Almonds
- **Snack:** Cottage Cheese with Sliced Peaches
- **Lunch:** Turkey and Avocado Wrap
- **Snack:** Celery Sticks with Almond Butter
- **Dinner:** Spaghetti Squash and Meatballs

**Day 22:**

- **Breakfast:** Kale and Mushroom Frittata
- **Snack:** Greek Yogurt with Mixed Berries
- **Lunch:** Asian Lettuce Wraps with Ground Turkey
- **Snack:** Celery Sticks with Almond Butter
- **Dinner:** Grilled Tofu with Quinoa and Green Beans

**Day 23:**

- **Breakfast:** Steel-Cut Oats with Cinnamon and Flaxseed
- **Snack:** Baked Kale Chips
- **Lunch:** Balsamic Grilled Vegetable Plate
- **Snack:** Sliced Apples with Peanut Butter
- **Dinner:** Eggplant and Chickpea Stew

**Day 24:**

- **Breakfast:** Savory Mashed Cauliflower with Poached Eggs
- **Snack:** Cherry Tomatoes Stuffed with Cottage Cheese
- **Lunch:** Salmon Nicoise Salad
- **Snack:** Roasted Chickpeas with Paprika
- **Dinner:** Beef and Broccoli Stir-Fry with Brown Rice
- **Dessert:** Dark Chocolate and Almond Clusters

**Day 25:**

- **Breakfast:** Quinoa and Berry Porridge
- **Snack:** Cucumber and Hummus Bites
- **Lunch:** Turkey and Vegetable Skewers
- **Snack:** Greek Yogurt with Honey and Cinnamon
- **Dinner:** Vegetable Curry with Brown Basmati Rice

**Day 26:**

- **Breakfast:** Whole Grain Toast with Ricotta and Berries
- **Snack:** Mixed Nuts and Seeds
- **Lunch:** Chicken, Apple, and Walnut Salad
- **Snack:** Edamame with Sea Salt
- **Dinner:** Pan-Seared Tilapia with Lemon and Capers

**Day 27:**

- **Breakfast:** Buckwheat Porridge with Almonds
- **Snack:** Carrot Sticks with Guacamole
- **Lunch:** Grilled Chicken Caesar Salad with Kale
- **Snack:** Celery Sticks with Almond Butter
- **Dinner:** Spaghetti Squash and Meatballs
- **Dessert:** Baked Apples with Cinnamon and Walnuts

**Day 28:**

- **Breakfast:** Protein-Packed Lentil Pancakes
- **Snack:** Avocado and Egg Salad on Whole Grain Crackers
- **Lunch:** Mixed Bean Salad with a Lemon-Tahini Dressing
- **Snack:** Greek Yogurt with Mixed Berries
- **Dinner:** Grilled Lemon-Garlic Salmon with Asparagus

**Day 29:**

- **Breakfast:** Zucchini and Carrot Breakfast Muffins
- **Snack:** Baked Kale Chips
- **Lunch:** Grilled Shrimp and Mango Salad
- **Snack:** Sliced Apples with Peanut Butter
- **Dinner**: Baked Cod with Roasted Vegetables

**Day 30:**

- **Breakfast:** Almond Butter and Banana Whole Grain Pancakes
- **Snack:** Greek Yogurt with Mixed Berries
- **Lunch:** Vegetable Stir-Fry with Tofu and Brown Rice
- **Snack:** Celery Sticks with Almond Butter
- **Dinner:** Eggplant Parmesan with Whole Wheat Pasta
- **Dessert:** Peach Cobbler with Oatmeal Crust

**Day 31:**

- **Breakfast:** Whole Wheat Vegetable Upma
- **Snack:** Cherry Tomatoes Stuffed with Cottage Cheese
- **Lunch**: Mediterranean Chickpea and Feta Salad
- **Snack:** Roasted Chickpeas with Paprika
- **Dinner:** Vegetable and Bean Casserole

**Day 32:**

- **Breakfast:** Mushroom and Spinach Breakfast Skillet
- **Snack:** Greek Yogurt with Honey and Cinnamon
- **Lunch:** Balsamic Grilled Vegetable Plate
- **Snack:** Edamame with Sea Salt
- **Dinner:** Grilled Lemon-Garlic Salmon with Asparagus

**Day 33:**

- **Breakfast:** Quinoa Breakfast Bowl with Mixed Berries
- **Snack:** Cucumber and Hummus Bites
- **Lunch:** Spicy Black Bean and Quinoa Bowl
- **Snack:** Carrot Sticks with Guacamole
- **Dinner:** Roasted Chicken with Sweet Potatoes and Brussels Sprouts

- **Dessert:** Almond Flour Chocolate Chip Cookies

**Day 34:**

- **Breakfast:** Savory Mashed Cauliflower with Poached Eggs
- **Snack:** Mixed Nuts and Seeds
- **Lunch:** Turkey and Avocado Wrap
- **Snack:** Celery Sticks with Almond Butter
- **Dinner:** Zucchini Lasagna with Ground Turkey

**Day 35:**

- **Breakfast:** Scrambled Tofu with Spinach and Tomatoes
- **Snack:** Avocado and Egg Salad on Whole Grain Crackers
- **Lunch:** Grilled Chicken Caesar Salad with Kale
- **Snack:** Greek Yogurt with Mixed Berries
- **Dinner:** Stir-Fried Chicken and Broccoli with Brown Rice

# Week 6

**Day 36:**

- **Breakfast:** Buckwheat Porridge with Almonds
- **Snack:** Greek Yogurt with Walnut and Apple
- **Lunch:** Spicy Tofu and Kale Breakfast Stir-Fry
- **Snack:** Roasted Cauliflower Bites with Curry Powder
- **Dinner:** Grilled Tofu with Quinoa and Green Beans

**Day 37:**

- **Breakfast:** Steel-Cut Oats with Cinnamon and Flaxseed
- **Snack**: Mixed Nuts and Seeds
- **Lunch:** Stuffed Acorn Squash with Quinoa and Kale
- **Snack**: Sliced Pears with Cheese
- **Dinner:** Stir-Fried Chicken and Broccoli with Brown Rice
- **Dessert:** Raspberry Sorbet

**Day 38:**

- **Breakfast:** Protein-Packed Lentil Pancakes
- **Snack:** Frozen Grapes
- **Lunch:** Salmon Nicoise Salad
- **Snack:** Cherry Tomatoes Stuffed with Cottage Cheese
- **Dinner:** Lamb Chops with Mint Pesto

**Day 39:**

- **Breakfast:** Whole Grain Avocado Toast
- **Snack**: Greek Yogurt with Mixed Berries
- **Lunch**: Balsamic Grilled Vegetable Plate
- **Snack:** Carrot Sticks with Guacamole
- **Dinner:** Eggplant and Chickpea Stew

**Day 40:**

- **Breakfast**: Quinoa and Berry Porridge
- **Snack**: Cucumber and Hummus Bites
- **Lunch**: Mediterranean Chickpea and Feta Salad
- **Snack:** Baked Kale Chips
- **Dinner:** Vegetable Curry with Brown Basmati Rice

- Dessert: Baked Pears with Honey and Greek Yogurt

## Day 41:

- **Breakfast**: Savory Mashed Cauliflower with Poached Eggs
- **Snack:** Almond and Date Energy Balls
- **Lunch:** Grilled Chicken Caesar Salad with Kale
- **Snack:** Edamame with Sea Salt
- **Dinner:** Vegetable and Bean Casserole

## Day 42:

- **Breakfast:** Almond Flour Blueberry Muffins
- **Snack**: Greek Yogurt with Mixed Berries
- **Lunch:** Asian Lettuce Wraps with Ground Turkey
- **Snack:** Sliced Apples with Peanut Butter
- **Dinner:** Grilled Lemon-Garlic Salmon with Asparagus

**Day 43:**

- **Breakfast:** Scrambled Tofu with Spinach and Tomatoes
- **Snack:** Almond and Date Energy Balls
- **Lunch:** Spaghetti Squash with Tomato Sauce and Meatballs
- **Snack:** Sliced Pears with Cheese
- **Dinner:** Baked Cod with Roasted Vegetables
- **Dessert:** Peach Cobbler with Oatmeal Crust

**Day 44:**

- **Breakfast:** Egg White Omelet with Mixed Vegetables
- **Snack:** Roasted Chickpeas with Paprika
- **Lunch:** Mediterranean Chickpea and Feta Salad
- **Snack:** Greek Yogurt with Walnut and Apple
- **Dinner:** Grilled Tofu with Quinoa and Green Beans

**Day 45:**

- **Breakfast:** Quinoa Breakfast Bowl with Mixed Berries
- **Snack:** Celery Sticks with Almond Butter
- **Lunch:** Balsamic Grilled Vegetable Plate
- **Snack:** Cherry Tomatoes Stuffed with Cottage Cheese
- **Dinner:** Stir-Fried Chicken and Broccoli with Brown Rice
- **Dessert:** Baked Apples with Cinnamon and Walnuts

**Day 46:**

- **Breakfast:** Whole Grain Avocado Toast
- **Snack:** Mixed Nuts and Seeds
- **Lunch:** Grilled Chicken Caesar Salad with Kale
- **Snack:** Cucumber and Hummus Bites
- **Dinner:** Eggplant Parmesan with Whole Wheat Pasta

**Day 47:**

- **Breakfast:** Greek Yogurt with Walnut and Apple
- **Snack:** Edamame with Sea Salt
- **Lunch:** Salmon Nicoise Salad
- **Snack:** Greek Yogurt with Mixed Berries

- **Dinner:** Zucchini Lasagna with Ground Turkey

**Day 48:**

- **Breakfast:** Spinach and Feta Egg Muffins
- **Snack:** Frozen Grapes
- **Lunch:** Quinoa Tabbouleh with Chickpeas
- **Snack:** Carrot Sticks with Guacamole
- **Dinner:** Pan-Seared Tilapia with Lemon and Capers
- **Dessert:** Dark Chocolate and Almond Clusters

**Day 49:**

- **Breakfast:** Oatmeal with Almonds and Berries
- **Snack:** Baked Kale Chips
- **Lunch:** Vegetable Stir-Fry with Tofu and Brown Rice
- **Snack:** Sliced Apples with Peanut Butter
- **Dinner:** Grilled Lemon-Garlic Salmon with Asparagus

**Day 50:**

- **Breakfast:** Steel-Cut Oats with Cinnamon and Flaxseed
- **Snack:** Greek Yogurt with Honey and Cinnamon
- **Lunch:** Asian Cabbage Salad with Grilled Chicken
- **Snack:** Cherry Tomatoes Stuffed with Cottage Cheese
- **Dinner:** Vegetable Curry with Brown Basmati Rice

**Day 51:**

- **Breakfast:** Mushroom and Spinach Breakfast Skillet
- **Snack:** Almond and Date Energy Balls
- **Lunch:** Spiced Lentil Tacos with Avocado Cream
- **Snack:** Sliced Pears with Cheese
- **Dinner:** Beef Stir-Fry with Broccoli and Bell Peppers
- **Dessert:** Baked Pears with Honey and Greek Yogurt

**Day 52:**

- **Breakfast:** Buckwheat Porridge with Almonds
- **Snack:** Edamame with Sea Salt
- **Lunch:** Zucchini Noodles with Pesto and Cherry Tomatoes
- **Snack:** Celery Sticks with Almond Butter
- **Dinner:** Baked Trout with Walnut Crust

**Day 53:**

- **Breakfast:** Low-GI Mango and Chia Seed Smoothie
- **Snack:** Mixed Nuts and Seeds
- **Lunch:** Roasted Vegetable and Quinoa Salad
- **Snack:** Greek Yogurt with Mixed Berries
- **Dinner:** Lamb Chops with Mint Pesto

**Day 54:**

- **Breakfast:** Savory Mashed Cauliflower with Poached Eggs
- **Snack:** Baked Kale Chips
- **Lunch:** Turkey and Avocado Wrap
- **Snack:** Cucumber and Hummus Bites
- **Dinner:** Pan-Seared Tilapia with Lemon and Capers

- **Dessert:** Dark Chocolate and Almond Clusters

**Day 55:**

- **Breakfast:** Almond Butter and Banana Whole Grain Pancakes
- **Snack:** Roasted Chickpeas with Paprika
- **Lunch:** Mediterranean Chickpea and Feta Salad
- **Snack:** Sliced Apples with Peanut Butter
- **Dinner:** Grilled Shrimp and Mango Salad
- **Dessert:** Berry and Chia Seed Compote

**Day 56:**

- **Breakfast:** Whole Wheat Vegetable Upma
- **Snack:** Carrot Sticks with Guacamole
- **Lunch:** Grilled Chicken Caesar Salad with Kale
- **Snack:** Almond and Date Energy Balls
- **Dinner:** Eggplant Parmesan with Whole Wheat Pasta

# Week 9

**Day 57:**

- **Breakfast:** Kale and Mushroom Frittata
- **Snack:** Mini Bell Peppers with Tuna Salad
- **Lunch:** Cold Quinoa Salad with Edamame and Carrots
- **Snack:** Greek Yogurt with Honey and Cinnamon
- **Dinner:** Vegetable and Bean Casserole
- **Dessert:** *None*

**Day 58:**

- **Breakfast:** Quinoa and Berry Porridge
- **Snack:** Cherry Tomatoes Stuffed with Cottage Cheese
- **Lunch:** Spicy Black Bean and Quinoa Bowl
- **Snack:** Sliced Pears with Cheese
- **Dinner:** Pan-Fried Cod with Slaw
- **Dessert:** Baked Apples with Cinnamon and Walnuts

**Day 59:**

- **Breakfast:** Scrambled Tofu with Spinach and Tomatoes
- **Snack:** Almond and Date Energy Balls
- **Lunch:** Tuna Salad Stuffed Avocados
- **Snack:** Celery Sticks with Almond Butter
- **Dinner:** Stir-Fried Chicken and Broccoli with Brown Rice
- **Dessert:** *None*

**Day 60:**

- **Breakfast:** Whole Grain Avocado Toast
- **Snack:** Roasted Chickpeas with Paprika
- **Lunch:** Grilled Shrimp and Mango Salad
- **Snack:** Greek Yogurt with Mixed Berries
- **Dinner:** Baked Chicken with Ratatouille
- **Dessert:** Dark Chocolate and Almond Clusters

# Conclusions

Embarking on a journey to manage type 2 diabetes through nutrition and lifestyle adjustments is an empowering step toward reclaiming your health. It requires commitment, education, and a willingness to transform your relationship with food. The path laid out in this book aims to guide you through understanding how the choices you make at the dining table can influence your blood sugar levels and overall well-being.

Navigating the world of diabetes doesn't have to be a solitary journey nor a daunting one. By arming yourself with knowledge and practical strategies, you can make informed decisions that lead to lasting changes in your health. Remember, each small step you take is a victory in its own right. Whether it's swapping out white bread for a whole-grain alternative, incorporating more leafy greens into your meals, or dedicating a portion of your day to physical activity, these changes accumulate over time to yield significant benefits.

## Empowerment Through Education

Understanding the nature of type 2 diabetes is the foundation upon which you can build a healthier lifestyle. Knowledge about how different foods affect your blood sugar levels enables you to make choices that can prevent spikes and dips. This understanding also demystifies the condition, making it more manageable and less intimidating.

## The Power of Choice

The power to improve your health lies in the daily choices you make. Each meal is an opportunity to nourish your body and support your diabetes management goals. Embrace this power with enthusiasm, knowing that you have the tools and knowledge to make choices that benefit your health.

## Small Changes, Big Impact

It's easy to become overwhelmed by the prospect of overhauling your diet and lifestyle. However, the approach advocated in this book emphasizes the impact of incremental changes. Small, sustainable adjustments to your eating habits and activity levels can have a profound effect on your health. These changes are more manageable and less daunting, making them easier to implement and stick with over the long term.

## Building a Supportive Community

You don't have to navigate this journey alone. Seek out supportive communities, whether online or in person, where you can share experiences, challenges, and successes with others who understand what you're going through. These communities can provide encouragement, advice, and a sense of belonging, all of which are invaluable resources on your path to better health.

## Celebrating Progress

Remember to celebrate your progress, no matter how small. Acknowledging your achievements reinforces your motivation and commitment to your health goals. Whether it's reaching a blood sugar target, successfully incorporating more vegetables into your diet, or consistently engaging in physical activity, each accomplishment is a step toward a healthier you.

## Looking Ahead

As you continue on this journey, keep in mind that managing type 2 diabetes is an ongoing process of learning and adaptation. New challenges may arise, but with the foundation you've built through education, mindful choices, and gradual changes, you're well-equipped to face them. Embrace the journey with optimism, knowing that you're empowering yourself to live a healthier, fuller life.

Your journey towards health is a testament to your strength and determination. Armed with knowledge, supported by a community, and motivated by progress, you are capable of navigating the challenges of type 2 diabetes and thriving despite them.

# Recipe Index

bbd566bb-e48f-4728-8781-7c42f2ba6f98R01